The American Consul

ADST-DACOR Diplomats and Diplomacy Series

Series Editor: Margery Boichel Thompson

Since 1776, extraordinary men and women have represented the United States abroad under widely varying circumstances. What they did and how and why they did it remain little known to their compatriots. In 1995, the Association for Diplomatic Studies and Training (ADST) and DACOR, an organization of foreign affairs professionals, created the Diplomats and Diplomacy book series to increase public knowledge and appreciation of the professionalism of American diplomats and their involvement in world history. The second edition of Charles Stuart Kennedy's history of the U.S. consular service, the definitive work on the subject, is the fifty-fifth volume in the series.

OTHER TITLES IN THE SERIES

Jonathan Addleton, *Mongolia and the United States: A Diplomatic History*
ADST, *A Brief History of U.S. Diplomacy*
Gordon S. Brown, *Toussaint's Clause: The Founding Fathers and the Haitian Revolution*
Charles T. Cross, *Born a Foreigner: A Memoir of the American Presence in Asia*
Peter D. Eicher, ed., *"Emperor Dead" and Other Historic American Diplomatic Dispatches*
Hermann F. Eilts, *Early American Diplomacy in the Near and Far East: The Diplomatic and Personal History of Edmund Q. Roberts (1784–1836)*
Stephen H. Grant, *Peter Strickland: New London Shipmaster, Boston Merchant, First Consul to Senegal*
Michael P. E. Hoyt, *Captive in the Congo: A Consul's Return to the Heart of Darkness*
Dennis C. Jett, *American Ambassadors: The Past, Present, and Future of America's Diplomats*
David D. Newsom, *Witness to a Changing World*
Richard B. Parker, *Uncle Sam in Barbary: A Diplomatic History*
Nicholas Platt, *China Boys: How U.S. Relations with the PRC Began and Grew*
James W. Spain, *In Those Days: A Diplomat Remembers*
Nancy Bernkopf Tucker, ed., *China Confidential: American Diplomats and Sino-American Relations, 1945–1996*

For a complete list of series titles, visit <adst.org/publications>

The American Consul

A History of the United States Consular Service, 1776–1924

Revised 2nd Edition

Charles Stuart Kennedy

An ADST-DACOR Diplomats and Diplomacy Book

NEW ACADEMIA PUBLISHING

Washington, DC

New Academia Publishing 2015
First edition, *The American Consul: A History of the United States Consular Service, 1776–1914* (Greenwood, 1990)

Printed in the United States of America

Library of Congress Control Number: 2015930109
ISBN 978-0-9906939-7-0 paperback (alk. paper)

NEW ACADEMIA
PUBLISHING

New Academia Publishing
PO Box 27420, Washington, DC 20038-7420
info@newacademia.com - www.newacademia.com

Contents

Preface to the Second Edition

In the intervening years following the publication of this book's first edition, *The American Consul: A History of the United States Consular Service, 1776–1914* (Greenwood, 1990), I hoped that historians would pick up on the important role of American consuls in the development of U.S. relations with the rest of the world. But that did not happen. As the first edition is no longer in print and had been published with a virtually prohibitive price by a firm that caters to the academic library market, I decided to bring out a new edition in paperback.

This new edition adds the period 1914 to 1924, when the Consular Service was integrated with the Diplomatic Service to form the present-day Foreign Service of the United States. This volume thus adds the work of the Consular Service through the end of World War I, the Greek disaster in Turkey, and Germany in the early years of the Weimar Republic.

On a personal note, I discovered with some chagrin that I had left out a family member in this tribute to the American Consular Service. A few years ago, well after I had published the book, I was playing with the Internet and noted that an entry regarding my grandfather, a Civil War veteran, referred to his father-in-law—my great grandfather Edmund Jüssen—as a fellow veteran. Checking further I found that Great Granddad had been consul general in Vienna between 1885 and 1889. So this obscure title runs in the family: I was consul general four times.

I want to thank the Association for Diplomatic Studies and Training, Kenneth Brown, Margery Thompson, and Marilyn Bentley for their support in encouraging me to bring out this new edition. The Association generously assigned the following interns to help with the editing of the book, and I thank them all: Jennifer Ricketts, Caroline Lemp, Brad Walvert, Biola Ijadare, Mary Larson, and especially Whitney Kipps, who gave particular attention to polishing the work.

1

Consular Antecedents

The origin of consuls predates that of permanent ambassadors by almost two millennia. The first ambassadors set up residence in foreign countries during the late Middle Ages. An establishment closely approximating a consular service had been created in Egypt in the sixth century B.C. during the reign of the pharaoh Amasis, who, wishing to encourage trade with the Greeks, set aside Naucratis, a city in the Nile Delta, where they could live under their own governors.[1] Those governors had many of the characteristics of modern consuls in that their principal functions were to encourage trade, act as magistrates for their citizens living in Egypt, serve as intermediaries with the Egyptian authorities, and report back to their city-states on political and economic conditions in Egypt. Naucratis was not a Greek colony but existed at the sufferance of the Egyptian Pharaoh, who delegated certain powers to the Greek governors in the manner that countries today will allow foreign consuls to perform certain legal functions for their own citizens.

Having foreign officials in a sovereign country exercising certain authority over their own citizens has a logic that was evident centuries before the exchange of resident ambassadors. The Pharaoh gave the Greeks a place where they were both isolated and protected. Removing them from too much contact with Egyptians also spared the Pharaoh's officials from having to deal with disputatious foreign traders and kept the foreigners from corrupting his subjects.

The Greek city-state system, and later that of the Romans, had their versions of consuls. But, with the collapse of the Roman Empire and the advent of the Dark Ages, it was not until the eleventh and twelfth centuries that the trading states of Europe began to reassemble their systems of laws, codes, and commercial practices. Gradually merchants in northern Europe (especially members of the Hanseatic League) and the Mediterranean were enabled to enjoy a certain security in knowing that their goods and agents were not completely at the mercy of capricious local magistrates. With the codification of mercantile practices, consuls began to reappear to help merchants of their cities or states on foreign shores. By the thirteenth century Venice had more than thirty consuls placed abroad in Tunis, Alexandria, Cairo, and Damascus, as well as in all of the major European ports.[2]

As commerce grew, countries and city-states began to send their ambassadors to reside at courts of foreign rulers, rather than to perform a specific mission and then return. These resident ambassadors took away some work consuls had performed, especially in dealing with major problems affecting large numbers of their subjects, but few ambassadors had the interest, experience, or authority to deal with commercial matters, or intercede for merchants or sailors in trouble. Courts and ports were two different worlds, and it took different types of men to deal with each. Even today, although there are attempts to meld professional diplomats with consuls, individual differences in personality and outlook sharply affect preferences for one or the other field of work.

By the eighteenth century the consular network of the major trading nations was well established; consuls in the ports and commercial cities of Europe were gaining respect for their abilities in seeing that the wheels of commerce turning at a proper rate. Some countries appointed their own merchants as consuls, permitting them to continue in private trade while looking after their countries' interests and collecting fees for their services. Others appointed foreigners as consuls; attracting men who found it worthwhile to represent a foreign power, either because of the honor or because occupying a quasi-legal position gave them certain trade advantages. A few countries, notably France, the dominant European power, had established a professional consular service.

While consuls in European cities enjoyed prestige and often monetary advantages, their colleagues along the north coast of Africa were in a perpetually precarious position. By the seventeenth century the Ottoman Empire had lost much of its control over it's supposedly subject states of Tunis, Tripoli, Algiers, and Morocco. The rule of the Sublime Porte was nominal, but because the Barbary States acknowledged the sovereignty of the Ottoman sultan, other nations wishing to deal with them could not send ambassadors since they could go only to the court of an acknowledged ruler. The consul's position was well suited for this type of situation. A consul could act almost as an ambassador without upsetting the dignity of the sultan in Constantinople. Another reason to put consuls on those inhospitable shores was that they were expendable. In diplomatic usage, endangering or taking the life of an ambassador could be a mortal insult, since the ambassador was the personal representative of the sending ruler. A consul was no more or less than a governmental official; if something happened to him, it might be a matter of concern or even outrage, but not a matter of war.

The European consuls to the Barbary states played a key role in helping clients caught in impossible circumstances. The states of Algiers, Morocco, Tunis, and Tripoli survived by means of war and tribute. Each state had a small navy and vessels fitted out as privateers. These ships preyed on the merchant ships of one or more of the European countries that did not pay tribute to the Barbary rulers.

The consuls helped negotiate and pay the tribute, and arranged for the ransom of their countrymen who had been captured and enslaved during times of war. The consuls might continue their appointed work even while their country was at war with the Barbary states[3], or they might be thrown in jail.[4] None of these Barbary states were as powerful as Spain, France, England, or a combination of the Italian trading states, such as Venice and Genoa, but they were not put out of business until the nineteenth century. "Beggar your neighbor" was considered a smart policy.

By the mid-eighteenth century the European consular corps in the Barbary states had become quite professional. Most members were paid salaries by their governments and were experienced in dealing with the autocratic rulers in the face of great hazards, such as being tied to cannons and blown apart if capricious demands of the rulers were not met.[5] Although it was not unknown for a French consul to urge the corsairs to attack English ships and for the English consul to reciprocate, there was a genuine esprit de corps in the consular ranks. At one point, when France and England were at war, both consuls in a Barbary state joined with other members of the corps to protest when one of their number was badly treated.[6]

The long travail of the European consuls on the Barbary Coast was perhaps salutary to the profession at large. The need to have competent men posted to such a difficult area brought the importance of selection of consuls home to their respective governments. This was a lesson the United States learned slowly; it would take over a hundred years for it to sink in.

By the time of the American Revolution, the French had a highly organized consular service. Elaborate rules were drawn up by Louis XIV's officials: requiring a consul to be over thirty years old, to have served over three years as a vice consul, and to have proved himself worthy of further advancement.[7] The consul received a salary and could not engage in trade. More authority was given to French consuls over their king's subjects abroad than was given by the British to their English counterparts. A British consul in Algiers once complained to London that an English merchant was hurting his country's interests, but he could do nothing. . Had that merchant been French, his consul could have sent him packing back to France.[8]

British consuls were selected from merchants, naval or military officers, or other men of responsibility and experience.[9] They were given a salary while serving abroad. The consul's authority resembled that of a chamber of commerce in that he "has the power to call a general meeting of British merchants and factors for the discussion of commercial affairs; and for the purpose of levying sums on trading ships, for the relief of shipwrecked mariners and charitable purposes. All matters are decided by the majority at such meetings."[10]

The British consuls' duties were spelled out in a series of instructions. The king's consul was to learn the local language; acquaint himself with the laws, ordinances, and customs of the area; and maintain the dignity of his office. He was to protect British subjects, seeking redress for injuries or insults they might suffer and acting as their advocate should they injure or insult a native. British subjects charged with crimes committed at sea were to be transported to Great Britain for trial. The consul was to relieve distressed British mariners and send penniless subjects home on British ships. He was also to see that British ships paid their bills before leaving port, claim and recover what he could from the wrecks of British ships, arbitrate trade disputes between British merchants and ship captains, and put disorderly seamen and captains into prison. Further, he was to complain against any oppressive regulations, arbitrary actions, or infractions of treaties in relation to the commerce of his country, and he was to transmit periodic reports on trade. Finally, in a Catholic country, he was to defend Protestants in the free exercise of their faith.[11] With the exceptions of putting seamen and their captains in a consular jail and protecting the Protestant faith in Catholic countries, these instructions given out in the time of George I (1714–27) cover the major responsibilities of the modern consuls of most countries today, including those of the United States.

Until the colonial Americans severed their ties to Great Britain in 1776, American merchants and seamen benefited from the British consular system, which looked after the interests of all British subjects. By 1776 any country with major shipping interests and markets abroad recognized the need to have a consular service and the value of having one that recruited and kept men who were knowledgeable in trade and in dealing with foreign governments.

2

Revolution and Confederation
(1776–1789)

The Revolutionary War period (1775–83) was not the time for the creation of a well-structured consular service. It was a period of ad hoc diplomacy with the niceties of diplomatic and consular titles and their functions being left to agents of Congress. This new Congress itself was in constant danger of being snuffed out by the powerful British armies prowling through the rebelling thirteen colonies. American interests abroad were limited to securing foreign backing, financial and military, obtaining munitions and other essential supplies, and gaining support for the small American naval forces, including privateers, in European waters. During the war foreign affairs were the direct responsibility of Congress; questions of both major and minor importance had to be settled by a vote.

In March 1776, four months prior to the Declaration of Independence, Congress sent one of its members, Silas Deane, to France. He was initially given the designation of "commercial agent," but he was also to sound out the French as to a possible alliance, thus mixing consular and diplomatic functions, an assignment that would happen often in the American consular service.[1]

The term "commercial agent" will be encountered again. The duties of commercial agents for the American colonies were almost indistinguishable in most matters from those of consuls, but during the hectic times of the American Revolution commercial agents, starting with Silas Deane, bore greater responsibilities than just seeing to American mercantile interests.

Deane eventually settled in Paris as one of three commissioners; the others were Arthur Lee and Benjamin Franklin, who acted as unofficial American ministers to the court of Louis XVI. As the first American commercial agent, Deane was instrumental in establishing the machinery that would funnel French aid to the Americans.[2] Prior to the entry of France into the war with Great Britain in 1778, the French king's ministers not only allowed American commercial agents to assist the fledgling Continental Navy but also permitted American privateers to fit out in French ports and use those same ports to sell off the proceeds from the prizes they had taken. Deane and the agents who followed him were a combination of military purchasing agents, naval storekeepers, and consuls. They acted as consular officers when dealing with local authorities and as sharp businessmen in purchasing supplies for the American cause taking a percentage of the procurement costs to put in their own pockets. The system was full of flaws, hastily organized by desperate men with little experience in obtaining and shipping government supplies. Both French and American suppliers and agents undoubtedly took full advantage of the makeshift channel, but the fact remains that Silas Deane and his successors were able to pump vital supplies to the revolutionary armies. Ninety percent of the powder used by the American revolutionaries in the first two and a half years of the war came from Europe, mainly from France.[3]

One of the first American commercial agents in France was Thomas Morris. His appointment was based on nepotism and arranged by Robert Morris, one of the wealthiest men in the American colonies, a member of Congress who was known as "the financier of the American Revolution" for his astute management of the meager financial resources of the former colonies. Thomas Morris was his illegitimate half-brother and had been reared by him. But young Thomas had acquired both bad companions and dissipated habits.[4] A change of scene was felt to be the solution to Thomas's problems; his brother sent him to the French port of Nantes as the American commercial agent and as agent for the Philadelphia firm of Willing and Morris. This firm had control over vessels taken as prizes and brought to Nantes by the small but effective Continental Navy and American privateers. The firm also purchased and shipped supplies and munitions to the rebellious colonies. Morris was in charge of what amounted to a gold mine since the family firm took a commission, quite legitimately, from transactions dealing with prizes, supplies, and munitions. The Atlantic crossing, however, had not changed Thomas; he kept his profligate habits and acquired a new set of bad companions in the French port.

By the spring of 1778 the two American commissioners then in Paris, Deane and Franklin, concerned about the situation in Nantes, asked Franklin's nephew Jonathan Williams, who was visiting his uncle, to go to the port and put matters right. Williams was to take prize-vessel cases out of the hands of Thomas Morris and deal directly with the privateer and naval captains.[5] The matter became more confused when William Lee, one of the Lees of Virginia and brother of Arthur Lee, the third commissioner in Paris, arrived in Nantes. Lee, who was to have been the commissioner of Congress to the courts of Vienna and Berlin but had not been accepted by them, stayed on in Nantes to lend a "helping hand." Instead of assisting Jonathan Williams, William Lee sided with Thomas Morris against Williams.

Silas Deane had left Paris under a cloud and was replaced by John Adams. The three American commissioners, Franklin, Arthur Lee and Adams, backed away from a confrontation over who had authority over commercial agents and left William Lee in charge.[6] Lee appointed two agents, Jean-Daniel Schweighauser in Nantes and John Bonfield in Bordeaux.[7] Meanwhile Thomas Morris died, perhaps of dissipation. William Lee eventually settled in Paris, leaving his agents to work in the port cities.

The Nantes affair demonstrated major weaknesses that were to plague the American consular service for the next 130 years. These flaws were patronage and profit. Men with political influence, such as Lee, Morris, and Franklin, had no qualms about placing family members in positions of public service where they could make a commission off the government goods and services that had to pass through their hands.

Article XXXI of the 1778 Treaty of Amity and Commerce between the America and France stated: "The two contracting parties grant, mutually, the liberty of having each in the ports of the other, consuls, vice-consuls, agents and commissioners, whose functions shall be regulated by a particular agreement." Franklin and his colleagues expected that Congress would soon appoint some consuls to put American affairs in order in the ports. Franklin, Lee, and Adams suggested in a letter to the president of Congress that in selecting consuls "the choice will fall most justly as well as naturally on Americans, who are, in our opinion, better qualified for this business than any others, and the reputation of such an office, together with a moderate commission on the business they must transact, and the advantages to be derived from trade, will be a sufficient inducement to undertake it, and a sufficient reward for discharging the duties of it."

Enclosed with this joint letter was a short piece labeled "The Functions of Consuls." Among the functions described was "to have inspection and jurisdiction, civil as well as criminal, over all the subjects of their states who happen to be in their department, and particularly over commerce and merchants." A consul should be over thirty. When there were questions that affected "the general affairs of the commerce of his nation," he should call general assemblies of all merchants and ships' captains in the port, with penalties for nonattendance. The commissioners went on to describe the consul's judicial authority. A consul was to be able to "oblige any of his nation to depart if they behave scandalously, and captains are obliged to take them, under a penalty." There were other provisions for dealing with disputes between consuls and merchants. The piece ended on probably the one practical note, at least in the American context: "If war happens, the Consuls retire."[8]

If Franklin and the other two commissioners had really wanted consuls soon, this description of the functions of consuls, obviously taken from the highly authoritarian French instructions, was a serious tactical error. The commissioners had been in France too long and apparently had forgotten that Congress was running a revolution against a distant ruler who had sent his appointed officials to lord it over American colonials. The men in Philadelphia would not tolerate little American Caesars strutting around major ports.

Franklin desperately needed someone to take the problems of the ports and the commercial agents off his hands. In 1779 he wrote the Marine Committee of Congress, asking that no more Continental Navy ships be sent to work out of France, as the prizes they seized only caused "Lawsuits and all the Embarrassment and Solicitation and Vexation attending Suits in this Country." If, however, the navy was "still ordered to cruise in these seas, a Consul or Consuls may be appointed to the several Sea Ports, who will thereby be more at hand to transact maritime Business expeditiously, will understand it better, relieve your Minister at this court from a great deal of Trouble, and leave him at liberty to attend affairs of more general importance."[9] In other words, no consul, no navy. Franklin, however, did not get his consul until a year later, but John Paul Jones and other American naval commanders continued their activities in European waters.

While Congress procrastinated in naming consular officers to France, the court of Louis XVI lost no time in sending its men to its new ally. By early 1779 French consuls were established in Boston, Philadelphia, Baltimore, and the Carolinas. New York was not on the list, but only because the occupying British army precluded French consular activity there. During the American Revolutionary War the French consuls had diverse duties. Their naval support activities included acting as purchasing agents for the French fleet, which put into American ports to be revictualed and to obtain naval stores. Moreover, these consuls were discreetly distributed about the thirteen ex-colonies to report on and influence political matters in the separate regions, since each ex-colony was an almost independent political entity with its own commercial interests. France hoped to take the lucrative American market away from Great Britain after the war and channel it into the French system. Their consuls were well placed to aid in this endeavor.

In 1780 John Adams was sent back to Europe to be on hand to negotiate a peace treaty with Great Britain whenever the time became propitious. In Paris Adams observed that "many of the disputes, delays and other inconveniences that have attended our affairs in this kingdom, have arisen from blending the offices of political Minister, Board of Admiralty, Chamber of Commerce, and Commercial Agent together." He wrote that the business of the minister (Franklin) was to negotiate with the court, and that was enough to keep one man fully occupied. He urged Congress to put a consul in Nantes. "I think it should be an American, some merchant of known character, ability, and industry, who would consent to serve his country for moderate emoluments. Such persons are to be found in great number in America. There are many applications from French gentlemen. But I think that a want of knowledge of our language, our laws, customs, and even humors of our people, for even these must be considered, would prevent them from giving satisfaction, or doing justice." Adams went on to extol the virtues of having consuls abroad who could report on political and commercial matters, which "in future times may be a rich treasure of the United States."[10]

Later in 1780 the American minister in Madrid, John Jay, voiced his own complaint about the lack of American consuls abroad. Jay said that he was not able to write freely, as letters were routinely inspected at ports and post offices in Spain and France:

Is it not Time for America like other Nations to provide against these Inconveniences by proper Regulations and Establishments? They ought in my opinion have an American

Consul or agent in some Port here [Spain] and in France. Their public Dispatches should be sent by Packet Boats to these Agents, and should on no account be delivered to any other Person. I have a very good Reason to suspect that the french Consuls in America are very watchful and attentive to these Matters, and good Care should be taken to keep american Letters out of their Way.[11]

Finally, on 4 November 1780 Congress appointed Lt. Col. William Palfrey a consul for France. Palfrey was the former paymaster general of the Continental army. But Palfrey never enjoyed his status as the first American consul, since his ship bound for France was lost in a storm. While awaiting confirmation that Palfrey had indeed drowned, Congress in June 1781 appointed Thomas Barclay of Pennsylvania as the vice consul to "perform the services required of William Palfrey, during his absence from the kingdom."[12] In October Barclay was named as consul to succeed Palfrey with a salary of $1,500 per year.

Congress refused to appoint other consuls but did appoint a commercial agent, Robert Smith, to reside in Havana "to manage the occasional concerns of Congress, to assist the American traders with his advice, and to solicit their affairs with the Spanish government, and to govern himself according to the orders he may from time to time, receive from the United States in Congress assembled, or the superintendent of Finance."[13]

As the war subsided in the period between the battle of Yorktown in 1781 and the peace treaty of 1783, there was only one American consul, Thomas Barclay, and a handful of commercial agents helping American seamen stranded in foreign ports, purchasing and forwarding supplies to the relatively inactive and shrinking American military forces. Barclay's activities were not confined to France; he was also in the Netherlands buying munitions for American forces. While making these purchases, Barclay and the commercial agents were taking their commissions and engaging in trade on their own behalf. Such activities were not forbidden by Congress: this was how the consuls supported themselves.

After Yorktown it was evident that the Revolution was a success and that the United States of America would enter the ranks of established nations as a minor power. Congress, however, still showed little enthusiasm for setting its diplomatic and consular affairs in order. Conrad Alexandre Géard, the French minister to the United States, prodded Congress to end the makeshift arrangement for accepting consuls without a consular treaty. At last Congress instructed Franklin in Paris to negotiate a consular convention, including a proposed draft written by a three-man congressional committee, using a model based on the French consular service as suggested by the French minister. Congress did not overwhelmingly support the proposed consular convention; four of the thirteen states had not approved the draft. But at least Franklin had permission to proceed with negotiations.

With the war over, Franklin was anxious for Congress to send him a consul to ease his work. He must have thought that with a consular convention signed in Paris, Congress would quickly appoint consuls to help commerce abroad. Elias Boudinot, a member of Congress, encouraged Franklin's optimism when he wrote, "as far as I can judge of the peace establishment, it will be to employ two or three Ministers in Europe and those not higher in Character than Residents, or simply Minister – The business in other places to be done by Consuls. Our Finances are so very low as to require every economical measure."[14] Here was the nub of the matter governing consuls: they were cheaper than diplomats. All members of Congress recognized that since American ministers sent to foreign courts could not engage in private trade they had to be paid. But consuls could support themselves by trade and act as part-time consular officers, taking a small portion of the fees they charged.

Franklin had little difficulty with Charles Graves, Comte de Vergennes, the French minister of foreign affairs, in negotiating the consular convention. They signed the convention on 29 July 1784 in Paris. The pact was sent to Philadelphia for the expected swift approval by Congress.

Unfortunately, Franklin did not reckon on John Jay. At the time Franklin was completing the negotiations with Vergennes on the consular convention; Jay became the secretary of the Office for Foreign Affairs and played a major role in directing Congress on matters concerning treaties and conventions. Jay was no Francophile. His Huguenot forefathers had been forced out of France by the Bourbons, the family that still occupied the throne of France. While acting as minister to Spain, Jay had considered French consuls in the United States to be little more than spies and was not eager to legitimize their status.[15]

When Franklin's signed consular convention came into the hands of Jay for his recommendation to Congress on ratification,

Jay easily assumed the role of a lawyer attacking a contract detrimental to his client. There may have been some jealousy in the zeal with which Jay set upon Franklin's work. He had had a miserable time in Spain as the American minister, with little to show for his efforts. Franklin, on the contrary, was the darling of the French and was considered the premier American diplomat. It may have given Jay some satisfaction to make it appear that Franklin had erred in not conforming exactly to the instructions of Congress in negotiating the consular convention.

On 4 July 1786 Jay sent a long report to Congress pointing out the flaws of the consular convention in great detail. Much of Jay's attack amounted to quibbling, but he had a point. Congress's instructions included too much of the original French draft proposal. For example, French consuls were granted great authority in the United States and might have prevented French subjects from becoming American citizens. The upshot of Jay's report was that Congress rejected the Franco-American convention. [16]

The French were unhappy. After giving the United States years to work on a consular convention, not an earthshaking proposition, and having made what they must have considered one-sided concessions to Franklin, they were to have all this overturned by a Congress guided by the Francophobe Jay. The French foreign minister showed remarkable restraint in dealing with his volatile ally and awaited a new round of negotiations while French consuls, still in a legal limbo, went about their business in the thirteen states.

Thomas Jefferson replaced Franklin as minister to France in 1785 and, among other matters, waited for instructions from Congress for renegotiating the consular convention. [17] Congress moved in its usual deliberate manner. It was not until the summer of 1788, the last year of the Confederation and ten years after the Treaty of Amity and Commerce with France, that Jefferson was able to negotiate a new convention. In opening the negotiations Jefferson wrote the French foreign minister, by then the Count de Montmorin:

> We carry on commerce with good success, in all parts of the world, yet we have not a Consul in a single port, nor a complaint for the want of one, except from the persons who want to be consuls themselves. Though these considerations may not be strong enough to establish the absolute inutility of Consuls, they may make us less anxious to extend their privileges and jurisdictions, so as to render them objects

of jealousy, and irritation in the places of their residence. The English allow to foreign Consuls scarcely any functions within their ports. This proceeds, in great measure, from the character of their laws, which eye with peculiar jealousy, every exemption from their control. Ours are the same in their general character, and rendered still more unpliant by our having thirteen parliaments to relax, instead of one.[18]

Jefferson was an excellent negotiator; his studied indifference to the need for consuls made it easier to wring some major concessions from the French in the reworked consular convention. By November 1788 he reported that he had signed a convention with France that met the objections Jay had raised in 1784. Jefferson took away most of the coercive powers that the French consuls exercised over their subjects and vessels in the United States. He also took away the right of consuls to have their testimony unchallenged in courts. The consular convention was ratified under the brand-new Constitution by the brand-new Senate in 1789. The final pact had a more "American cast" in refusing to give too much power to government officials, a reflection of the recent colonial experience.

During the Confederation period the French had their consuls well placed in the various states to deal with the local governments and maintained a minister in the capital, New York. After the peace treaty of 1783 the British accepted John Adams as the American minister in 1785, but they did not reciprocate. Instead, British-American relations were left in the hands of a consul general and his subordinates, similar to what was done in the Barbary states. The British foreign minister, when asked about the lack of a British diplomat in the United States, remarked that if he sent one representative, he would have to send thirteen.[19] Despite the lack of a treaty between Great Britain and the United States regarding consuls, Congress accepted Consul General Sir John Temple in 1785, as it would "be proper for the United States, on this and every other occasion, to observe as great a degree of liberality as may consist with a due regard to their national honor and welfare".[20] A year later Britain sent a consul to deal with the mid-Atlantic states, while Temple stayed in New York.

The two major European powers, France and Great Britain, were making effective use of consuls within the United States, but Congress was not tempted to emulate them. The only American consul, Thomas Barclay, was diverted from France to negotiate a treaty with the emperor of Morocco, leaving Thomas Jefferson once again without consular help. John Adams, in London as minister, hoped that the acceptance of a British consul general to the United States would open the way for an American consul general in England with vice consuls in Scotland and Ireland. In writing to Jay, Adams noted, "Consuls and Vice Consuls are very useful to Ambassadors and Ministers in many ways that I need not explain to you. Consuls would explore new channels of commerce and new markets for our produce."[21] Adams, alas, was not to get any such assistance.

Jay had been asked by Congress in 1785 to report what his department considered the number of consuls necessary to give the United States adequate representation. He replied that it would be expedient to have consuls in Russia, Sweden, Denmark, Germany, the Netherlands, Britain, Ireland, France, Portugal, Spain, the Canaries, Madeira, and certain ports in the Mediterranean.[22] Congress asked the question, had its answer, then pigeonholed Jay's ideas and went on to other business.

The only exception to congressional indifference to a consular service was with China. Prior to the Revolution, American colonial trade had been directed toward the mother country, European ports, and the West Indies. British trade with China was in the hands of British trading companies, and colonials had little opportunity to expand their trade in that direction. Now, with independence, American traders were looking forward to new and lucrative markets in the Far East, important markets since trade with Great Britain and her remaining colonies had become difficult with American ships no longer part of the British system. With no commercial treaty to grant reciprocal privileges, the British could play the thirteen separate states against each other regarding trading rights. At a time when it was becoming clear to Yankee merchants and traders that British markets were not going to be as open as before the Revolution there was good news from the Far East. An American ship, the *Empress of China*, returned to New York in May 1785, after a successful trading voyage to Canton. As soon as the ship returned to port, the business agent of the ship, Samuel Shaw, wrote to John Jay. Shaw addressed the letter "for the information of the fathers of the country, an account of the reception their subjects have met with, and the respect with which their flag has been treated in that distant region."[23]

Shaw described his voyage and meeting with a French squadron that welcomed the ship and escorted it to Macao. There the French consul gave friendly assistance and congratulations to the Yankee crew on America's entering the China trade. In Canton Shaw found that Chinese merchants were quite receptive to the newcomers, but had some difficulty comprehending the distinction between Englishmen and Americans. The Chinese finally distinguished the Americans as the "new people."

Chinese authorities carefully controlled trading with outsiders. Canton was the only port open to foreign ships, and the Western merchants were confined to compounds, called factories, along the river. There was a brief trading season of several months, then all foreign merchants had to leave until the next year's season. The Chinese, fearing the spread of Western influence, kept tight control over the port and enforced their stern code of justice, including the dictum that "blood must answer for blood."[24]

While in Canton Shaw became a participant in a drama demonstrating this rule of Chinese law. An English ship in harbor had fired a salute to honor some guests, accidentally killing a Chinese bystander. The port authorities demanded the gunner for retribution. When the English resisted turning him over to certain death the Chinese seized a ship's officer who was in the city on business. The Europeans in the port armed themselves and demanded the return of the captive. The Chinese refused and brought up warships and troops. At this point the Chinese head magistrate asked for a deputation of all the trading nations except the English. Shaw joined the deputation as the representative from America, an act inaugurating the entry of the United States into Far Eastern affairs. In negotiations with the delegation the magistrate agreed that if the English turned over the gunner he would have an impartial trial, and if the killing were proved to be accidental, he would be released. The English saw no alternative and agreed. The seaman was eventually released.

Shaw noted in his letter that the English rather begrudgingly thanked the ex-colonial for his assistance in serving on the delegation. In contrast to the coolness of the British, there was harmony between the French and the Americans. This cordial relationship "was particularly noted by the English, who more than once observed, that it was a matter of astonishment to them that the descendants of Britons would so soon divest themselves of prejudices, which they had thought to be not only hereditary, but inherent in our nature."[25]

Jay sent Shaw's letter to Congress with the recommendation that a consul and vice consul be appointed to Canton, expressing his feeling that "such officers would have a degree of weight and respect which private adventurers cannot readily acquire, and which would enable them to render essential services to their countrymen."[26] Within ten days Samuel Shaw had a consular commission from Congress. Jay then asked that his friend Thomas Randall, another former artillery officer, be appointed vice consul for Canton, advising that his ship would be leaving shortly. The President and Congress responded with unaccustomed speed, and the new consul and vice consul sailed to Canton a week later. They were to serve "with neither salary nor perquisites but with the confidence and esteem of the United States."

The only other significant appointment the Continental Congress made to help American trade abroad was that of Oliver Pollock to replace Robert Smith as the commercial agent in Havana, which was the center of Spanish colonial rule in the Caribbean. Smith, a resident in Havana and recommended to Congress by Robert Morris,[27] had been appointed to the position during the Revolution in 1781. When Smith died two years later, Congress replaced him with Pollock, carefully stipulating that "no commercial agent of the United States in foreign ports shall be entitled to a salary, unless such salary is expressed in the resolution appointing the agent."[28] Congress did not so express.

Pollock had been a major figure in the Revolutionary War, purchasing ammunition from the Spanish for American troops. He had also been an advisor to Bernado De Gálvez, the Spanish governor of Louisiana, who had attacked the British once Spain entered the war. Pollock, acting as a purchasing agent for Congress, had extended his own credit to get crucial supplies and owed some $140,000, an immense sum for the time. Pollock had depended on Congress to repay him, but Congress was not responsive to his expectations. The appointment as commercial agent to Havana was considered to be a form of unpaid recompense to help Pollock make some money. The scheme did not work out. The Spanish, never enthusiastic about the upstart Americans, clamped down on their trade in Cuba and Louisiana, even throwing some American merchants into the Havana dungeon to discourage compromise. Congress protested and retaliated by passing in 1784 a resolution terminating the commercial agent's appointment to Havana. Pollock was shortly thereafter put in Spanish debtors' prison in New Orleans for eighteen months. Eventually Congress helped him pay his debts, and he became a successful trader in the West Indies.

Congress operated on the principle of avoiding problems whenever possible. Dealing with the rulers of the Barbary states ranked high on the list of problems to be avoided. There were really only three approaches for a government trying to protect its citizens from these scoundrels: pay a hefty tribute, maintain a strong naval presence off the North African coast, or keep one's citizens away from the area. In the first years of the Republic, Congress had little choice but to hope that American ships would not venture into the Mediterranean.

From the beginning of the Revolutionary War in 1776 the British took away the Mediterranean passes that had been issued to British and colonial ships to provide immunity from attack by Barbary corsairs. These passes were the result of a mix of British naval might and substantial "gifts" to the Barbary rulers by British consuls. Due to the Revolution American trade to the Mediterranean dwindled away. Because this trade recovered slowly after the war, there was a temporary easing of the pressure on Congress to deal with the Barbary problem. Nothing, however, inhibited the Yankee trader. American ships began to test out Mediterranean markets in Spain, France, and Italy. The British consul general in New York wrote John Jay in 1786 to warn him that many American ships were sailing with British passes counterfeited in Philadelphia, and that he could "but lament the misery that such of your mariners will probably meet with, should they, with such counterfeit passes, fall into the hands of the Barbary corsairs."[29]

The British consul general's insincere lament was a good example of the duplicity that permitted the Barbary pirates to ply their vocation for so long. The British were delighted to see their former colonial charges in difficulty because the protection of His Majesty King George III had been withdrawn. The harm dealt to the Americans was good for British trade. "What is bad for you is good for me." The result of this policy was that a growing number of American seamen were falling into the hands of Algerian, Tripolitan, and Moroccan masters. The Yankees were held for ransom and worked as slaves until ransom arrived or they died.

Congress asked its diplomatic agents abroad to see whether friendly countries could help the United States in dealing with the Barbary states. France and Spain initiated some contacts between American representatives and Barbary agents, but for the most part it was up to each country to make its own arrangements with each Barbary ruler, always to the ruler's advantage.[30]

The United States was fortunate in securing a favorable treaty with Morocco at a reasonable cost. For some reason the emperor of Morocco had shown particular friendship toward the new country across the Atlantic and as early as 1778 had forbidden his corsairs to attack American ships.[31] After the Revolution, in 1783, the emperor attempted to open negotiations for a treaty with the United States, but Congress was so slow in responding that Morocco seized an American ship, the *Betsey*, and held it to encourage Congress to get on with the treaty process.

At last, in 1785 Congress authorized its representatives in Europe, Adams and Jefferson, to negotiate treaties with all the Barbary states, appropriating $80,000 for this purpose. Adams and Jefferson sent Thomas Barclay, the American consul in France, to deal with the emperor of Morocco. Barclay's treaty of 1786 with the ruler of Morocco reflected the goodwill of that potentate toward the United States. While these negotiations used up $25,000 of the money allocated for all the Barbary states, Barclay's success was evidently worth the cost: no annual tribute was demanded, American ships were given safe passage by Moroccan corsairs, and American consuls had certain extraterritorial powers in Morocco.[32]

Congress commended Barclay for having done an excellent job as a negotiator. Since no American consul was sent to Morocco during the remaining years of the Confederation, Barclay appointed two members of the Chiappi family, Italians settled in Morocco, to serve as deputy consular agents in Mogador and Tangiers. Each of the Chiappis was already a consul in his respective district, one for Genoa and one for Venice. As an ad hoc arrangement the United States at least had experienced men to represent its interests.

Despite the high favor shown Barclay by Congress, soon after he returned to France from Morocco, he was arrested for debt. While acting as a consul and diplomatic agent, Barclay had continued his personal activities as a businessman. Creditors from his business endeavors had instigated the arrest. He was shortly released and returned to America. John Jay, writing from his Office of Foreign Affairs, confirmed that no American "Consuls should be exempt from Suits and Arrests for their own proper Debts," but he acknowledged that such arrest and imprisonment "must hurt the Feelings of the United States and in some degree would injure their Dignity."[33] Jay urged Barclay to settle his affairs so that he could return to France. Apparently the debts were discharged, since Barclay was later active again in Europe.

With the Moroccan treaty made, Congress hoped that similar treaties with Algiers, Tripoli, and Tunis would be forthcoming, but American diplomatic agents had no success. The cruel reality was that none of the other Barbary states had any interest in helping the United States; they only wanted as much tribute as they could extract. Congress under the Confederation simply could not raise the money necessary for tribute and ransom, nor was there money to try the "iron fist" approach, for there was no American navy to speak of. Because of this helpless situation Americans were falling into the rapacious hands of the Barbary rulers. Mediterranean trade under the Stars and Stripes was badly stunted, and there were no consuls in the respective quasi-hostile states to help their countrymen.

In looking back on the six years of the peacetime Confederation (1783–89) with regard to consular developments, one finds that they were sparse years indeed: one consul assigned to France (but he was either negotiating elsewhere or trying to stay out of debtors' jail), a consul and vice consul in Canton, a few commercial agents, one consular convention that was not even finally ratified until after the Confederation ended, and some foreign consuls operating on an interim arrangement in the United States.

Although there were but few concrete steps during this time toward developing an American consular service, the Confederation period was one of intense debate by Congress and its diplomatic agents abroad over the structure and role of consuls. Four of the major founding fathers, Franklin, Adams, Jefferson, and Jay, were especially concerned with laying the groundwork for the consular service, a foundation that was to last almost unchanged for over a century. Unfortunately, despite the talent concentrated upon the role and structure of the future consular service, the consular corps that emerged was defective by being nonprofessional and wide open to patronage and corruption. That despite its flaws it would work relatively well was due to the individual talents, dedication, and courage of most of the men selected to serve as American consuls abroad.

3

Birth of the Consular Service
(1789–1800)

One of the immediate beneficiaries of the new American constitutional form of government was the consular service. The Congress of the Confederation had refused to do more than make a few token appointments of consuls and consular agents. But in 1789, with the creation of an executive branch of government, there were now a President and a Secretary of State able to take the initiative in dealing with foreign affairs and commerce. Although it was not much noted at the time, the President and his Secretary of State presided over the start of an impressive expansion of one small branch of the new federal government, the consular service.

During Washington's administration the American army was kept at shadow strength, the navy was literally nonexistent, and the diplomatic service was limited to a few capitals. The consular service, however, spread itself throughout Europe, the West Indies, and North Africa and maintained its representation in China. .

Two factors caused this remarkable growth. The first was the appointment of Thomas Jefferson to the new position of Secretary of State, the ideal person to preside over the inauguration of the consular service. He was a man of great intellect and diverse interests with a practical experience in consular matters that no other figure in the formative years of the Republic had. Jefferson had served in France for five years and knew the value of consuls. Jefferson had successfully negotiated the first American consular convention with a foreign power; thus he understood both the domestic and foreign concerns that consular operations raised. As a congressman he had learned what was possible from that deliberative body and – more important – what was not possible. As a tobacco planter and former governor of Virginia, Jefferson was attuned to the dynamics of American trade abroad and knew how consuls could help that vital export trade. All this knowledge and experience were put to use as Jefferson shepherded the consular service through its early years.

The other reason for the growth of consular appointments in the first decade of the United States under the Constitution was that the service expanded without cost to the government. There were no attempts by Washington, Jefferson, or Congress to make the consular service into a professional body with salaries, rotation in posts, or promotion upward. It was agreed that the United States could have an adequate distribution of consuls abroad by using those who would serve for whatever compensation they might personally extract from their positions as consuls. It cost money to maintain an army or navy, but the American flag could be flying from consuls' offices throughout the world with little expense except that of the ink and paper to print their commissions. The only drawback to this favorable fiscal situation was that the men appointed were often not experienced or trained for their new positions.

The prodigious growth of the American consular service after the adoption of the Constitution is revealed in the listing of consular posts (in order of creation) in the first ten years of the new Republic (1790–99), showing the remarkable dispersion of these offices throughout the world of commerce. All positions given had the rank of consul unless otherwise noted. Approximately half of them were originally staffed by non-Americans.

> Canton, (Shaw reappointed), Island of Madeira, Liverpool, Dublin, Bordeaux, Nantes, Rouen, Island of Hispaniola, Martinique, Bilbao, Cowes (vice consul), Marseille (vice consul), Hamburg (vice consul), Le Havre (vice consul), London, Fayal (Azores) (vice consul), Surinam, Poole (vice consul), Island of St. Croix, Tangier, Copenhagen, Bristol, Lisbon, Algiers, Calcutta. Cadiz, Alicante, Curaçao, St. Eustatius (Netherlands Antilles), Demerara (Georgetown), Malaga, Amsterdam, Bremen, Franconia (Duchy of Franconia), Tenerife (Canary Islands), Isle de France (Mauritius), Gibraltar, Falmouth, St. Petersburg, Dunkirk, Morlaix, Leghorn, Tunis, Tripoli, Hull, Naples, Belfast, Cap François, Brest, Genoa, Trieste, Gothenburg, Aux

Cayes, New Orleans, St. Bartholomew, Rome, Rotterdam, Venice, Cork, Santo Domingo, Barcelona, Madrid, Stettin, Santiago de Cuba, Edinburgh, Cape Town, Port-au-Prince, Santander, La Guaira.[1]

This list of America's first consular posts not only demonstrates the early growth of the service but also shows where American trading and shipping interests lay in the 1790s. In contrast to the consular net cast by Thomas Jefferson and his immediate successors, by 1800 the United States had diplomats only in Paris, Berlin, The Hague, Lisbon, Madrid, and London. The French Foreign Ministry must have been amused when it received reports of the spread of the consular service that Thomas Jefferson had inaugurated, the same man who had noted "the absolute inutility of Consuls" when negotiating for the Franco-American consular convention.[2]

Not all consular posts were filled immediately. It took time for the men appointed to sail to their posts; some had second thoughts and did not go, leaving a post unfilled, sometimes for several years. But by the end of ten years the United States was well represented abroad by part-time consuls. It is worth noting that no American consuls were sent to the British possessions in Canada or to British islands, such as Jamaica, Bermuda, or the Bahamas. The British prohibited American trade with their colonies in the West Indies. There were, however, consulates in Cape Town and Calcutta. The Spanish to the south were also cool to American consular penetration of their colonial empire, limiting representation to Cuba and one post on the coast of Venezuela, La Guaira, while allowing the United States to have as many consuls as wanted in Spain. The rest of the Latin American continent, including the Portuguese possession of Brazil, was closed to American consuls. All the Middle East was terra incognita to the American consul. The United States had to deal with the Barbary powers but made little effort at this early stage to establish links to the rest of the Ottoman Empire. In the Far East Japan was barred to all but the Dutch.

The new Senate and House of Representatives took some time to enact the necessary legislation to guide consuls. Secretary of State Jefferson, becoming impatient, sent his consuls and vice consuls a message on 26 August 1790: "I expected ere this, to have been able to send you an act of Congress, prescribing some special duties and regulations for the exercise of the consular offices of the United States; but Congress not having been able to mature the act sufficiently, it lies over to their next session."[3] He asked the consuls to send him a report every six months on the number of American vessels entering their respective ports, giving a full description of the ships and cargoes. Consuls were to report on military preparations and indications of war. The consuls were to warn American ships of dangerous situations so that "they may be duly on their guard."[4] The consuls were asked to report political and commercial intelligence that would be of interest to the United States. Jefferson gave the consuls permission, without encouraging them, to wear the navy uniform: a deep-blue coat with red facings, lining, and slashed cuffs, a red waistcoat, blue breeches, yellow buttons with a fouled anchor, a black cockade, and a small sword.

Jefferson then gave some sound advice to his subordinates. "It will be best not to fatigue the government in which you reside, or those in authority under it, with applications in unimportant cases. Husband their good dispositions for occasions of some moment, and let all representations to them be couched in the most temperate and friendly terms, never indulging in any case whatever, a single expression which may irritate."[5]

In his second annual address to Congress, 8 December 1790, Washington tried to nudge that body into legislation concerning the consular service. "The patronage of our commerce, of our merchants and seamen, has called for the appointment of consuls in foreign countries. It seems expedient, to regulate by law, the exercise of that jurisdiction, and those functions which are permitted them, either by express convention, or by a friendly indulgence, in the places of their residence."[6]

Despite Jefferson's impatience, Washington's pleas, and the fact that a score of consuls were already at their posts waiting for legal status, Congress procrastinated, not enacting the necessary legislation until 14 April 1792. The 1792 act was to remain the basic legislation for the consular service for the next century. Some provisions of this act derived from the 1788 consular convention with France that put French consuls stationed in the United States on a legal basis.

The body of the 1792 act spelled out the duties of American consuls. These officials were to:

A. receive protests or declarations regarding American shipping matters;

B. take provisional possession of the estates of American citizens dying abroad if there were no legal representative present, and notify the Secretary of State of the death;

C. take charge of stranded American ships and endeavor to save them and their cargoes until the owners could take charge; and

D. collect certain fees for taking statements and holding and inventorying estates.

Section 5 of the act provided for salaries for consuls assigned to the Barbary States, not to exceed $2,000 per person. Congress, it seemed, at last realized that consuls to Morocco, Tunis, Tripoli, and Algiers would be fully occupied, with neither the time nor the opportunity to act as traders in those difficult posts.

Sections 7 and 8 of the 1792 act clearly detailed the duties of consuls assisting American seamen in cases of sickness, shipwreck, or captivity, all common occurrences in those days. They were to provide for the care of such men stranded in their districts at a rate not to exceed twelve cents per day, which the U.S. government would provide. Consuls might require the masters of American ships to take on stranded seamen for transport back to the United States if they were bound in that direction. They were given sanction to fine those masters who refused. Consuls were to supervise the sale of any American ship in their districts to assure that the seller be provided enough money from the sale to send the crew home.[7]

From the beginning American consuls were set apart from American diplomats in that they had judicial duties prescribed by law regarding notarial acts and estates and what amounted to police functions over American shipowners and their masters. American diplomats did not have these responsibilities. If there was a conflict between a minister and a consul over a legal matter involving consular duties, the judgment of the consul was to supersede, a fact that did not always please an aggressive minister. For the most part, however, American ministers (and later ambassadors) and their secretaries were only too happy to concern themselves with court life and leave estates, shipping, and other such business to their consuls.

The Consular Act of 1792 contains nothing about assisting distressed American civilians abroad, but the care of seamen was spelled out in detail. Even in the laissez-faire time of the early Republic it was recognized that sailors needed special care and treatment, almost as wards of the government. On board a ship the master and his mates were absolute rulers; there was no challenge to this right by Congress. But the American government and other seafaring nations had to be concerned when their seamen were stranded without money on an alien shore. Foreign governments were wary of penniless alien sailors in their port cities, for these restless men often wound up in jail. Sailors were always vulnerable because they had to depend upon captains who were often irresponsible in paying them and seeing that they got home. Sailors were well known for squandering their money at the first port of call and then depending on someone to help them out, usually the consul.

The period from 1790 to 1815 was a time when the services of consuls abroad were most needed to help American seamen and shipping. For most of that time France and Britain were waging a battle for naval supremacy over the shipping lanes of the world. In such battles neutral ships were often the prime victims. Good money was to be made by merchants who could slip a ship through a blockade. Even if only one of several ships sent off made it to a belligerent port, the profit would be such as to make the enterprise worthwhile. The real loser in this game of "break the blockade" often was the ordinary seaman of a neutral country.

The rules of blockade were that a neutral ship could be stopped at sea by belligerent naval vessels or privateers, its papers and cargo could be examined, and if it were found that the ship was going to or from an enemy port or carrying a cargo that was contraband or of enemy origin, the ship could be taken as a prize. Prizes were taken to friendly ports where a prize court would determine if the ship had indeed been a legitimate prize; if so, ship and cargo were confiscated, and the cargo was sold to the highest bidder, with some of the prize money going to the crew of the capturing vessel. Prizes were lucrative, and captains were not overly scrupulous in selecting ships to be taken. Crews of seized ships were thrown upon the shore destitute.

American consuls in Britain, France, and other European countries and in the West Indies spent much of their time representing American shipping interests at prize courts and helping the crews of confiscated ships return to the United States, where they usually signed on another vessel to try again. Because of shifting alliances and varying periods of peace and war, the consul was important to the master of an American vessel. The consul could explain the existing situation to a master who might have been months at sea, a vital service for a man who had to decide whether or not to sail for certain ports. Consuls could give informed estimates of where the naval forces and privateers of belligerents might be active and hence of areas to be avoided.

The newly appointed American consuls arrived on the international scene at a time of great turbulence in shipping and commerce due to the French-English hostilities, and they also had to deal with unrest or even war within their consular districts. One of the first consuls to find himself in a difficult post was Fulwar Skipwith. Only twenty-five, a scion of one of the old Virginia families, Skipwith was better prepared for consular duties than many of his older colleagues, for at twenty-one he had been busy in the tobacco trade both in Richmond and London, where he acted for Virginian tobacco merchants.[8] After a fire had destroyed his trading company and left him in strained financial circumstances, Skipwith spent some time in Paris. He needed a position to help him regain his financial standing after the disastrous fire and seized upon the new consular service as the answer. By the time he applied for a consular appointment, Skipwith was fluent in French and well acquainted with the European scene. He wrote Jefferson, describing his present position as "a gloomy one, & leads me to seek for favours which I had hoped to have lived without."[9] He asked for a consular appointment to Lisbon, Bordeaux, Cadiz, or Marseille, but received instead a commission as consul to the island of Martinique in the French West Indies.

In no position to refuse, Skipwith sailed for Martinique in 1790, arriving just in time to experience the turmoil there that had rippled out from Paris starting from the fall of the Bastille the year before. The new American consul was more or less dumped on the unfriendly shores of Martinique with no official status because the colonial French governor would not recognize Skipwith as consul, not having received instructions from the Foreign Ministry in Paris, which was otherwise occupied. But Skipwith was expected by the Secretary of State to report on the effects of the French Revolution both on the island and on the other nearby French possessions. He was also to record the claims of Americans losing property or goods because of the upheaval on the islands and to generate goodwill toward the United States.[10] Moreover, he was warned not to take sides in the fighting between the forces of the French government and wealthy planters and those of the revolutionaries or "patriotic party."[11]

Skipwith had hoped that as consul he would be salaried, but Secretary of State Jefferson disabused him of that idea.[12] The American consul was expected to support himself by acting as an agent for American firms dealing with Martinique; but, with what amounted to a civil war going on in the French West Indies, prudent merchants were reluctant to risk their ships and cargoes. Skipwith's case was a clear example of the difficulty of using part-time, unpaid consuls. The more dangerous the situation, the more American interests needed consular support; yet as political situations got worse, there were fewer opportunities for a consul to earn a living.

Jefferson was unsympathetic to the pleas of consuls for pay. He wrote the U.S. consul in Santo Domingo: "Those appointments are given to gentlemen who are satisfied to perform their duties in consideration of the respect and accidental advantages they may derive from them. When the consideration ceases to be sufficient, the government cannot insist on a continuance of service because this would found claims which it does not mean to authorize."[13]

Skipwith took care of what business he had, but unable to make a living, he left Martinique in 1794 while the government and patriotic forces were still fighting. A British privateer captured the American ship on which he was bound for the United States and seized his private papers. Using his experience as a consular officer, Skipwith managed to help the stranded American crew return home.[14] Not discouraged by the dangers he had faced or the lack of pay, Skipwith set off for Paris a year later as the new American consul general, where he was to remain for fourteen years of revolution and reaction.

By 1793, when France declared war on England and Holland, the European situation had become dangerous for American seamen. The belligerents seized neutral ships dealing with their enemies. Joseph Fenwick, the American consul in Bordeaux, did what he could to help stranded American seamen off ships taken by French privateers, or those who were held by the French government. He was able to get the American brig Sally released after its capture by a privateer. This was unusual, for there seldom was a reprieve for seized American ships.[15]

Consular business in Bordeaux involved distressed seamen and the problems of privateers, but the consul also had to attend to more mundane tasks such as making inventories of the effects of deceased Americans, a tedious task; in one case Fenwick listed "five flowerpots and forty two snuff boxes."[16] He was also chairman of an inquest on the death by beating of a ship's cook by his captain, with other American merchant captains idled in Bordeaux at the time sitting on the inquest panel. The panel's decision was to send the murderer back to the United States under arrest.[17]

Fenwick, feigning optimism, wrote that the problems with the French might have resulted from the "new organization rather than the want of good will."[18] The attitude of the French did not improve toward neutrals, especially the United States, which was considered a fat goose that could be plucked with impunity by French officials and French privateers. This would eventually push the United States and France into their quasi-war of 1798–1800.

The new consular service quickly proved its worth to the United States. American shipping firms and captains were able to get accurate information regarding foreign markets, regulations, and the dangers of war and piracy, as well as legal support, from their consuls in major ports. The secretary of state received reports on local political conditions and trading opportunities and advice on foreign policy matters from experienced men in the field at a time when the European scene was in a dangerous state of flux. The U.S. consular service was given little time to settle into the routine of new work before some of its officers became active participants in the naval war with France (1798–1800) and then the Barbary Wars (1800–1805).

Frustrated by their inability to challenge the British fleet directly, the French unleashed swarms of privateers and exercised little control over their actions, especially those that working out of the French West Indies. American ships were the easy targets of those privateers, as they rarely traveled in convoys and there was no protective American navy.

Indicative of the bad situation, from July 1796 to June 1797 some 316 American ships were seized by the French.[19] Although British privateers were also taking American ships; the French were far more effective and dangerous. Sometimes American consuls could help, but not often. The consul in Marseille, a French citizen, reported that he had secured the release of the American ship Flora of Gloucester, which had been taken by a French privateer owned by Lucien Bonaparte,"a brother of the great General Buonoparte [sic]" .[20] In doing his duty, this Frenchman acting for American interests against those of the powerful Corsican family was taking an obvious political risk.

Although President John Adams tried to settle American difficulties with the French by diplomacy, French Foreign Minister

Talleyrand demanded a bribe from the special envoys Adams had sent in 1797. This incident, dubbed the XYZ affair, caused considerable outrage in the United States when it became public, strengthening the hands of those who wanted to re-create the United States Navy, which had been dormant since the Revolution. The first positive result was that a number of frigates were commissioned.

The young United States Navy and the consular service were often involved in mutual activity that fostered a strong alliance. In times of peace the American consul in a port was surely heartened to see a warship enter the harbor flying the Stars and Stripes. The round of official calls between the naval vessel and the local authorities helped the standing of the American consul. For many foreign officials and civil leaders in Europe and elsewhere the United States was as yet a little-known country. A well-turned-out warship represented a country to be reckoned with. The American consul became more important in their eyes. American naval officers benefited from the consul's services. He helped them resupply their ships, introduced them to the social delights of the port city after perhaps months at sea, and could get their crews out of the hands of the local authorities if they overindulged in celebrating their shore leave.

In time of unrest or war the close proximity of a frigate might relieve a consul's mind and make his work easier as the protector of American interests. Mobs had far more respect for cannon than for consular credentials. Local authorities understood the threat a hostile ship presented to the city's commerce. If a situation came to the worst, the American naval ship could pluck the consul and his family out of danger.

For the captain of an American naval ship, a consul available in a trouble spot was a godsend. Naval commanders out of touch with their superiors for months at a time and often politically unskilled might find almost insurmountable difficulties upon arriving in a foreign port where there was tension, civil unrest, or war. As a commander, the captain was expected to show initiative in protecting American interests, usually shipping. The ability to consult with the consul on the scene eased his burden and his responsibility.

During the time of the American difficulties with the French, the island of Santo Domingo (then called St. Dominique) was of major importance to the United States because of its sugar trade and its controlling position in the Caribbean. As the United States flexed its new naval muscles to put down the French privateers and any regular French naval vessels that might intervene, it was the obvious policy to deny those privateers haven in Caribbean harbors as well as to catch them at sea.

In 1791 there had been a bloody insurrection against the French colonial planters in the part of Santo Domingo that now comprises Haiti. After some ineffectual efforts to put the European overseers back in control, the French in Paris, inspired by their new motto "*liberté, egalité, et fraternité*," had made the African inhabitants of the island full citizens. They had been led by Toussaint L'Ouverture, who steered an independent course but never declared independence from French colonial rule.

At this time the United States had moved closer to the British as the French privateers had become more ferocious. Nowhere was the cooperation between the two former enemies more in evidence than in the West Indies, especially in dealing with Toussaint. The new American consul to Santo Domingo, Dr. Edward Stevens of Pennsylvania, arriving in 1799 under instructions from the Secretary of State, proceeded to give Toussaint support to preserve his virtual independence from France.[21]

Stevens consulted often with the British general in command in the West Indies, and by agreement with the local British naval commander the American consul was allowed to grant passes to ships going through the British blockade.[22] France, uneasy with the independence of Toussaint, supported an uprising against him. The leader Riguard, had encouraged French privateers, while Toussaint had kept the ports he controlled clear of these semi-pirates. The United States took the side of Toussaint, as did the British.

Stevens was in a sensitive political situation. He must further American interests without interfering with British, French, Haitian, or even American naval activities. Toussaint needed to have supplies come to his island. The French merchants were concerned that the American navy was scaring away neutral trading ships. Stevens worked closely with the United States Navy, including the captain of the Constitution, to "quiet the Apprehensions of the People here, and prevent any interruptions of Harmony between this Colony and the U. States."[23]

Fortunately, Stevens got on well with Toussaint, finding the black leader "so candid - so prudent & liberal that we will do everything that can contribute to supporting the Dignity & Interest of the U. States. It is a happy circumstance for me to have a man of his Character to cooperate with."[24] Cooperation between the United States and Toussaint became increasingly close, with

Stevens lending a small American ship under his control to take Toussaint to his army on the coast. Later the American frigate General Greene actually helped force the surrender of Riguard's troops by bombarding the forts at the town of Jacmel in February 1800.[25] Secretary of State Pickering recognized Consul Stevens's difficult role and wrote him that his work on the troubled island was "distinguished by that intelligence and attention to the interests of the United States which were expected when you accepted your appointment."[26]

By the end of 1800 the situation in Santo Domingo had calmed down for a while with Toussaint in full control. The quasi-war with France also began to wind down after Napoleon became first consul in France and was in all but name the new French monarch. The new first consul saw no point in needlessly antagonizing a major neutral, at least at that time.

4

The Barbary Consuls
(1794–1815)

Several years prior to the deterioration of relations with France that led to outright naval hostilities, the United States had made settlements of sorts with the Barbary States. The pressure on the President and Congress to remedy the intolerable condition was severe and getting worse, when in 1794 the United States entered into a second round of negotiations with Algiers, then the most powerful state on the Barbary Coast. The diplomatic process was slow, difficult, and painful, since it required the payment of tribute. Without this annual "payoff" no American shipping could be safe, no captives released, and no consuls installed. American ships were being taken in the Mediterranean and the Atlantic. Not only were ships and cargoes lost, but Americans were captured and used as slaves in the Barbary ports.

Responding to the concerns of shipping interests and the pleas of the families of those Americans held as slaves, President Washington authorized David Humphreys, his minister to Portugal, to see what he could do to bring about peace with Algiers and have the American captives released. At the same time Washington asked Congress to authorize the building of a navy, comprising six frigates, in case military force became necessary.

An approach to the Algerians had been made two years earlier in 1792, when Secretary of State Jefferson appointed the Revolutionary War naval hero John Paul Jones, then residing in Paris, to be the consul in Algiers.[1] He was authorized to go as high as $25,000 to negotiate a peace agreement with that state, a laughable sum when compared to what it actually cost the United States several years later. But by the time his commission arrived in France, Jones was dead. The commission was then transferred to Consul General

Thomas Barclay in Paris, who had previously served as the successful negotiator with Morocco, but he too died before he could set sail for Algiers. The ill-fated commission then devolved upon David Humphreys, minister to Portugal. Humphreys' attempt to negotiate with the dey of Algiers was a complete failure. According to the Swedish consul acting as intermediary, the dey would not receive Humphreys because of pending peace treaties with the Dutch and Portuguese. That ruler could not afford to be at peace with the United States at the same time.[2] The dey needed employment for his corsairs, because if there was no prospect of booty and slaves, they might turn on him. Humphreys conceded at this point.

Two years later Humphreys was to try again, this time with permission to expend up to $800,000 for a treaty and ransom of the American captives, a more realistic sum than the $25,000 allocated before.[3] Humphreys recruited Joseph Donaldson to carry on the negotiations in Algiers and Joel Barlow in Paris to help Humphreys get French support. Acting as an intermediary between Donaldson and the dey was a captive slave, James Cathcart, one of the first Americans to fall into the hands of the Algerians. He had been captured in 1785. In fact, Cathcart had been captured twice, once as a young midshipman on an American naval vessel taken by the British in the Revolutionary War. He escaped from the British, but not from the Algerians. He had worked his way up in the slave hierarchy, starting as a keeper in the dey's zoo, then moving through the clerical ranks. He was manager of the prison tavern until he became chief Christian secretary to the dey.[4] Cathcart was fluent in Arabic and privy to the dey's confidence, which made him a useful ally. He also had a personal stake in the negotiations; he would be one of the first freed if things went well for the American side.

The treaty and ransom for the captives were not cheap; the United States paid a total of $642,500 and an annual tribute of $21,600 in naval stores.[5] The treaty, sent back to America, was ratified by the Senate in March 1796 but could not go into effect until the dey had his tribute in hand, to be paid in gold and silver coins. To obtain the money as soon as possible, the dey sent another American slave, Richard O'Brien, to collect it from the Barings, British bankers, who had the note of the United States. Unfortunately, because of the unsettled conditions in Europe at the time, the Barings did not have the necessary specie on hand. O'Brien then went to Humphreys for instructions and was sent scouting for specie among Italian bankers.

The dey threatened to renew hostilities if he did not get his money at once. Joel Barlow, who had been working with Humphreys in Paris, hurried down to Algiers with gifts he had bought on behalf of the United States to present to the dey as part of the treaty; Barbary rulers insisted on their douceurs, lavish "sweeteners" before they would sign any agreement.

Barlow was one of a series of remarkable Americans who were to serve as consular officers on the Barbary Coast during the early days of the Republic. A graduate of Yale College and a classmate and lifelong friend of Noah Webster, the lexicographer, Barlow was a leading intellectual and a poet well known as a political and social critic of his time. He went to France in 1788 primarily to sell land in Ohio to Frenchmen. He was popular in intellectual circles, both in England and France, but he had little success as a land salesman. Excited by the ferment in France after the Revolution, he wrote several political tracts that led to his being made a French citizen. He even ran, unsuccessfully, for a seat in the Chamber of Deputies.[6]

David Humphreys, also a Yale graduate and mentor of Barlow's, sought to draw Barlow back into the orbit of his native country by recruiting his help with the Algerian negotiations. In Algiers Barlow quickly put the treaty process in its proper framework as he reported to the Secretary of State on the dey and his principal officers. He noted that the Algerians' pattern in making a treaty was to allow the nation to enjoy free navigation for a time, and then make a frivolous or unjust excuse for abrogating the treaty. Thereupon the cycle would recommence with the "offending" nation paying enormous tribute to the dey in order to restore peace and free use of the seas. Even England and France, whose naval strength exempted them from this cycle, deemed it expedient to spend great amounts of money on "occasional presents."[7] It was Barlow's opinion that no peace with Algiers would last more than seven years.

Despite his justified pessimism about the duration of any peace, Barlow had to deal with the immediate problem. There were about a hundred American captives to be redeemed. If the treaty were rejected due to the lack of specie to pay for it, the cost, Barlow believed, would be greater the next time the Americans came to deal with the dey, and by that time more Americans would have been captured.[8] In desperation and responding to hints emanating from the ruler's court, Barlow offered the dey a thirty-six-gun frigate to be built in America to be "presented to his daughter" if the dey would delay for six months more before abrogating the treaty, with the expectation that the tribute would arrive before that time.[9] Barlow made other commitments, including increasing the traditional "consular present" given to the rulers when a new consul arrived from $17,000 to $27,500.[10] He won the extension of time and the treaty. The dey got his gold and silver coins, and eventually his daughter became the owner of a brand-new frigate, the *Crescent*. The American prisoners were released, including Cathcart and O'Brien, and, for the time being, the Algerian corsairs preyed on ships of other nations.

Getting the money to the dey, even when it had been collected from Italian bankers, was not without difficulty. O'Brien, who was still technically a slave of the dey, was finally able to put together the agreed sum and set sail for Algiers, but his ship was captured by a Tripolitan corsair and released only after some delay on the part of the pasha of Tripoli, who must have lusted after his brother ruler's gold and silver but did not dare to cross him."[11]

Barlow's achievements in signing a treaty with Algiers, obtaining the release of the captive Americans, and gaining permission to have an American consul in residence in Algiers, were significant, but the cost was immense. Ransoms, presents, and other forms of tribute came to almost a million dollars. Even more, a dangerous precedent was set in equipping the dey's fleet with a powerful frigate. The other rulers of the Barbary States, the emperor, pasha, bey, and dey all had daughters who might want their own frigates. Frigates would figure in future negotiations with other rulers and their successors. A thirty-six-gun frigate was a powerful warship for a small country. The 1794 naval bill Washington had sponsored to give the United States a navy (if the Algerian negotiations broke down) called for four forty-four-gun and two thirty-six-gun frigates, and that was the total navy. What Barlow had done was to arm Algiers better than his own country, since Congress had stipulated that its naval construction was to cease if there was an Algerian peace.

While negotiations were dragging on in Algiers, there was a threat that the peace made with Morocco in 1787 by Thomas Barclay would fall apart. The emperor had died, and after a fight for the succession was followed by his son Mulcy Soliman. The new emperor asked for tribute. The Secretary of State delegated James Simpson, his consul in Gibraltar, to deal with the new ruler. Simpson sailed across the Straits to Morocco with gifts for the emperor, mostly military equipment such as cannons, small arms, and gunpowder, but refused to consider annual tribute.[12] Good fortune was again on the side of the United States in dealing with Morocco, for the emperor was called away from his negotiations to deal with an insurrection elsewhere in his country. To settle the matter before leaving, the emperor told Simpson: "The Americans, I find, are the Christian nation my father, who is in glory, most esteemed. I am the same with them as my father was; and I trust they will be so with me."[13] He thereupon agreed to the renewal of the favorable 1787 treaty, which did not call for tribute. Simpson was then moved from Gibraltar to Morocco in order that the Americans might have a consular presence there.

Having made a new Algerian treaty and having renewed the Moroccan treaty, the United States turned next to the Barbary state of Tripoli. President Washington commissioned David Humphreys to negotiate the treaty. Humphreys passed the commission to Joseph Donaldson and Joel Barlow, who in turn commissioned O'Brien, the recently released slave of the dey of Algiers.

Richard O'Brien was born in Maine, but as a child his family took him to Ireland. When his father, died he went to sea at an early age and during the American Revolution served both on as a privateer and in the Continental navy as a lieutenant. After the war he became the master of a ship out of Philadelphia, which was captured in 1785 by the Algerians. As with Cathcart, his fellow slave, O'Brien worked his way into the esteem of his Algerian masters, becoming a supervisor in the port's naval yard.[14] During the negotiations with the United States the dey trusted O'Brien's integrity and sent him to Europe to bring home the tribute.

In bargaining with the pasha in Tripoli, O'Brien drew upon all the skills he had acquired in his ten years of captivity in Algiers. The Tripolitan ruler was familiar with the dey's success in extracting money from the Americans, but did not have as powerful a fleet of corsairs or nearly as many American prisoners as the Algerian. A treaty in 1796 was agreed upon at a cost to the United States of approximately $57,000.[15] Although the negotiation seemed cheap, compared to the nearly one million dollars paid to the Algerians, the treaty with Tripoli soon collapsed. For years the United Slates engaged in an off-and-on war with Tripoli.

Barlow, the American consul in Algiers, took on the negotiations with the bey of Tunis, who rejected Barlow's offer of as much as $80,000 to conclude a peace, but through an intermediary an agreement was reached at a cost to the United States of about $107,000.

There were problems with parts of the treaty and in 1798 the Senate required certain modifications. The negotiators tasked with settling the American objections to the treaty were James Cathcart, now the new American consul to Tripoli, and William Eaton, a new man to the Barbary Coast, who had been appointed consul to Tunis. After much haggling, Cathcart and Eaton received the dey's reluctant agreement to alterations in the Tunisian treaty, which the Senate approved in 1800.[16]

The year 1800 saw U.S. consuls established in Morocco, Tripoli, Algiers, and Tunis and the Barbary corsairs under instructions to refrain from capturing American ships. The work of the American consuls on the Barbary Coast, however, remained difficult. Joel Barlow had left Algiers, succeeded by Richard O'Brien as supervising consul general for the Barbary States. The Barbary rulers were not comfortable with Cathcart and O'Brien, who, because of their years of slavery, were far more knowledgeable about Barbary ways than their European consular counterparts. Both spoke fluent Arabic and presumably knew some embarrassing secrets, which made them formidable representatives of the United States. The two ex-slaves turned consuls detested each other. O'Brien was a rough-and-ready, self-educated seafaring man who had worked his way up in the dey's shipyards, while Cathcart, better educated, had risen in the ruler's administrative ranks as a clerk. Eaton and Cathcart looked down upon O'Brien; having him as their consul general did not enhance the relationship among the three, especially as both Eaton and Cathcart had hot tempers and were difficult to work with.[17] The tension created by their relative social positions was not lessened when O'Brien married an Englishwoman who had been a maidservant in Cathcart's household.[18]

The work of the consuls was difficult since peace treaty commitments rested lightly with the Barbary rulers. They were continually testing the Americans and the consuls of other nations to see what they could extract from them as tribute or gifts. Going to war with a nation was a purely economic decision; a pretext could always be found. As the youngest maritime nation and with almost no navy, the United States was a particular target for the whims of the various rulers, agreeing to stiff tribute payments, especially to Algiers. There were a growing number of American merchant ships ripe for the plucking in the Mediterranean and the approaching waters.

A serious incident occurred in September 1800 when the American frigate *George Washington*, fresh from the quasi-war with France, appeared at Algiers, carrying the annual tribute. The dey needed to send an ambassador to Constantinople with gifts to maintain the sultan's favor. Arrogantly, the dey demanded that the *George Washington* carry his ambassador with gifts to the Sublime Porte. Consul General O'Brien and Captain William Bainbridge of the frigate at first refused, but the situation was precarious. The *George Washington* had unsuspectingly moored and was vulnerable if the capricious ruler were to order an attack, which would surely bring an end to the costly peace that had taken so long for the United States to achieve.

Bowing to *force majeure,* Bainbridge took the Algerian ambassador to Constantinople, flying the Algerian banner instead of the American flag as he entered that port. Still, it was the first U.S. naval vessel to call at that port. When the *George Washington* returned with the ambassador, Bainbridge prudently anchored out of range of the dey's batteries. The Jefferson administration, which had recently come to power, quite properly considered the commandeering of the *George Washington* as a major humiliation to the United States. The Secretary of the Navy warned Consul General O'Brien not to let such a thing happen again.[19] American patience was running out.

In the spring of 1801, with the French naval war over, the United States sent its first naval squadron, consisting of four ships under Commodore Richard Dale, to the Mediterranean to show the flag and demonstrate that America was not an eagle without talons. The squadron of observation, as it was termed, arrived at Gibraltar only to learn that the pasha of Tripoli had declared war on the United States. The pasha had increased his demands on Consul Cathcart for more tribute and, getting nowhere, had decided that war would be more profitable. Cathcart reported to the secretary of state that the pasha "declared war against the United States and would take down our flag staff on Thursday the 14th inst. of May 1801. That if I pleased to remain in Tripoli I should be treated with respect but if I pleased I might so go away."[20] Cathcart left after the pasha's men chopped down the consular flagpole as a symbolic gesture, meaning that a state of war existed between Tripoli and America. The pasha unleashed his corsairs, two of which were shortly trapped in the port of Gibraltar by the arrival of the American squadron of observation.

Before proceeding to Tripoli, Commodore Dale stopped in Tunis. The arrival of the small squadron was fortuitous for Consul

Eaton because the dey had been demanding more military equipment and threatening war if he did not get it. The presence of the American frigates stilled the demands for a time.[24] Off Tripoli Dale communicated with the pasha through the Danish consul but was unable to settle matters. A few Tripolitans were captured and exchanged for some American prisoners, but when Dale ran short of supplies, he sailed back to Gibraltar. This was to be the pattern for most of the war with Tripoli. Although the pasha did not have the ships to challenge the American fleet, the United States Navy could not keep a tight blockade on Tripoli because of frequent storms and the need to replenish supplies. There were some ship actions when American naval vessels encountered corsairs in the Mediterranean. The United States Navy always triumphed in these skirmishes, but Tripoli was not mortally wounded.

At the beginning of this war, William Eaton in Tunis, declared that Tripoli was blockaded, a declaration that for a time kept Tunisian ships from supplying Tripoli. It soon became apparent that this was only a paper blockade, for Dale's ships were in Gibraltar. Not only was Eaton bluffing the Tunisians with a blockade that did not exist, he was hatching a plot with Cathcart to unseat the pasha of Tripoli. The pasha's brother Hamet could claim the rulership if his brother Yusuf were deposed.[22] The prospect of using Hamet to get rid of Yusuf was first raised by Eaton and Cathcart in the spring of 1802. Nothing came of the idea at that time, but the seed had been planted back in the new Capitol in Washington.

The Tripolitan war was to drag on until 1805. The American consuls in Morocco, Algiers, and Tunis were busy trying to keep their respective rulers friendly, not an easy task since the sporadic activity of the United States Navy was interfering with their trade with Tripoli. For example, in 1802 the Emperor of Morocco asked the American Consul James Simpson to allow him to send grain to Tripoli since the Moroccans had a surplus and a profit was to be made. Simpson tried to get the naval commander to permit this breach of the less-than-complete blockade. The commodore's reply was that a blockade was a blockade.[23] The Emperor responded with a declaration of war, but withdrew the declaration after receiving presents from the United States. Later, when the blockade was temporarily abandoned, the Emperor was able to ship grain to Tripoli.

The American consuls in the Barbary States and the Mediterranean ports of Spain, France, and Italy came up against an American trait that plagues consuls to this day. Freeborn Americans do not take kindly to officials of their government telling them what to do, even if it is for their own good. The consuls desperately wanted to keep American merchant ships out of the reach of the corsairs from Tripoli and warned them away. Americans held captive in the pasha's prison would strengthen the pasha's hand, prolong the war, and make negotiations that much more difficult and expensive. The masters of American ships resented the advice of their consuls and continued to be captured by Tripoli.

There were changes in the consular ranks on the Barbary Coast. In 1802 O'Brien left Algiers, and James Cathcart, more or less at loose ends when he had to leave Tripoli, was named as his replacement. The dey of Algiers would not accept Cathcart, claiming that his character was not suitable, which may have meant that the dey did not want someone as familiar with the Algerian scene as the former chief Christian clerk. When Eaton, who was always difficult, was ordered out of Tunis by the dey because of a dispute over money, he designated George Davis, a doctor off a U.S. naval vessel, to be acting consul. Later the Secretary of State sent Tobias Lear to relieve O'Brien, who remained along with Cathcart as an advisor to the navy.

Lear was experienced, having served as consul at Santo Domingo, replacing Edward Stevens. Prior to his first appointment as consul, Lear had been George Washington's private secretary for the last seven years of the leader's life (1792–99). He had the distinction of marrying two of Martha Washington's nieces (the first niece died prior to his marriage to the second).[24]

Lear arrived in Algiers at a critical time. Disaster had struck the American cause. In October 1803 the thirty-six-gun frigate *Philadelphia* ran aground under the guns of the pasha of Tripoli while chasing a Tripolitan ship. The captain was compelled to surrender. The pasha had three hundred American naval officers and seamen as his prisoners and a frigate at his disposal. Later, in a daring exploit, young Lieutenant Stephen Decatur and a small crew of seamen were able to slip past the pasha's guards and set fire to the *Philadelphia*, destroying it. But the pasha still had his American captives, an advantage that weighed heavily in later negotiations.

The American fleet made several efforts to bombard the pasha into a peace treaty, but with little success, although the blockade became more effective as the number of American naval ships in the Mediterranean increased. While these actions were taking place, the former consul to Tunis, William Eaton, had turned to the United

States (after the dey had expelled him) to push his and Cathcart's plan for a land campaign against Tripoli, using the pasha's brother Hamet as the lever. Hamet, however, proved an ineffectual tool on which to base any political scheme or military campaign, for he was indecisive, willing one day to compromise with his brother, ready the next to unseat him.

Eaton was a man of determination who had worked his way up in the small American army, performing some difficult missions that earned him the attention of Secretary of State Timothy Pickering, who appointed him consul in Tunis. In the United States, Eaton won the approval of President Jefferson to pursue his plan to use Hamet, but if Samuel Barron, the naval commander in the Mediterranean, thought it practical.

Barron, caught by some of Eaton's enthusiasm, helped him launch one of the strangest campaigns ever sponsored by the United States. Eaton, now a "naval agent," landed in Egypt with a squad of U.S. marines, money, and weapons to help recruit an army, which was made up of about 300 Arabs, 38 Greeks, and a few men of other nationalities, giving him a force of around 400. Hamet was reluctantly persuaded to join. The bellicose Eaton then attacked Tripoli from the rear, driving this motley army across 500 miles of almost impassable desert. At one point there was an attempted mutiny; Eaton personally beheaded the ringleaders, which inspired his men to continue the march. His campaign reached a climax when he took the Tripolitan town of Derne from the rear while a squadron of American ships bombarded it from the sea. [25]

As a military march this was a magnificent achievement and earned immortality in the phrase "to the shores of Tripoli" in the well-known "Marines' Hymn". As a military campaign it was a more modest accomplishment; Eaton and his little army were soon besieged in Derne and were dependent on American naval support to keep from being overwhelmed.

While "General" Eaton was conducting his cross-desert campaign, Commodore Barron and Consul General Lear were examining more coldblooded options for peace. To them it became apparent that Hamet was a person too weak to support with any expectation that he could last as a ruler; he would be useless as the keystone for building a foundation of peace. The 300 captives off the *Philadelphia* were in jeopardy with Yusuf threatening to kill them, which probably was a bluff, but it was unwise to risk so many American lives. For his part, the pasha was ready to come to some sort of an agreement; he found that the Americans were taking his declaration of war far more seriously than had the Europeans. Even worse, the war was dragging on with that madman Eaton attacking from across the desert.

Lear and the Pasha Yusuf, after some negotiations using the Spanish consul in Tripoli as intermediary, reached an agreement in June 1805. The treaty called for the exchange of all prisoners, a payment to Yusuf of $60,000 because he had more Americans than the United States Navy had Tripolitans, and a restoration of peace between the two countries. Included in the treaty was the withdrawal of Eaton's force from Derne.[26] Eaton was angry when he heard of the treaty and the $60,000 to be paid. He felt that with the proper backing he could have taken Tripoli and installed Hamet as the ruler. It is doubtful whether Eaton could have broken the siege of Derne with his unreliable force, marched to Tripoli, and taken it from Yusuf. In his negotiations Lear had made a bad mistake in allowing Yusuf to keep Hamet's family under his control for at least four more years.[27] This clause in the treaty was originally kept secret for good reason, since it virtually abandoned Hamet after he had been dragooned into joining Eaton's campaign against Yusuf.

The peace with Tripoli held, despite the unhappiness of Eaton and others in the United States over the money paid, the chance for further military glory lost, and the desertion of Hamet. George Davis, who had been acting consul in Tunis before he was transferred to Tripoli in 1807, was able to get Harriet's family released. When Eaton returned to the United States, he denounced the treaty but soon suffered eclipse as American attention turned from the coast of North Africa to problems with Great Britain.[28]

American relations with the Barbary States after the end of the war with Tripoli in 1805 continued to be troubled. The bey of Tunis threatened war over the seizure of a Tunisian ship trying to run the blockade of Tripoli in the waning days of the war. Lear and the now quite large American squadron in North African waters in an impressive show of strength sailed to Tunis and were able to settle matters peacefully.

After the peace with Tripoli, the United States began to keep its small fleet closer to home because of increasing difficulties caused by Great Britain's interference with American shipping and the impressments of American seamen. In 1812, as relations between America and Britain moved toward conflict, the dey of Algiers expelled Consul General Lear, claiming that the United States had not lived up to its treaty commitments, and ordered his corsairs to attack American shipping. The timing could not have been worse for the Algerian side, since war had now begun between the United States and Britain, with the British navy picking up almost all American merchantmen in the Mediterranean. An Algerian ship captured one American vessel, the brig *Edwin* out of Salem, and twelve captives ended up in the dey's hands. The American consuls in Tunis and Cadiz, with the surprising assistance of the British consul in Algiers, were able to get some of the captives ransomed in 1814, but the rest remained captives until after the war.

Although the British navy had bottled up the much smaller American one in its harbors by the end of the 1812–15 war, the American navy had acquitted itself well in a series of frigate encounters in the earlier part of the war. Most of the United States Navy was intact when hostilities ceased in 1815.

With the conflict with England out of the way, President Madison turned American attention to the dey of Algiers and his fellow Barbary rulers. At Madison's request Congress declared war on Algiers on 2 March 1815, Commodore Stephen Decatur set sail from New York with a squadron of three frigates, two sloops of war, three brigs, two schooners, and one new consul general to the Barbary States, William Shaler. The consul general designate, a former sea captain in the China trade, had served some years before as the American consul in Havana. He had also been sent on diplomatic missions in Europe during the War of 1812.[29] Stephen Decatur was returning with zeal to the scene where he had earned international fame in burning the captive frigate *Philadelphia* under the guns of the pasha of Tripoli. He would not shrink from the task of bringing the corsair leaders to heel. Madison was sending a tough team to deal with the dey.

Decatur's squadron, arriving off Gibraltar, captured the flagship and one other ship of the Algerian fleet and took more than 400 Algerians captive.[30] When the American fleet anchored off the harbor of Algiers, the new dey found the defenses of his port in disrepair and what was left of his navy in poor shape; he was ready to listen to whatever Decatur and Shaler had to propose. The Americans demanded that all tributes cease, that all American prisoners be released without ransom, and that the dey pay an indemnity of $10,000 for seizing the *Edwin* in 1812. The dey would get back the prisoners and ships taken by the United States. The very idea that a Barbary ruler should actually pay indemnification was unprecedented, but forced to yield to superior power, the dey signed the treaty, and Shaler landed to take up his duties as consul general. He was to remain at the difficult post in Algiers for twelve years.

Decatur then took his fleet to Tunis and after consulting with the consul there, Mordecai Noah,[31] demanded of the dey $46,000 in indemnity because, during the War of 1812, the dey had permitted the British navy to retake prizes brought into the supposedly neutral port of Tunis by American privateers. The dey of Tunis was as reluctant as the dey of Algiers to pay money to a Christian power, but he paid, and Decatur sailed to Tripoli with his fleet. During the British-American War the pasha had allowed American prizes to be retaken, and Decatur, with obvious relish, forced Yusuf to pay $25,000 and release some Christian captives.[32]

When the War of 1812 began, the British assured the dey of Algiers that they would sweep the American navy from the seas and that the Algerians had nothing to worry about in helping England. Three years later Decatur appeared with his flagship, the *Guerriere*, a former British frigate captured in a famous duel with the *Constitution* during 1812. The dey reportedly said to the British consul in Algiers: "You told us that the Americans would be swept from the seas in six months by your navy, and now they make war upon us with some of your own vessels which they have taken."[33]

In 1816 the Algerian dey tried to change the unfavorable treaty concluded with Decatur and revert to the 1795 agreement that provided for tribute. He expelled the American consul general. Time, however, had run out for the Barbary corsairs, not only because the United States Navy was on the prowl, but because the end of the wars between England and France after the battle of Waterloo lessened the European tolerance for the rapacious acts of the corsairs. A large British-Dutch fleet in July 1816 bombarded Algiers, destroying most of its ships and the port area. The dey was forced to release all his Christian captives and abolish Christian slavery. Later in the same year Consul General Shaler returned to Algiers supported by a naval show of force and was able to make the dey accept Decatur's treaty. As far as the United States was concerned, the power of the Barbary rulers had been broken, and Tripoli, Tunis, and Algiers became backwater port cities where American consuls' main worry was the plague and not the men of the pasha, or dey coming to the consulate to chop down the flagpole.

After 300 years of dominating the North African coast, the Barbary rulers were brought into line by a country across the Atlantic that did not even have a navy until the turn of the century, and had seemed willing to pay tribute rather than fight. In a short fifteen years, from 1800 to 1815, a former American consul had led an expedition across an impassable desert and taken one of their towns, and an American fleet had dictated a harsh peace including indemnities. These North African potentates found that the United States was different from European nations in that it did not encourage corsairs to attack commercial rivals. Tribute was bribery and was perhaps more repugnant to the Americans than to the sophisticated Europeans. Moral indignation was a powerful motivating force for the American naval commodores and consuls, a force Barbary rulers never quite understood.

During the time that relations with the Barbary States were of major concern to the United States, consuls were appointed for their demonstrated merit and accomplishments, not for domestic political reasons. This was a state of affairs that would not continue as partisan politics became predominant. The appointments of Cathcart and O'Brien brought into the consular service the two Americans most knowledgeable about the Barbary Coast. Joel Barlow was already a major intellectual figure at the time of his appointment, and while there could have been reasonable concern that he might be too sophisticated for Barbary tastes, he proved to be a tough negotiator. Tobias Lear had already served as a consul in a difficult post and was familiar with the political scene before he came to Algiers. William Eaton won his spurs in the army and was known as a bold and resourceful leader. William Shaler served as a consul in Havana and had diplomatic experience in Europe before going to North Africa. While these men did not always get on well together, they were as professional a team as any nation could have sent to such a trouble spot.

5

Free Trade and Seamen's Rights
(1800–1815)

In the first decade of the nineteenth century the United States had a sizeable consular service covering sixty-two cities, mainly in Europe and the West Indies. There were ten American consular posts in Great Britain and its dominions, including Malta and Gibraltar; in French territories there were thirteen, including Mauritius in the Indian Ocean and French Guiana in South America. In the period 1800–15 American consuls on French territory were not called consuls but commercial agents, apparently because when Napoleon seized power and called himself first consul, the United States wanted to avoid the confusion of having a consul general in Paris when the French head of state was first consul. But in practice everyone involved, including French officials, called the commercial agents consuls.

Portugal had four American consular posts, one on the mainland, one in the Azores, another on the island of Madeira, and another in San Salvador, Brazil. Spain had nine posts, but none on the mainland of South America. Other posts were in Denmark and its possessions in the West Indies. Prussia, Sweden, and Russia had one post each. Ten American consuls were scattered throughout the German and Italian states.

There were the four Barbary consulates established with such difficulty. In China a post was created in Canton, and the first post in the Middle East was in Smyrna, in the Ottoman Empire. It is noteworthy that there was no American consul in Halifax to the north, or in Mexico, or other parts of the Spanish domain in South America. Despite this consular expansion American diplomatic missions were still limited to the major courts of Europe.

American consular officers' main responsibilities remained looking out for their seamen and shipping, precisely the two areas directly challenged during the long series of wars between England and France. With these two powers dominating the rights of neutral shipping, the U.S. consuls could do little in the greater problem of securing immunity for ships and seamen under the American flag. That was up to their diplomatic colleagues, who were equally impotent. Consuls could only report to the secretary of state the latest outrages against American neutral rights and try to protect their charges as best they could within their consular districts. Each consul was left to struggle with the twin evils of impressment and the seizure of American ships.

The British were by far the greater offenders in impressment. The French sometimes imprisoned crews of American ships seized by their navy or privateers for alleged blockade violations. The honors were fairly even between the two powers for taking ships and confiscating their cargoes.[1]

Caught between two devils, Americans had to pick their enemies carefully or try to avoid them completely. In the quasi-war with France (1798–1800), whose privateers were the main source of provocation, American consuls in the Caribbean cooperated with the British military commanders to put down French privateering in that sea. Following the turn of the century came a period of attempts to navigate between the two conflicting European powers (1800–1807) while ship seizures and impressment waxed and waned, depending on the military situation and whims of the English and French. President Jefferson then tried the "plague on both your houses" policy at the end of 1807 by having Congress declare an embargo, which virtually prohibited the export of goods from the United States.

The embargo was designed both to keep American ships and seamen out of the reach of the French and British, and to place economic pressure on those warring states to respect neutral rights. An embargo has often been a favorite tool of American Presidents. Wherever there was a situation abroad about which the United States could do little without actually fighting, placing an embargo gave the appearance of retaliation, without the costly side effect of warfare.

The embargo of 1807 was as ineffective as most of its successors.[2] The main losers were the American merchant marine and the farmers who raised the principal exports of the United States. The embargo also had a disastrous effect on American consuls abroad, who received no salaries but depended upon commissions earned in assisting and documenting trade with the United States. While earnings were drastically cut due to the curtailment of trade, the consuls' work was not, since there were still seamen stranded abroad, as they signed on and off ships of other nations, including those of France and Britain. Sailors had to make a living, embargo or not.

The embargo lasted little more than a year. Congress repealed the act in March 1809 and substituted it with one that forbade trade only with ports under British or French control, but this also was unsuceessful.[3] There were profits to be made, American seamen needed jobs, and shipping interests did not take direction from their government supinely.

Through all the twists and turns of America's policy toward the belligerent powers, the consuls' work changed little. The major problem was what to do about seamen left destitute in a foreign port, put into a French prison, or impressed into the British navy. That many American sailors ended up on the beach with no money was not always the fault of the belligerent powers. American ships were well built; sometimes a captain found it profitable to sell both cargo and vessel when he docked in a European port. Even if he paid off his crew and gave them money for passage home, which was not always the case, sailors and their wages were often quickly separated in the taverns and brothels of a port city. American crews were well paid; unscrupulous ship masters, once in European ports, found excuses to leave some of their men behind and sign on less expensive French, British, Dutch, Portuguese, or Scandinavian seamen.

Desertion compounded the difficulties of consuls. Although Americans expected high wages because they were known as good and healthy seamen (scarce in wartime Europe), they were sought after not only by British press gangs but by both French and British recruiters for privateers.

The consuls had the power to call on the local authorities to assist them in catching and holding deserters from American ships. William Lee, consul in Bordeaux, in reply to a charge that he had arrested Americans who refused to serve on his own ships (he was in the shipping business), reported that "the principal reason for the arrestation of so many of our seamen in this port is desertion. The privateers of those who are fitting out French bottoms offer any price for American seamen who will quit their vessels they engaged on board of the U. States. I have always from fifteen to twenty of these deserters to lock up. This very morning I have dispatched a party of soldiers after seventeen sailors who have left their vessels, shipped on board a privateer."[4] Surprisingly, Lee obtained the help of the French military to arrest the deserters when they were going on a French privateer. The French were seldom so obliging to American requests. Lee must have been both diligent and persuasive.

Congress and the executive branch quite early did what they could to help the plight of seamen. On 28 May 1796 an Act for the Relief and Protection of American Seamen was passed, which provided for two agents to reside overseas "to inquire into the situation of such American citizens, or others sailing under the protection of the American flag, as have been impressed or may hereafter be impressed or detained by a foreign Power; to endeavor by all legal means to obtain the release of such American citizens or others and to render an account of all impressments and detentions."[5] One agent for seamen was to work in Great Britain and the other elsewhere, at the discretion of the President. Because of the volume of shipping in the Caribbean and the impressment activities of the British navy there, the second agent was posted in Kingston, Jamaica, a British colony in the West Indies. These agents were, in effect, specialized consuls paid for their work to allow them to devote full time to the serious business of helping American seamen. Consuls in other ports were not absolved from their duty toward the distressed sailors in their districts; agents and consuls worked together on the problem, but with only moderate success.

Impressment was the problem that would not go away in events that led to the War of 1812. The confiscation of cargoes and ships by the belligerent powers was provoking, but American shippers could balance their ledgers if only some of their ships were able to slip into a European port; the profit from even a few would offset the losses. Protection of shipping interests was not a cause to die for. The impressment of seamen was a graver matter. Native-born Americans dragged off ships flying the Stars and Stripes by boarding parties led by zealous junior officers of the British navy were forced to serve in those ships in virtual slavery. There was often little difference between being the slave of a Barbary ruler or a seaman in the British navy.

The issue of impressment was not always clear-cut. Many deserters from the British navy served on American ships; pay and working conditions were far better on the Yankee vessels, and

American shipmasters were not particular about whom they signed on board.[6] Also, many of the seamen were naturalized Americans, having been born British subjects, and the British at that time adhered to the rule "once an Englishman, always an Englishman." The British were fighting a long, hard war for survival against Napoleonic France and desperately needed men for their navy. For the most part the captain of a British warship was the final judge as to who might be a British subject. There was little love lost between the British officer class and American merchant mariners; neither the boarding officer nor his captain was scrupulous in seeing that only true British subjects were taken.[7] The British Admiralty usually backed up its officers' arbitrary decisions and refused to discipline even gross cases of wrongful impressment.

The first agent for seamen in Kingston was Silas Talbot, who had been an officer in the Continental navy. During his service (1796–98) Talbot had some success in using his powers of persuasion with British governors, admirals, and captains on the West Indies station to effect the release of some seamen whom he could verify as Americans.[8] He was able to use the colonial courts to obtain writs of habeas corpus, but the British commander in chief in the West Indies, Admiral Sir Hyde Parker, put a stop to that by ordering his officers not to obey writs issued by British civilian courts. Depending on the admiral in charge and on the naval manpower situation, the agents who followed had varying degrees of success but were unable to change the basic situation, and Americans continued to be impressed off their merchant ships.

David Lenox, a former comptroller of the United States Treasury, was the first agent for seamen sent to London. He spent five years (1797–1802) in that demanding post. Initially he succeeded in persuading the Admiralty to release those Americans whose citizenship could be proved without dispute. Such documentation in that era was difficult, especially for men whose background was uncertain because of their itinerant lives as seamen. A market flourished for false citizenship documents, making it easier for press gangs to dismiss any piece of paper shown to them by an able-bodied seaman.[9]

One agent for seamen in London, George W. Erving, reported: "American captains expelled American seamen who had regular certificates, either to avoid payment of their wages, or to secure other seamen for lower wages." He accused the British of having invented methods of their own to discredit American certificates, a notable example being a "game" in which they would find an American seaman whom they could bribe to make affidavit that he was in fact a British subject and had obtained his certificate by direct purchase or by some other fraudulent method. Another practice of the British "was that of enlisting American seamen whom they had impressed under false names so that applications for their release would be of no avail."[10] Despite the work of agents and consuls, impressment of Americans continued and was to lessen only when the British navy had enough men for its ships during periods of peace or when Napoleon was no longer able to challenge British dominance of the seas.

Bordeaux was the most active American consular post in France, being comfortably removed from the main naval bases of the British blockaders. Despite the importance of Bordeaux, the State Department did not deem it necessary to keep in touch. The consul, Cox Barnet, complained in 1801 that he had not heard from the department for twenty-one months.[11] Bordeaux was a magnet for out-of-work American sailors because it was active in trade with the United States. Consuls in other cities in France and Spain sent their charges there. The Bordeaux consul reported in 1802 that he had 20 seamen in hospitals and 150 on the streets in distress. The French police were complaining, and the consul was trying to put as many men on American ships as their masters would accept.[12]

In 1807 the British initiated a licensing system allowing some trade with France under the supervision of the Board of Trade, but this easing of the blockade did not really help American-carried trade. As one historian described the situation: "Theoretically American ships were not discriminated against in the issue of licenses. In actual practice the Board of Trade found European flags far more useful and more amenable to control. Since no trade to the French Empire could be safely carried on without them, licenses were extremely valuable, worth sometimes as much as £15,000 on the open market, where they were freely traded."[13] The French had their own system of controls and were ruthless in enforcing them, not only in France but in other ports of Europe where Napoleon held sway. The U.S. consul in Bremen reported that the French authorities controlling that German port were seizing American ships, which had certificates of origin of their cargoes that the French did not consider in order.[14]

American consuls were in a potentially profitable position with the imposition of various licenses, certificates of origin, and other controls working to their advantage, together with the excellent money to be made from having the proper papers to permit loading or unloading of cargo to and from the United States. But a consul's position could also arouse animosity among American shipping firms if their ships were seized by one of the belligerents, but those of the consuls were not.

Although the contempt of France for the rights of neutrals, especially those of Americans, was a grave concern, the outrages committed by the British on American seamen and British support of hostile Indians along the Canadian border aroused greater animosity in the American people. A British-American war might even offer the opportunity to capture Canada. For a variety of reasons and motives, the United States declared war on Britain in June 1812. Even war with France was considered by both the President and Congress, but common sense prevailed, and the young United States took on only the nation with the greatest navy and not the one with the greatest army.

As the news of war reached the American consulates in the British Isles and its dominions, consuls who were American citizens packed up and left, as did the British consuls in the United States. In London the American consul and agent for seamen, Reuben Beasley, was permitted to stay on by the British authorities in the capacity of "United States agent for prisoners of war" to help with exchanges of prisoners. When the war was over he reverted to being the consul.[15]

Robert Ware Fox, U.S. consul at Falmouth, did not leave Britain. He was a British subject appointed to the post in 1793 by George Washington. When the war came, Consul Fox took down the American coat of arms, stored away the American flag, and waited for the war to run its course. At its conclusion, up went the coat of arms and the American flag, and Mr. Fox resumed his duties. A prominent Quaker, Fox may have had the distinction of being the only consul to use the familiar "thou" in his dispatches to the Secretary of State. The consular position in Falmouth was passed down from generation to generation in the Fox family, with only a short break, until 1908, when the post was closed.

The declaration of war by the United States on Great Britain caught the American merchant fleet in European waters by surprise, and the British navy had easy plucking. Levitt Harris, the American consul in St. Petersburg, Russia, reported that thirty American ships were part of a convoy being protected by the British navy as they sailed through the Baltic from Russia to England. When the convoy commander heard that America was now at war with his country, he informed the Yankee skippers that their protectors were now their captors.[16]

Seventeen American merchant ships that had not joined the ill-fated convoy were trapped in St. Petersburg during the war. Consul Harris later wrote the Secretary of State that there were seventy seamen off the American ships with no employment and that "in order to preserve the morals and maintain good conduct among so great a number of idle people for so long a time, I promoted the establishment of a school at Cronstadt, the project for which it must be mentioned to the honor of the seamen, originated with themselves. At this school between forty and fifty American sailors are occupied during ten hours in the day in learning to read and cypher."[17]

Although the United States was at war with Great Britain, its relations with France remained strained. Normally in wartime the code of "my enemy's enemy is my friend" prevails, but Franco-American relations did not improve. In October 1812, that fateful year for Napoleon, Consul William Lee in Bordeaux wrote that French officials were still detaining American vessels in port for three to six months because of questions over their ships' papers. Lee hoped that the American minister to France, Joel Barlow, former consul general in Algiers, would set matters right. Barlow set off for Russia to see Napoleon, who was on his way to what appeared to be a certain victory over the tsar.[18] Things did not happen as Lee had predicted. Napoleon's army was destroyed, and Barlow died of a fever in Poland before being able to discuss shipping matters with the French emperor.

In June 1813 Commodore William Rodgers, cruising in the Atlantic on the U.S. frigate *President*, captured the British brig *Maria* laden with a cargo of codfish. Putting a prize crew on board, he directed them to take the *Maria* to the port of Bordeaux where the cargo could be sold. The *Maria* arrived in late June, and Consul Lee took charge to arrange the sale of both ship and cargo. This was the normal practice, as a United States Navy vessel had captured the brig and the consul was the U.S. representative on hand.

Both the crew of the *President* and Lee stood to make some profit from the sale. Lee immediately wrote the director of customs in Bordeaux asking for permission to sell the codfish, which he noted he had stored in a warehouse "adjoining my house."[19] When the director did not reply, Lee wrote again stating that it was essential to have the sale soon, "viewing the perishable nature of the cargo, particularly at this season."[20] It was then mid-July; Lee, in his residence next to the codfish, must have been very much aware of the urgency. The director of customs finally informed Lee that the sale of prizes and their cargoes was delegated to some French merchants, not to the American consul.[21] Lee then received a sharp reprimand from the French minister of commerce in Paris that he, Lee, had acted improperly and that David Warden, the American consul general in Paris, was in charge of all prizes and had ordered French merchants to take care of the prize sale.[22]

William Lee was not a man to take a rebuke lightly, especially when it concerned his dignity as a consul and his ability to turn a profit. With some heat, Lee wrote William H. Crawford, the American minister in Paris: "Mr. Warden has not only stated to the Minister that he is consul general and special agent for all prizes! but has made it appear that I have acted improperly and without authority in the case of the *Maria*. This is to carry personal animosity so far as to merit the severe animadversion of all good men. I will confess to your Excellency that as a native American educated in my country, descending from one of the oldest and most respected families [he was of the Massachusetts Lees], and with more connections than perhaps any other man, to be thus calumniated by an adventurer who was obliged to fly from his own Country, and has not lived long enough in mine to be legally naturalized is insupportable."[23]

David Bailie Warden, born in Ireland, had at an early age ardently espoused the Irish cause. The British authorities, aware of Warden's activities, gave him the choice of arrest or departure to another country. He left in 1799 for the United States and accepted a teaching position at the Kingston Academy in Ulster County, New York. In 1804 he became a citizen and almost immediately joined General John Armstrong as private secretary when Armstrong went to Paris as the American minister. On Armstrong's departure in 1810 Warden was appointed consul in Paris and agent for prize cases, which apparently meant that he was to adjudicate disputes over prizes rather than to take charge of all prize cases in France.[24]

Minister Crawford, Armstrong's successor, unhappy over the consular discord, wrote Lee that the matter had given him

> great pain. The acrimony of the style [of correspondence] is of itself highly objectionable, but the charges of falsehood

and of crime on one side, and of ignorance and arrogance on the other, are extremely reprehensible. It is probable that this correspondence has been submitted to the Minister of Commerce. What opinion must he entertain on the character of persons whom the United States thought proper to clothe with a portion of their confidence and of their power? If Officers of the United States in France cannot think better of each other I hope they will cease to publish their opinions and that in their communications to me they will not indulge that asperity of language which I feel much reason to reprehend in this present case.[25]

Despite his rebuke to Lee, Crawford found that in the case of the *Maria* the conduct of the consul in Bordeaux had been correct. He noted that Warden was not the consul general in Paris. Warden was removed from his consular position under a cloud for claiming more authority than was rightfully his, but he stayed on in Paris. Later Warden performed a valuable service to the consular establishment by writing a book on the origin and history of consuls. For his part, Lee was almost successful in a plot with some French naval officers to spirit Napoleon to America after Waterloo and the emperor's flight from the British.

During the War of 1812 other consuls had more important matters than squabbling over the sale of rotting codfish. American privateers used neutral ports to sell their prizes or refit their own ships. As noted earlier, the consuls in Tunis and Tripoli were unable to prevent the British navy from sailing into these supposedly neutral harbors and, with the cooperation of the Barbary rulers, retaking ships that American privateers had sent there as prizes. Consuls' protests were in vain since the United States Navy had been driven from the Mediterranean.

When the war ended in 1815, American consuls returned to England and other ports they had been forced to leave in 1812. The war in Europe also ended after Waterloo; the systems of licenses and blockades were mercifully stopped so that trade could resume its normal pattern. Even the Barbary corsairs were no longer the menace they had been for centuries, and the Mediterranean was open for merchant ships of all nations.

American consuls returned to their more ordinary activities of promoting trade, reporting on both the quick recovery of the American merchant marine after its devastation during the war years and the growth of commerce between the United States and Europe. Sailors were still being stranded; they ran out of money and raised hell in the port bars and brothels, but these were now comparatively easy matters for consuls to settle with the local police, and there were plenty of American ships to take their wayward charges home.

The long period of the French-British wars, American involvement first with the French and then with the British, and the Barbary problems proved the value of having consuls throughout the trading world. American consuls themselves had shown their own worth at a difficult time. The link between U.S. consuls and their navy was stoutly forged, each dependent on the other when situations became tense abroad, one serving as the eyes and the other as the arms of the growing American influence beyond its territorial waters. The American merchant fleet was also dependent on its consuls for protecting its sailors and helping in trading activities. Considering that the U.S. government paid only the four Barbary consuls and the two agents for seamen in London and the West Indies, while all the other consuls worked for what fees they could derive from their office, the American people got a bargain.

6

Yankee Consuls in Latin America (1810–1860)

The armies of Napoleon in Spain created a quandary for the United States in South America. In 1808 the French deposed Charles IV, the king of Spain, and Napoleon made his brother, Joseph, the new monarch. With the French holding nearly all of the Iberian Peninsula, the Spanish bureaucratic network that had controlled its possessions in the New World was greatly weakened. The Spanish colonies in South America were already primed for an explosion; too much control remained in the hands of the now-unsupported Spanish-born officeholders to the exclusion of the Creoles, Spanish-stock colonials born in South America. The subsequent wars for independence that moved up and down the southern continent from 1810 to 1824 put the U.S. consular service on the front lines.

As the only successful democratic nation to have won its own war for independence, the attitude of the United States was one of kinship for its fellow American countries to the south, although they were almost as alien as Asia to most North Americans. But U.S. citizens had learned to be suspicious of revolutionary movements after the fall of the Bastille had led to the horrors of the guillotine and the dictatorship of Napoleon rather than French democracy. Nevertheless, the fight for freedom from Spanish rule was a popular cause.

The two American secretaries of state during most of the Latin American wars for independence, James Monroe and John Quincy Adams, had other considerations than bowing to national sentiment. The United States has not since seen such professional leaders in foreign policy as Monroe and Adams; between them they had served as the American ministers to France, Great Britain, Spain, the Netherlands, Russia, and Prussia. The problem facing these two professionals was the extent and timing of the United States' recognition of the independence of the Latin American colonies. Recognitions too precipitous could so antagonize Spain as to end the expectation of successful peaceful negotiations for acquiring the Florida territory. Both Monroe and Adams were aware of the enmity such recognitions might also engender against the United States in the courts of the major European powers, which for the most part were bitterly conservative as an aftermath of the French Revolution. Moreover, the United States had continuing problems with France and England during most of the period.

The only real interest the United States had in Latin America, other than fostering democracy, was developing commerce. For centuries Spain had purposefully excluded foreign merchants from dealing directly with its colonial subjects. The Spanish had never allowed consuls in their colonies, except in Cuba, where they were barely tolerated. The success of the liberation movements could open a vast new market for Yankee products and materials, and Yankee consuls would be needed. A prime consideration of the United States in dealing with South America in the first quarter of the nineteenth century was to be sure that the British did not get there first in developing commercial ties. Hesitancy to recognizing the emerging republics in the south might prejudice relations with their new leaders and damage the market for American goods, but the outcome was not certain. The United States took a pragmatic half-step and sent in its consuls or, as they were sometimes termed, agents for commerce and seamen, appointed ostensibly to work with local authorities to look after American interests.

The first official sent by the United States to one of the rebelling Latin American countries was Joel Roberts Poinsett, a wealthy 32-year-old, South Carolinian who had spent much of his adult life learning languages and touring Europe and Western Asia.[1] In 1810 he was appointed "special agent of the United States to South America." His orders by then Secretary of State Robert Smith were ambiguous, as befitted American policy:

> You will make it your object, wherever it may be proper, to diffuse the impression that the United States cherish the sincerest good will towards the people of Spanish America as neighbors, as belonging to the same portion of the globe, and as having a mutual interest in cultivating friendly intercourse: that this disposition will exist, whatever may be

their internal system or European relation, with respect to which no interference of any sort is pretended: and that, in the event of a political separation from the parent country, and of an independent system of National Government, it will coincide with the sentiments and policy of the United States to promote the most friendly relations, and the most liberal intercourse between the inhabitants of this hemisphere. The real as well as ostensible object of your mission is to explain the mutual advantages of commerce with the United States, to promote liberal and stable regulations, and to transmit seasonable information on the subject.[2]

Poinsett was sent to Buenos Aires. From here he would be reporting and promoting commerce with the United States in what was then called the Provinces of the Rio de la Plata (Buenos Aires and its neighboring territory) and Chile. Buenos Aires was a good place to put an agent/consul to observe the revolutionary movement, for it was the only major city not to be recaptured at one time or another by the Spanish loyalist forces. Such an event usually caused the American representative to be expelled posthaste. This city of 70,000 was healthful, well planned, and solidly anti-British in 1818. The British had attempted to capture it in 1806–7 but had been defeated by local levies.

In 1811 Poinsett's title of agent was changed to that of consul general, which meant that he had both the official appointment of the president and Senate approval. He also had a clearer set of instructions from the new secretary of state, James Monroe:

The disposition shewn by most of the Spanish provinces to separate from Europe and to erect themselves into independent States excites great interest here. As Inhabitants of the same Hemisphere, as Neighbors, the United States cannot be unfeeling Spectators of so important a moment. The destiny of those provinces must depend on themselves. Should such a revolution however take place, it cannot be doubted that our relations with them will be more intimate, and our friendship stronger than it can be while they are colonies of any European power.[3]

Poinsett stayed in Buenos Aires long enough to reach a commercial agreement with the governing junta. He appointed a vice consul, William Miller, and then went to Chile. In Santiago, Poinsett found the Creole forces in control but already dangerously weakened by factional disputes. Taking Monroe's comment about relations being more intimate and friendships stronger with independent republics than with colonies too much to heart, Poinsett plunged into the political life of Santiago. He became a close friend of the then Chilean dictator José Miguel Carrera and was forced to flee when the Spanish retook the colony.

Poinsett returned to Buenos Aires, and then left for the United States in 1814. He continued to have an eventful career in South Carolinian politics. Later, he was the first American minister to the new Republic of Mexico (1825–29), and then served as the secretary of war under President Van Buren. Poinsett was an ardent amateur botanist, and his most enduring contribution is seen every Christmas. The red flower that he cultivated from obscure Mexican wild flower is called the poinsettia.

At the northern end of the continent Robert K. Lowry of Baltimore, the first American citizen to be the commercial agent at La Guaira (or La Guayra), the port for Caracas, was well received by the junta when he arrived there in September 1810. He served off and on at that post until his death in 1826. Of major concern to Lowry was the nearby presence of the British (occupying the island of Curaçao), whose representatives were attempting to obtain "some exclusive privileges for the British Commerce in this Quarter; but [the Creoles] prefer connection with the United States." Lowry was also worried about the Spanish, who were arming privateers, working out of Puerto Rico, to intercept American merchant ships bringing supplies to the rebel colonists. Lowry asked for the U.S. navy to send a warship to protect "our commerce from such Pirates. It would put us on a footing with our competitors [the British], of whom there are at present two Brigs of War in this Port." [4]

The rebel junta wanted official recognition from the United States but got nowhere. One member of the junta chided the American secretary of state in 1811, noting that they had received nothing from their pleas that would "indicate sentiments of union and friendship notwithstanding that [the junta] generously received Robert Lowry in the capacity of Maritime and Commercial Agent at La Guayra for your Government." [5]

Lowry was not impressed with the progress of the first attempt of the rebels in Caracas and the neighboring provinces to establish an independent state. He reported: "From want of a proper application of the Public money, through the want of talent; and intrigue; the country is fast approaching to poverty, anarchy & imbecility."[6]

Lowry was soon to have more than anarchy and imbecility to deal with. On 26 March 1812 a severe earthquake destroyed most of La Guaira and Caracas and was followed almost immediately by a royalist invasion of the country. The Catholic priests told their people that the earthquake was the vengeance of God on those who had deserted the cause of the Spanish king.[7] Coincident with the earthquake and invasion, Lowry had received his commission as consul, but he had had no opportunity to gain official recognition of his new dignity, as the rebel junta had other preoccupations.

Shortly after sending Lowry his consular commission, Secretary of State Monroe appointed Alexander Scott as agent to Caracas, where he was expected to serve more as a diplomat than as a consul, since Lowry had matters well in hand in the port. Scott was also in charge of what may have been the first official American relief mission abroad. Congress had authorized the procurement of relief supplies for the victims of the earthquake in La Guaira and Caracas, which were to be presented to the junta by Scott. When he arrived in June 1812, Scott found it prudent to represent himself as "agent of the United States for the relief of earthquake sufferers in La Guayra" since the royalists, resuming power in Caracas, were hostile to the United States because of the unofficial support that had come from both the American government and people for the cause of liberation. Scott and Lowry tried to protect Americans, especially the crews of ships seized by Spanish privateers, but as Scott reported, "the seizure and detention of our vessels, and imprisonment of American citizens, have evinced a spirit not only of injustice, but hostility towards our government."[8] When in December 1812 the Spanish authorities ordered the expulsion of all Americans from the areas that they controlled, Scott and Lowry had to leave.

As it was dangerous to sail in the Caribbean with the United States at war with Great Britain and Spanish privateers and freebooters on the prowl, Lowry and Scott chartered a vessel to take them to the nearest non-Spanish port on the island of Curaçao, but the British governor of that island's occupying forces would not allow the Americans to land. They "had to return again to the Spanish Main" but finally managed to reach the United States.[9]

The republican forces of Simón Bolivar did not succeed in liberating most of the northern portion of South America until 1821.

That same year Lowry was again in La Guaira as the American consul, where he soon found himself involved with the nemesis of all consuls: privateers. This time he was trying to protect Americans from their own folly. He reported:

> On board of Privateers under the flag of this Govt., are many Americans decoyed into their present unhappy situations, & in fact groaning under the heaviest tyranny. Numerous applications have been made to me by Americans in this situation, & of a few whose liberation I have procured, it has been professedly more as a matter of personal favor to myself [from the local authorities], than as a right due to these unfortunate men as individuals and Americans, or to my character as agent of the Government of the United States. [10]

To the south, during the War of 1812, Poinsett's successor Thomas Lloyd Halsey of Rhode Island had great difficulty in getting to his post. He had to avoid the British blockade, first going to New York City, catching a ship for Spain or Portugal, and from there sailing to Buenos Aires. He did not arrive at his post until more than a year had passed. Once at his post, Halsey found the usual problem: stranded American seamen with no means to get home. With almost all shipping cut off to and from the United States, the seamen had to stay on shore or depart via foreign vessels.

Halsey finally ran afoul of the factional disputes endemic to the various liberation movements in South America. The supreme director of the then United Provinces of South America (Argentina) expelled Halsey on the grounds that he had been dealing with José Artigas, the chief opponent of the supreme director. Artigas represented the provinces outside Buenos Aires and wanted to have a loose federal system, while Supreme Director Juan Martin de Pucyrredon wanted, as his title implied, a centralized government under his control. Halsey was accused of bordering "on the abuse of power, [and] did not hesitate to promote the insidious attempts of the malcontents and disturbers of the peace."[11] Halsey was also accused of having a personal interest in privateers attacking Spanish commerce and of selling blank privateering commissions to friends in Baltimore, which apparently he did, but for which he was never admonished.

The United States acknowledged the official independence of the Latin American republics in the spring of 1822. More consular officers for the area were appointed. One was William Tudor, a Boston-born Harvard graduate and a less-than-successful businessman who turned to the field of arts and became an essayist and historian, founding the periodical *North American Review*.[12] Appointed consul at Callao in Peru, Tudor arrived after a trip of 120 days from Boston to find his appointment somewhat premature. The Spanish were still in control of the port.

Uncertain as to how he should proceed (it might take 240 days to send for instructions and receive them), Tudor on his own initiative tried to present his consular credentials to the Spanish authorities thus: "The probability of my being received is not great, and however small the inducements may be to enter on the duties of my office in respect to my personal advantage, I thought myself bound to ask for a recognition as I might in the absence of all other official agents render some service to my countrymen."[13] While waiting for the viceroy's reply, Tudor was allowed to stay in Callao and make periodic reports on the uncertain military situation.

It was a confusing and dangerous time for a man whose main accomplishments hitherto had been as a literary editor and as founder of the Boston Athenaeum, a library and art museum, but Consul Tudor plunged into his work, obviously enjoying being part of history rather than merely writing about it. There was a surprising amount of American shipping along the coast of Peru despite the blockades, privateers, and the distance from the United States, a voyage that required the rounding of Cape Horn.

The new consul found that the blockade of the royalist ports of Peru by the patriot ships was a cynical method of exacting revenue. Blockaders stopped neutral ships trying to enter the port of Callao, letting them go in only if their captains paid 25 percent of the value of the cargoes. "Here is a blockade established on the new system, not to distress an enemy but to pillage neutrals."[14]

Concerned for the safety of American ships, Tudor called for more U.S. navy warships to protect merchant ships from privateers and the blockaders of the rebel (or patriot) forces. The navy kept a small squadron on station in Peru under Commodore Isaac Hull. American warships helped by escorting their countrymen's vessels through the troubled waters of the eastern South Pacific, as did naval contingents of the French and British.

As it often happens, difficult times bring people together. The former enemies, the British and Americans in Peru, were drawn closer by a mutual disapproval, and even disdain, for the excesses of both sides of the Spanish royalist/patriot struggle. Tudor sent copies of his official dispatches to the United States on British naval ships heading in that direction. He wrote: "On our glorious <u>Fourth</u>, the few Americans in Lima dined by invitation on board this ship [U.S. frigate *United States*], as did all the English commanders & some of their lieutenants, the awning under which we dined, was composed of the American & English flags, the first time I presume that they were ever blended on that day. The experiment was a delicate one but succeeded most harmoniously and seemed to give mutual satisfaction" [15]

British, French, and U.S. naval vessels kept a close watch in the port of Callao. The patriot blockading ships darted in from time to time, attempting to pick off a prize. The neutral naval contingents were there to keep their merchant ships safe. The small Spanish navy was able to seize several American ships trading with the liberated areas during the Spanish counter-blockade. Tudor did what he could to free the crews and have the ships released, but here he was thwarted by a maddening characteristic of Spanish colonial rule: when in doubt, or even if mildly unsure, refer to Madrid. While the Spanish candle was flickering out in the South American continent, American consuls in Cuba, Puerto Rico, and the Philippines were to continue to deal with the "refer to Madrid" reflex on most problems until Spain's loss of those colonies in 1898.

The seas around Callao were not the only danger spots for neutrals; patriot guerrilla forces consisting of irregular cavalry intermittently raided the outskirts of the city. There was increasing concern in the foreign community as the Spanish withdrew most of their forces to the forts of Callao, leaving the city unprotected. The Spanish commanding general proposed that the British and American naval commanders land some men to guard the foreign community. The British responded immediately by sending 3 officers and 110 marines ashore, where they remained as a protecting force until Bolívar's army took over the city some weeks later. But, as Tudor wrote, "Commodore Hull declined taking the same course for several reasons, but he offered to send up a few sailors under the charge of an officer to be distributed in the houses of his countrymen; on consulting with [the U.S. naval officers] I found they were afraid they could not manage the sailors, and have therefore only requested the loan of some arms and ammunition." [16] There was an obvious contrast between British and American discipline.

The concern for the safety of foreigners was not unreasonable. The British consul in Callao died of wounds received when the guerrillas entered the city as the advance guard of Bolívar's army. The consul had once been the commanding officer of a regiment of volunteer cavalry in London; in honor of the occasion he had put on his uniform to greet the occupying patriot forces. It was dusk; he was mistaken for a Spanish officer and shot.[17]

Tudor had the sense to keep out of the way of contending armies. At the end of 1824 he was at last able to report that he had "received the exequatur of General Bolivar to my Commission as Consul of the U.S. for Peru; and I shall now be able to enter more regularly into the business of my office."[18]

The collapse of the Spanish empire in Latin America by the mid-1820s ended a period of independent U.S. consular operations. Instead of being the only official American representative in a country, the consul, with the arrival of U.S. ministers to the various capitals, lost some autonomy and settled into what should have been normal consular work but seldom was. The continent was huge, communications were poor, and there was an almost unending series of wars, revolutions, provinces breaking away, civil unrest, and natural disasters, which left each consul to deal with the situation on his own and protect American lives and property as best he could with the means at hand.

A warship in harbor flying the Stars and Stripes was often a great help to the consul in persuading the authorities to release an American from the local jail or lower an unreasonable local duty on American imports. Yet the combination of an impetuous consul and the availability of a U.S. frigate commanded by an aggressive commander could be dangerous. In the 1820s the Falkland Islands off the coast of the United Provinces (Argentina) had as a governor Louis Vernet, French by birth but owing allegiance to the United Provinces. From time to time, foreign vessels visited the islands to kill seals for their furs. When depredation of the stock of seals got out of control, Vernet, who had the United Provinces concession for sealing operations, vowed to put a stop to the poachers. After warning a number of these predatory ships, including the American schooner *Harriet* in 1829, Vernet took action: he seized the *Harriet* when it returned to the islands in 1831 and sent the schooner to Buenos Aires, where a hearing was to be held regarding the captain's and ship's liability.

By chance, the United States had no diplomatic representative in the country. The minister there, John M. Forbes (who had formerly been the consul in the city) had died, leaving Consul George W. Slacum as the ranking American official. Slacum had already shown some intemperance in dealing with the authorities of Buenos Aires; the arrival of the *Harriet* under arrest further incensed the consul. He challenged the right of the Buenos Aires government to regulate the fishing or sealing rights of Americans anywhere and demanded the release of the *Harriet*, but got nowhere with the officials, who not only rejected his argument but also his right as a consul and not an accredited diplomat to make such sweeping charges and demands.[19]

At this point the U.S. frigate *Lexington* under the command of Commander Silas Duncan put into Buenos Aires. After a meeting with Commander Duncan, Slacum warned the Buenos Aires government of the U.S. navy's duty to protect its citizens in the Falkland Islands and that the Lexington would sail there if the government did not order "the immediate suspension of the right of capture of vessels of the United States" and release the *Harriet*.[20]

British Consul General Sir Woodbine Parrish may have had a hand in subtly pushing Slacum to make this ill-considered ultimatum. Parrish had told Slacum that Great Britain had never given up its claim to the Falkland Islands, so the action of Vernet was possibly illegal.

Commander Duncan, with the blessing of Consul Slacum, set sail from Buenos Aires for the Falklands. There he put a landing party ashore, spiked the few cannon on the island, burned all the gunpowder, and arrested nearly all the inhabitants. He then declared the islands free of all government and sailed back to the mainland with seven islanders in irons.[21] Apparently realizing that he had gone too far, Duncan prudently did not put into Buenos Aires but went into Montevideo, where he released the Falkland prisoners and sailed away.

Slacum, left to face an outraged government and populace, was informed that the authorities of the United Provinces would no longer deal with him. The American government, when informed of the actions of its fire-breathing consul, revoked his commission.

While Consul Slacum was testing the temper of the Argentineans in 1831, the U.S. consular establishment in South America had grown to maturity. By 1830 there were 22 consular posts scattered throughout the southern continent, 2 in Central America, 10 in Mexico proper, 1 in Santa Fe, New Mexico, and 2 in Texas (Galveston and San Antonio). The islands of the Caribbean had another

22 posts; out of the 146 American consular posts throughout the world, one-third were in the Western Hemisphere.

The United States had not been able to put a consul into a Mexican port before that country became independent in 1821. Mexico differed from most other parts of Latin America in that there had not been a long period of semi-independence from Spanish colonial rulers. With independence the American government began to open consular posts in Mexico. The first commercial agent (made a consul a few months later) was William Taylor of Virginia, sent to Vera Cruz, the country's major port on the Gulf of Mexico. Taylor's appointment was soon followed by that of James Smith Wilcocks to Mexico City and Nathanael Ingraham to the other gulf port of Tampico. By 1830 there were ten American consular representatives throughout Mexico, including Chihuahua in the north, the Pacific ports of Mazatlán and Acapulco, and Compeche in the Yucatan Peninsula.

Wilcocks, the consul in Mexico City, was already well experienced in Mexican affairs, having lived there during the final stages of the Spanish collapse. He had taken it upon himself to write Secretary of State John Quincy Adams a detailed and valuable report on Mexico as it emerged as an independent country. He noted that he had traveled throughout the country and that "few foreigners have perhaps, had an opportunity of seeing as much of the Kingdom as myself"[22] His initiative and obvious knowledge of the country resulted in Adams's appointment of Wilcocks, an appointment that illustrates a process evident in administrations until that of Andrew Jackson. By and large, consuls who were appointed were qualified for their positions. Many were merchants dealing in international trade; others had good connections in the country in which they were to serve or already had a record of public service.

Mexico was in a state of continuous civil unrest. American interests there were growing rapidly, bringing more Americans to live in the country. U.S. consular officers often had to intervene, frequently with danger to themselves, in protecting the lives and property of their charges.

American consuls in Mexico kept a careful watch over the endemic insurrectionary movements in their districts. For example, the consul in Vera Cruz in 1832 reported disturbances there. Expecting the city to be besieged by government troops, he requested naval protection for American citizens and their property.[23] Three years later another occupant of that consular position wrote, "It becomes my duty to communicate to the Department, that the tranquility of Mexico is again interrupted. The troops stationed in the Castle of San Juan de Ulloa revolted on the night of the 26th ult. and captured that Fortress. The Commerce at Vera Cruz in consequence of the late disturbances has been entirely interrupted." The consul noted that shipping was diverted to the nearby port at Sacrifice, which was "declared by the government the present port of Vera Cruz."[24] There was an extensive bombardment of the city, but no Americans were injured, and a U.S. naval ship was standing by in case American interests were threatened. Six days later the consul reported, "I beg leave to inform you that the late disturbances at this place have terminated and tranquility is again restored."[25]

Tranquility was never to be restored for long in Mexico. It was a big country rent by a variety of disputes between rich and poor and between centralists and loose federalists, all of which allowed military and bandit leaders to run amok. American consuls could not be indifferent to these insurrections or revolutionary movements. The other American citizens in the country and their business interests were threatened whenever the status quo was broken. Assignment to a Mexican consular post was what would later euphemistically be called "challenging."

Staffing some consular posts was not always easy. The position at Galveston when Texas was under Mexican rule went begging. David G. Burnet, the incumbent in 1834, was appointed a judge by the Mexican authorities, having become a Mexican citizen, as had most of the other settlers from the United States; he thought that he could not be both judge and consul. His efforts to get someone to apply for the position of consul were unsuccessful. Taking the job could jeopardize one's Mexican citizenship, a prerequisite for settling in Texas. Burnet said that possible applicants were not interested in an "office of so little worth."[26] Ex-consul Burnet later became the first president of the infant Texas Republic until Sam Houston replaced him in the fall of 1836. There were also problems in the late 1830s getting a consul into Monterey in the Mexican province of California. At least two men nominated did not take up the post, failures that were to have unfortunate consequences.

American consuls at some Mexican posts tended to be casual about their fiscal responsibilities. When the consul in Mazatlán was questioned about the yearly statement of fees he had sent to the department in 1837, he informed Washington: "I also beg leave to add that neither my predecessor nor myself have ever been in the habit of making any charge in our official capacity, to the Masters of American Vessels visiting this Port, the fees which might have been derived from that source, never have been deemed worth the trouble of collecting." [27]

Mazatlán was a key post in the events that led to the annexation of California by the United States. Its location just below the Gulf of California made it a convenient port of call for ships California-bound from South America. Beginning in the 1820s, the United States had kept a Pacific Squadron on station to cruise the long Pacific coastline of South and North America. Valparaiso in Chile, Callao in Peru, and Mazatlán in Mexico were frequent stopovers for this force, whose mission was to show the flag, protect Americans and their property, and put down piracy.

The consulate at Mazatlán was an important communications link with both Mexico and the United States because it was on the couriers' road that ran from Vera Cruz to Mexico City to Mazatlán to California. The commodore of the Pacific Squadron, months away from messages sent him by a U.S. navy ship going around the Horn, depended on the consul to keep him informed of the always-troubled relationship between Mexico and the United States, especially after the Texas Revolution and its independence in 1836.

In 1842 Thomas Catesby Jones was the commodore of the Pacific Squadron. His command consisted of the flagship, the frigate *United States*, the sloops of war *Cynne*, *Dale*, and *Yorktown*, the schooner *Shark*, and the storeship *Relief*. While at anchor in the harbor of Callao, Jones received disquieting news from John Parrott, consul at Mazatlán, to the effect that war was imminent between the United States and Mexico over Texas, which Mexico had not recognized as an independent country and which the United States had not yet accepted as a new part of the United States.[28] At the same time the commodore learned that a French naval squadron had left Valparaiso some time before for an unknown destination. Added to this uncertainty was another: a British squadron had sailed out of Callao on 5 September 1842, also without announcing its destination.

The cause of Jones's concern was California. As one historian has written: "It was obvious even before 1840 that the Mexican Republic was too weak internally to maintain her sway over a province so remote. Local revolutions in California had destroyed all but a slight resemblance of government. By 1841 authority in California had almost vanished."[29] California was a ripe plum; the United States and Great Britain kept wary eyes on each other. The

French were known to aim at targets of colonial opportunity; their naval squadron that had left Callao had taken for France the Marquesas Islands in the South Seas. As for the British, there had been serious proposals by influential persons in Great Britain to accept California from Mexico in exchange for the considerable debt that country owed Britain, and in the 1840s, with its possession of British Columbia and claims to part of the Oregon Territory of the United States, Great Britain was a close neighbor to California.[30] The United States also bordered California after making the Louisiana Purchase, which included Oregon. There were not enough Spanish settlers in California to form a lasting, independent country. Another country would end up with the prize.

After receiving Parrott's message and believing that he was in a race for California with the British squadron, Commodore Jones crowded on all sail and set his course directly for Monterey, capital of Upper California. Two ships that could not keep up were detached while Jones sailed on with his flagship *United States* and the *Cynne*. Because beating the British to the goal seemed all-important, Jones did not put in at Mazatlán to verify Consul Parrott's prediction about war. In fact, the Texas dispute had subsided, leaving relations between the United States and Mexico on a fairly even keel. But the keels of Jones's ships were heeled over as the U.S. squadron of the Pacific pressed on for California.

On 19 October 1842 the U.S. navy entered Monterey harbor to find neither British nor French naval ships. The Americans had won the race, and California was theirs, or so they thought. The captains of several of the American merchant ships moored in the harbor had no new information about American-Mexican relations. At this point a U.S. consul *in situ* would have been invaluable to American interests, but the Department of State had not in five years been able to put one there. With no consul to serve as political advisor and observing what appeared to be the manning of the harbor defenses, such as they were, Jones sent an officer ashore under a flag of truce demanding the surrender of the district of Monterey and its adjoining territory, from San Juan Bautista in the north to San Luis Obispo in the south.[31]

The California authorities in Monterey had twenty-nine soldiers and no usable artillery. There was no knowledge about a war, but it was sometimes six months or more before they received instructions or news from Mexico. There was little the authorities could do but surrender peaceably on 20 October, and the Stars and

Stripes were hoisted. Acting as interpreter during the short negotiations was Thomas G. Larkin, an American merchant who had
lived in Monterey for ten years. Larkin, alone with Commodore
Jones, asked a hard question: "Which side had declared the war,
Mexico or the United States?" Jones had no answer.[32] The commodore had been acting on a June 1842 consular report from Mazatlán.
Newspapers and letters dated in August from Mexico that had just
arrived in Upper California in October made no mention of war
with the United States, a development that would not have been
overlooked.

Commodore Jones was decisive. Realizing that he had made a
monumental error, he wasted no time in putting matters right. The
day after the surrender he informed the deposed governor that a
mistake had been made, hauled down the American flag and hoisted the Mexican flag, firing a salute in honor, and set about a series
of courtesy calls befitting the friendly port visit of a foreign naval
squadron. There were parties and balls and men taking shore leave,
with the Californians showing their renowned hospitality.

Jones had the unpleasant task of reporting to the secretary of the
navy and the American minister in Mexico City the circumstances
of his unfortunate action in Monterey. To appease the Mexican government, which had protested strongly, Jones was relieved of his
command. He was not, however, censored by the U.S. government,
and two years later he was back as the commodore of the Pacific
Squadron.

With the precipitous departure of Jones, in Monterey Thomas
Larkin was left with $900 worth of potatoes that the U.S. navy had
ordered but never collected or paid for.[33] But Larkin was destined
to be more than a duped merchant left with too many potatoes. A
native of Massachusetts who had failed in business in North Carolina, he sailed around the Horn to seek his fortune in Monterey in
1832. Here he married a widow born in the United States and was
later to claim that their children were the first to be born in California to U.S. parents.[34]

This American invasion of California in 1842 sparked Thomas
Larkin's interest in matters other than mercantile. He became one of
the first California "boosters." He began to write back to the United
States about what a wonderful place California was for settlers. He
was soon the California correspondent for the *New York Herald*, the
Journal of Commerce, and the *Boston Daily Advertiser*.[35] Larkin's writings helped divert to California a significant part of the overland

immigration flow from the eastern states to the Oregon Territory, which had been the primary goal of settlers, especially since it was American land. The stories about "Golden California" attracted many who would prefer it to the rainier climate of Oregon.

Larkin's writings also attracted the attention of the secretary of state, and Larkin was appointed consul to Monterey in 1844. When he began his duties, he found that he was "without seal, stamp, press books, flag, or coat of arms."[36] Dubbing a man already *in situ* a consul was easy, but getting the accoutrements of office to him often lagged. Larkin was not daunted by lack of equipment; he settled quickly into his consular role, appointing as his vice consul in Yerba Buena (San Francisco) William A. Leidesdorff.[37] Larkin bombarded the State Department with reports on the state of affairs in his district. He was an optimist, seeing a positive side to the Jones episode:

> It was the opinion of many, both Natives and Foreigners in 1842 that the taking of Monterey by Com. Jones would be of serious injury to his country in California and leave a bad impression respecting our Government. I am happy to give as my opinion that the result has not been as anticipated, in fact I think it's proved to the reverse – but a few days after October 20, 1842, Com. Jones and his officers were treated in a remarkable kind manner by all on shore, their treatment towards me and my Countrymen has continued to this time in this Port.[38]

Larkin's reports gave the State Department some background on the ineptitude of Mexican rule in the Province of Alta California and on the various revolts against the rule from Mexico City as well as the Mexican counteractions. He was sending a flow of information back to Washington that made the following points:

1. California was rich territory, strategically located.
2. Mexican rule was on its last legs.
3. The French and British were up to no good.
4. Americans would be well received by the Californians.
5. Time was running out.

Larkin's official reports were a boon to Americans in the government with expansionist aspirations. In his reporting the consul helped set the stage for the ultimate takeover of California by the United States.

In the critical year of 1845, Larkin had little instruction from the department, having received only one letter from Secretary of State James Buchanan. Belatedly Buchanan wrote Larkin on 17 October 1845, expressing his appreciation for the information the consul had sent on California. "The future destiny of that country is a subject of anxious solicitude for the Government and the people of the United States should California assert and maintain her independence, we shall render her all the kind offices in our power, as a sister Republic. This Government has no ambitions to gratify and no desire to extend the federal system over more territory than we already possess, unless by the free and spontaneous wish of the independent people of adjoining territories." The secretary went on to say that the United States could not view with indifference the transfer of California to Great Britain or any other European power and that the United States would "vigorously oppose" any attempt to make California a British or French colony and would assist the Californians in resisting such a move. Continuing, he noted that if it were the wish of the Californians to join the Union, "they will be received as brethren, whenever this can be done without affording Mexico any just cause of complaint."[39] How Mexico would accede to the takeover of California without cause for complaint was not spelled out. Such is the language of diplomacy.

The secretary went on to inform Larkin that he was to be the president's confidential agent as well as consul in California and was to keep the department informed of the locations of settlements of Mexican, American, British, and French citizens and of their feelings toward the United States. For his duties as a confidential agent, Larkin was to be paid $6 a day, or $2,190 per annum, which was better than being an uncompensated consul, even if it was not up to the standard of $3,000 paid the French consul in California.[40] Being designated confidential agent added nothing to Larkin's duties, since he had given up his work as a regular merchant to devote himself to American affairs, except for his interest in land dealings. The confidential-agent designation seemed designed to circumvent the congressional prohibition on the payment of consuls, except those in the Barbary Coast. It also assured the full attention of the consul in what promised to be exciting times in California. When Buchanan wrote his instructions of October 1845 about receiving Californians "as brethren," he must have assumed that

Larkin could read between the lines. Larkin did his best to prepare his neighbors to be brethren.

As the territorial situation in California and Texas moved toward a climax, Captain John C. Fremont of the U.S. Army arrived in California in 1844 on an exploration trip with a party of fifty tough mountain men after a difficult passage through the Sierra Nevada mountains. The Mexican commander in Monterey asked Larkin to explain "the object & commission" of Fremont. Larkin replied that the army captain was surveying the most practical route to the West, and that the men with him were not soldiers, but simply men hired to help with the exploration.[41]

Supposedly the explorers were to stay in California only long enough to recuperate from their journey. Larkin tried to keep relations smooth between the American explorers and the Mexican authorities as Fremont lingered. Larkin must have intimated to Fremont that he was outwearing his welcome, even though he was following instructions, by staying on. Fremont eventually moved north and out of the way of direct confrontation with the Mexicans but kept within striking distance. He was an aggressive officer who saw opportunities of military glory if things fell apart in California.

The U.S. navy was also making its presence felt. The sloop-of-war *Portsmouth* under Commander John B. Montgomery arrived off Monterey in April 1846, bringing news from the consul in Mazatlán that war was imminent and that the rest of the Pacific Squadron could appear at any time on a nonpacific mission, the seizure of California.[42]

It was the situation in Texas that triggered both the Mexican War and the acquisition of California by the United States. When Texas won its independence in 183f>, it was expected by most Texans of American stock that the territory would join the United States, but slavery was the sticking point. Because of its location, soil, climate, and the many settlers from the slave states, there was no doubt that Texas would be a slave state too, but matters were stalled for years in Washington because of opposition from the free state representatives. Moreover, Mexico had not renounced its claim to Texas and made it clear that annexation by the United States could mean war.

James K. Polk was elected president of the United States in 1844 on a platform calling for the annexation of Texas. John Tyler, the lame-duck president, wanted the credit for bringing Texas into the Union. By the unusual procedure of a joint resolution in Congress, which only required a simple majority in both houses rather than the normal two-thirds, Tyler succeeded in annexing Texas. The measure was signed on 1 March 1845.

Mexico promptly broke diplomatic relations with the United States. The ministers in Washington and Mexico City took their passports and left. Although severing diplomatic relations usually meant expulsion of foreign consuls too, this was not always the case. The American consular network in Mexico remained intact, with free communication with the United States. John Black, the American consul in Mexico City, was to be the de facto American minister for the next two years. U.S. consuls in such vital spots as Mexico City, Vera Cruz, Tampico, Mazatlán, and Monterey during the events that led to hostilities and even after hostilities started, were able to supply invaluable intelligence to American political and military leaders.

During the latter half of 1845 American and Mexican land forces were concentrating along the disputed Texas border, but they were kept a prudent distance apart to avoid clashes while the process of diplomacy was at work. An American naval force was assembled off the ports of the Gulf of Mexico, and Commodore John D. Sloat of the Pacific Squadron was instructed to avoid aggression but to be ready to occupy the ports of California should Mexico declare war.[43]

Hope for peaceful settlement rested on serious negotiations taking place in Mexico City. It would be necessary to find an honorable way out for Mexico's irretrievable loss of Texas and the likely loss of other border areas, including California. There were also certain financial claims against Mexico by Americans.

Just as the reports and writings of the U.S. consul in California helped stoke the fires that burned within the expansionist wing of American politics, it is possible that the diplomatic ineptness of the U.S. consul in Mexico City was crucial in bringing on the war. Consul John Black arranged for a meeting between the Mexican foreign minister and someone to be sent by President Polk. The identity of that person, his official title, and the agenda of the meeting were to be absolutely crucial as to whether there would be peace or war. In September 1845 Black had received instructions from Secretary of State Buchanan to determine whether the Mexicans would "now be willing to restore diplomatic relations [and] would receive an Envoy from the United States entrusted with full power to adjust all questions in dispute between the two governments."[44] In his negotiations Black did not make the crucial points of restoring "diplomatic relations," sending an "envoy", and "adjust all questions" as clearly to the Mexican foreign minister Manuel de la Peña y Peña as he should have done. Peña, on his part, may have deliberately confused the issue too. Black and Peña reached an agreement that the United States could send a "commissioner," which was quite different from sending an "envoy." The agenda also was left vague. [45]

Many times in diplomacy it is necessary first to come to a general agreement and avoid being too precise. An early spelling-out of terms can raise problems best left undetailed until they can be worked out later. This was definitely not one of those times. Black did not press Peña on the restoration of relations or on the agenda. In reporting to Washington the consul failed to make clear that the term "commissioner" was not defined. Neither the secretary of state nor the president asked for clarification (the traveling time between Washington and Mexico City probably would have precluded this anyway), and Polk's minister plenipotentiary John Slidell was sent to Mexico posthaste.

Upon his arrival Slidell found that the Mexicans were willing to talk only about the Texas boundary and would not receive him as an accredited American minister. He angrily returned to the United States. The American army moved to the Rio Grande, and war resulted.

The consul in Mazatlán John Parrott, who had been instrumental in sending Commodore Jones off on his embarrassing attack in 1842 by reporting that war was then imminent, was once again to play a role in events in California. In May 1846 he sent almost the same message to Sloat, the new Pacific Squadron commander. On 25 April, during a major clash between American and Mexican troops along the Rio Grande, sixty-three Americans under Captain Seth Thornton were killed, wounded, or captured. Parrott, who happened to be in Guadalajara at the time, heard the news and reported to the secretary of state and at the same time sent an express message to Commodore Sloat urging his immediate departure for the coast of California "assuring him that not a moment should be lost in taking possession of that important country. I have every reason to believe that the Commodore will have acted upon my suggestion and can almost with a certainty venture to state that our flag may be flying over California at this very moment."[46]

With the example of his predecessor Commodore Jones before him, Commodore Sloat treated the message from the consul in

Mazatlán with understandable caution. Sloat also was not in good health and moved slowly. He stayed in Mazatlán until 7 June, four days after Parrott had written of his visions of the American flag flying over California. The Pacific Squadron finally left after receiving news of several more battles on the Rio Grande and of a naval blockade of Vera Cruz. The squadron arrived at Monterey on 2 July, but as Sloat was still unsure of the situation, he took the safer course of making the normal courtesy calls on the Mexican port authorities and then conferring with Consul Larkin.

Sloat and Larkin celebrated the Fourth of July on board the American naval ships. As it happened to be also a fiesta day in Monterey, there were celebrations all around. While the consul and commodore were assessing the situation, word came of an uprising, later known as the Bear Flag Revolt against Mexican rule, by American settlers north of San Francisco, with Captain Fremont and his men taking part. This was enough for Sloat; he called for the surrender of the Mexican forces in Monterey.[47] The Californians and Mexicans in Monterey, already aware of the fighting on the Rio Grande, were puzzled that the United States Navy, which had acted so precipitously two years earlier, had not moved sooner, but they accepted the strange ways of the "gringo." They enjoyed the fiesta, the Fourth of July, and then the surrender ceremonies on 7 July, complete with a marine landing force of one hundred men and a small band of six musicians. There was no resistance.

Larkin saw himself as a peacemaker. He sought both to keep California under the American flag and to stop American settlers, the U.S. military, the Mexican military, and native Californians of Spanish descent from fighting each other. He wrote all the leaders asking for a transition to American rule without bloodshed.

Although unable to stop the fighting, Larkin still exerted a moderating influence. He persuaded the Americans to release some of the captured Californian and Mexican leaders on pledges of friendship or neutrality. He then went with the navy, now under a new, much more energetic commodore, Robert F. Stockton, south to San Pedro, where he accompanied a naval landing force sent to Los Angeles. Stockton's army of 350 men, though small, was large enough to achieve its purpose, camping in front of Los Angeles while Larkin, a midshipman, and a servant entered the city to negotiate its surrender. The Mexican governor and his troops had already left. Although a more peaceful man than William Eaton of Tripoli, Larkin was following in his fellow consul's footsteps by having a city surrender to him.

By the middle of August 1846 the Americans had taken all of California without any real fighting. Larkin, of the opinion that he had done so well that he had worked himself out of the job as consul (since California was now under the United States), wrote the secretary of state to that effect but asked that he be kept on as a confidential agent. [48] But he was premature in thinking that matters were settled in California.

The native Californians, disliking Mexican rule, had revolted against it from time to time, but after only a month under the Stars and Stripes they found that they liked American rule no better and again revolted. The uprising was at first successful, catching the Americans by surprise and short of soldiers because combat troops had been sent to more active theaters of war. The revolt won back most of the cities and towns taken by the Americans, especially those in Southern California.

Larkin was regarded by some Californians not as a friendly consul and peacemaker but as the cause of all evils. This was essentially true, since Larkin had been instrumental in bringing the American troops to California. Although he knew that he was a marked man, Larkin took no precautions and was captured by a partisan force on 15 November 1846 when he was traveling without protection from Monterey to Yerba Buena. As a prisoner, he was present at a small battle between California partisans and American volunteers and was almost killed by an enraged partisan who blamed him for the death of a relative in the fighting. [49] Later Larkin, still a prisoner, was taken south to Los Angeles. He was released unharmed after the Americans won the battle of Los Angeles on 9 January 1847.

After the final conquest of California in 1847 Larkin was kept another year on the U.S. government payroll as a confidential agent and went as a delegate to the state constitutional convention in 1849 before resuming his business activities. Although his tenure as an American consul (1844–46) was short, it was one of the most significant in the history of the consular service.

The experience of the U.S. consuls in Mexico was quite different from that of the consul in California. After the Mexicans rejected Polk's envoy John Slidell and fighting broke out along the Rio Grande, Congress voted for war in May 1846. Mexico, however, did not declare war until 1 July, but American consuls and citizens were ordered out of the country in May, with the exception of the consul in Mexico City.

In his last dispatch prior to leaving his post, Francis M. Diamond, the consul in Vera Cruz, reported that two American ships had entered the harbor shortly before the expulsion order and were at anchor. The Vera Cruz authorities, at first inclined to seize the ships, finally agreed with Consul Diamond that since the ships had entered the port in good faith, it was only fair that they be allowed to depart unharmed.[50]

The Mexican government, for unknown reasons, did not expel John Black from Mexico City although all his colleagues had had to leave by the end of May 1846. He was to remain at his post for almost a full year, regularly sending and receiving dispatches to and from the secretary of state, an almost unprecedented situation. The cause may have been inertia on the part of the Mexican government or a hope that there would be some sort of settlement with the United States and hence no point in cutting off all lines of communication with the United States. Whatever the case, Black was reporting in July 1846 on developments in the wartime capital: "Things are dragging on here in their usual snail paced way. I was in hopes that ere this I should have been able to give the Department some information of a more positive character in relation to the operation of this Government, either in respect to their carrying on the war, or manifesting their willingness to make peace, but affairs remain in `status quo' – and notwithstanding the Government and its friends are fully satisfied, of their inability to carry on the war with any degree of advantage, and of the absolute necessity of making peace, yet they stand with their arms folded as if insensible to the impending storm." [51]

Black had to leave in April 1847, by which time all the major battles in the north, Palo Alto, Monterrey, and Buena Vista, had been fought and won by the Americans. Further to the south, General Winfield Scott had taken Vera Cruz, and his army was preparing for its march on Mexico City.

During this time of military activity Black was not only reporting on his contacts with the Mexican Foreign Ministry but also on details of Mexican troop movements. Apparently no effort was made to control Black's correspondence; his reports gave the secretary of state and the president a good picture of the mood in the enemy capital, although Black's reports on military activities were probably less useful because of the time factor for sending dispatches to Washington.

The war reached its climax with the capture of Mexico City in October 1847; the peace treaty was signed in February 1848, and shortly thereafter Black returned to his post in Mexico City, John Parrott went back to Mazatlán, and Diamond went back to Vera Cruz, as did the other consuls to their posts in that still-not-so-tranquil country. From the consular point of view, it was strictly *status quo ante bellum* with the exception of Consul Larkin, who had worked himself out of his job.

In Latin America during the momentous decades between 1810 and 1860 the consuls of the United States were the spearhead of American diplomacy, not mere spear carriers, the common conception of the role of American consuls, as contrasted to American diplomats. One reason the consuls were so important in Latin America was that they served in a turbulent era when power and influence were often transferred from the capitals to the provinces and the control of the capitals was frequently changing hands. Then too, because of the desire not to offend Spain unreasonably, the United States for much of this period avoided establishing diplomatic relations. Even when diplomats were sent in, the many local eruptions in the cities and provinces of the various countries in Latin America required that a man on the spot deal with whoever was temporarily in charge, and the man on the spot was usually the American consul.

Another reason the consuls played an unexpectedly large role in Latin American affairs was that in most cases the United States had sent capable men to represent its interests. Although personnel records for that period are nonexistent, an examination of the background of men sent to the major consular posts during the 1810–60 period shows that most of them were merchants who were familiar with Latin America and who spoke Spanish. There was also a degree of self-selection. Few men with political influence but with no experience in South America or Mexico would aspire to go to those countries that seemed always to be in a state of revolt and were, therefore, dangerous.

Because of the distance from Washington, the ever-changing political situation, and the danger in Latin America, a consul soon learned that he had to understand his environment in order to survive both financially and physically. These lessons often bred a self-sufficient, energetic, confident, and effective public official.

7

Consuls in Europe — Consular Reform (1815–1860)

The American consular presence in Latin America expanded in a logical order. As the Spanish empire crumbled away, the United States appointed consuls to the areas previously closed to foreign representation; the gradual expansion followed the battle lines. In Europe, however, between the end of the War of 1812 in 1815 and the start of the American Civil War in 1861, there was a different pattern. The boundaries of European countries were well established. The impetus for consular expansion was in the economic relationship between cities, both within Europe and the United States, and between European and American cities.

At the end of the Napoleonic Wars there was a major spurt in international trade; the long pent-up mercantile energies of both Europe and the United States at last had an outlet. Cities on both sides of the Atlantic were becoming manufacturing and trade centers dependent on the smooth flow of foodstuffs, raw materials, and manufactured goods across borders and seas. In addition to their responsibilities for merchant seamen, consuls had an important role in this expanding export/import trade by providing shipping documentation and information for exporters in their own countries and in their host cities. The growth of U.S. consular posts in Europe from 1815 to 1860 largely reflects American foreign commercial expansion. In 1830 there were sixty-two consular posts in Europe; by 1860 there were eighty-nine, scattered from Russia to Spain and Greece to Norway.

The increase in Trans-Atlantic trade in the post-Napoleonic years was not the only reason for the growth of the American consular establishment in Europe. Political patronage was the force greater than commercial necessity, which pushed for the opening

of new consulates. Some American businessmen, seeing opportunities in European cities with no American consul, wrote their
congressmen to have posts opened and secured such appointments
for themselves. A consulship could be a commercial advantage, a
social distinction, and a possible source of revenue. Since consuls
in Europe were not paid, neither Congress nor the secretary of state
worried much about consular proliferation.

Although consular appointments were virtually unchecked,
Congress was concerned about the growing number of American
diplomatic missions abroad. In 1832 the House suggested that
American ministers be limited to England, France, and Russia.[1]
Nothing came of this proposal, but later, in 1844, the House Committee on Foreign Affairs, aghast at the cost of maintaining diplomatic representation abroad ($200,000), suggested that certain
ministers combine several countries under their responsibility. Suggested combinations included Spain and Portugal; the Italian states
and Turkey; Brazil, Uruguay, and Argentina; and Bolivia, Peru, and
Chile.[2] Again, nothing evolved from this unworkable proposal.

Though appointments to government positions were increasingly politicized, especially after the election of Andrew Jackson in
1828, the consular service was not affected as much as postmaster-
ships or other domestic appointments. Thomas Aspinwall of Massachusetts, for example, held the prestigious post of consul in London from 1815 to 1853, Alexander Hammit of Maryland was consul
in Naples from 1809 to 1861, and members of the Sprague family,
American merchants settled in Gibraltar, were consuls there from
1815 to the end of the century, the position passing from generation
to generation. Incumbents of the more lucrative posts with the considerable number of fees generated by shipping, such as Liverpool,
Genoa, and Antwerp, more accurately reflected the political party
in power. It was not until after the end of the Civil War that appointments to the consular service, especially those in Europe, were
to feel the full weight of the spoils system.

There was a curious twist in the staffing of some new posts.
They became convenient assignments for authors, painters, or
other professionals in the arts. When the United States was established, there were complaints that the government did not have the
fancy "feathers" European courts had to hand out, such as knight-
hoods and other titles as rewards. It certainly was not envisaged
that the position of a consul, with the mundane duty of protecting
American seamen and documenting merchandise, would be used

to reward or encourage the arts, but the practice of appointing such writers and artists continued until early in the twentieth century. Consular positions were also available for gentlemen seeking a touch of European polish before returning to America.

An early example of the use of a consulship to reward achievement in the arts was the request by Governor De Witt Clinton of New York to Secretary of State Henry Clay in 1826, suggesting some such position for James Fenimore Cooper, Esq., of his state, "believing you disposed to encourage American talent, I have taken the liberty of commending him to your favorable notice as a gentleman every way worthy of it."[3] Cooper at thirty-seven was already a well-known author, having published several successful books, such as *The Spy*, *The Pioneers*, and *The Pilot*. He had just finished what was to be his most popular book, *The Last of the Mohicans*.

Cooper, by no means impoverished, was looking for a sinecure, a rationale to take his family on "the grand tour," and thought that an official title would help facilitate travel in Europe. He went to Washington to discuss such a position with Clay and, according to the author's daughter, was first offered the post of minister to Sweden, but declined. Clay then suggested opening a post at Lyons, France, and giving it to Cooper.[4] After thinking the matter over, Cooper accepted the position with the understanding that he would be only the nominal consul.

While Cooper played at being a consul, other consuls in Europe were hard at work, some finding that such appointments had their moments of danger, even in generally peaceful Europe. The American consul in Antwerp, still under the Dutch king at the beginning of 1830, found himself in the middle of the revolutionary creation of Belgium. Consul William D. Patterson reported to the State Department in August 1830 that there was fighting in Brussels and that fugitives were fleeing into Antwerp. "The merchants here treat it as the act of some hot headed men and that it will be pacified, yet from what I have seen there appears to be a strong dissatisfaction with the [Dutch] Government generally prevailing in the country."[5] The consul was right.

Trade fell off in Antwerp as the revolution grew. Patterson reported that citizens in the towns were arming themselves and that the merchants blamed the situation on the Catholic priests, who, they maintained, were stirring up the masses to reject their Protestant ruler. The consul remarked however, that it was difficult to wade through prejudices to get at the truth.[6]

By early October unrest was worsening, especially in Brussels. Although Antwerp was still quiet, Patterson advised American ships to get away as quickly as possible.[7] His advice was sound, for the revolt spread to Antwerp, where parts of the city came under the guns of the Dutch army. There was fighting in the city, even in front of the consulate, and Patterson's house was badly damaged by the bombardment. He moved to an American brig still in port, but when it left he returned to his post to stay as did the British and Hanseatic consuls; all the others had fled. These consuls went under a flag of truce to the fortress, where the Dutch garrison was holding out, in an attempt to protect neutral property and halt indiscriminate shelling of the city. They were successful.[8] The Dutch finally withdrew and Belgium became independent, leaving Consul Patterson to deal with the more intractable, yet more peaceable, problem of relations between American skippers and their seamen.

The professional consuls of France and Russia fled Antwerp when the situation became dangerous, but a nonsalaried U.S. government official stuck to his post and played an active and exposed role in achieving peace. Presumably, as one engaged in trade, Patterson had some financial stake in the issue. Nevertheless, he showed commendable courage and a sense of duty at a difficult time.

Despite the heroic actions of some consuls, such as Patterson in Antwerp, the problems of the consular service, especially the constant complaints about the quality of service abroad and the disparity in the fees charged by different consuls, caused Congress in 1830 to take a hard look at the system. Secretary of State Martin Van Buren was directed to report on the situation. He noted that

> fees which our consuls are authorized to charge for services rendered by them in the regular discharge of their official duties, are not well defined by law, and that consequently, no uniform rule is believed to be observed some consuls charging more and some less for the performance of the same specific acts. This dissimilitude in practice leads, likewise, in many instances, to unpleasant collisions between these agents of the Government of the United States and their fellow citizens and to endless criminations and recriminations on both sides.[9]

Secretary Van Buren further stated that there was no requirement on the part of consuls to report on the fees they collected and that the consular system was "susceptible of great and beneficial changes; but in what respects, my experience does not enable me to point out – the other important duties incident to the charge of this Department, of a more urgent nature, having almost exclusively occupied my attention since I was entrusted with it, [have] left me but very little time to devote to this highly necessary and interesting branch of the public business." [10] As he had been secretary of state for almost a year, Van Buren was honest in admitting his lack of attention to consular work, a lack that had been apparent in all secretaries after Thomas Jefferson.

The next year Van Buren was more helpful to the deliberations of Congress on the structure of the consular service. He had asked all the consuls to report on the fees they charged for official services and for their observations and suggestions for improving the consular system. These reports were turned over to a veteran consular officer then in Washington to use in preparing recommendations for Congress. The consular officer was Daniel Strobel of South Carolina, who had taken over the consulate at Bordeaux from the contentious William Lee in 1816.

The Strobel report of January 1831 was a thoughtful look at the consular service or, as it was often termed, the consular system that had developed in the 54 years of American independence. Strobel noted that foreign consular positions fell into two main categories, "one, consuls [appointed] from among opulent merchants of their respective nations, permanently residing in foreign ports, to whom they grant no further remuneration than what is derived from certain fees," the other being salaried officials who were not permitted to trade. The Dutch, Danes, Swedes, and Hanseatic towns used the merchant consuls, while Great Britain, France, Spain, Portugal, Russia, and most of the other commercial states had professional consuls. The problem with the United States copying the Dutch model, as Strobel saw it, was that there were few "opulent commercial houses of our nation permanently established in the ports to which we trade." There were not enough Americans settled abroad

whose circumstances enable them to hold the offices of consuls, and discharge the duties of that situation as they ought to be performed, for the slender and precarious emoluments to be derived from a few fees. Accordingly, experience has demonstrated, that, here and there an exception, our consulates have proved injurious to most of the individuals who have unwarily gone out to occupy them, and have done so under erroneous impressions of their value in a pecuniary point of view, which has plunged many of them into difficulties and embarrassments; whilst the struggles and shifts that some among them are consequently compelled to make for a livelihood, are often of a nature to derogate from their official character, and to injure its efficacy.[11]

Strobel pointed out that consuls should be able to mix socially with local authorities on an equal basis, but many could not afford to, limiting their effectiveness. He made a strong case for the British system of granting consuls salaries and prohibiting them from trade. Consuls in trade were likely to show favoritism to certain merchants and shipowners. "It is a fact generally admitted by those who had the opportunity for making observations and acquiring information on the subject, that the duty of the consul, and the interest of the merchant, where the two characters are united in the same individual, are, in many cases, totally irreconcilable."[12] Merchants needed to stand well with the masters of ships and their supercargoes. The consul, however, in the course of his duties often clashed with these same masters and supercargoes over crew matters and proper shipping documentation.

Strobel suggested a uniform system of fees based on the tonnage of ships, which would produce a fund from which the consuls could be paid modest salaries. The number of consuls in Europe could be reduced so that there would be little or no drain on the Treasury. He stated:

What we now call our consular system, is, in fact, a hasty sketch on the spur of the occasion, when it became indispensable, at the peace of 1783, to send consuls to some of the nations of Europe that were sending similar agents to reside among us. Such as it then was, it has continued to remain, without any attempt being made towards improving it, although its defects have long been felt, and occasionally exposed; whereas the British, with all their long experience and extensive practice, have found it expedient, of late years, to introduce changes and ameliorations in their consular system.[13]

As part of his plan for the improvement of the consular system, Strobel urged that there be better direction from the State Department, as consuls had little instruction as to exactly what their duties and authorities were. He proposed that a qualified person be attached to the department to carry on a regular and active correspondence with the consuls in the field to keep them informed, answer their questions promptly, and solicit their comments. Any laws passed by Congress pertaining to consular work would be sent expeditiously to the posts with comments on what these laws meant to consuls. He also suggested that all official forms be sent to consuls and that they not be allowed to deviate from the format unless there was evident need for an exception, in which case they should inform the department of the reason. Consuls would be informed of complaints about their work and be given an opportunity to respond. Finally, Strobel suggested that the consular authority in Washington be more responsive to the consuls in the field "in furnishing them with general or partial instructions, whenever requisite for their government in fulfilling their official duties."[14]

One is left with the ugly impression of masters and supercargoes of American merchant ships haggling over the fees charged in each port by the resident consuls. With no fixed schedule of fees, seemingly a simple matter for Congress to legislate or delegate to the State Department, consuls were free to charge what the traffic would bear. There was also the option of waiving the fees altogether when the consul might be given commercial advantages by the ships' captains.

Van Buren's successor as secretary of state, Edward Livingston (1831–1833), tried to bring some sense of order to the so-called consular system. After examining the staffing of consulates abroad and hearing complaints about some consuls, Livingston was quoted as saying, "For all the wonder is not that we have bad consuls, but that we have good ones – for we have taken great pains to settle on the worst consular system in the world – and no thanks to us, if we are not represented by men as universally bad as the system under which they serve."[15] In 1833 he issued a set of general Instructions to all consuls and commercial agents. Consular duties were spelled out regarding record keeping, citizenship documentation, estate settlement for American citizens dying abroad, and dealings with masters of American vessels. It is difficult to understand why this straightforward action had not been taken by some of the major figures who previously held the office of secretary of state.

Livingston then called upon consuls to transmit to the department copies of laws or regulations enacted in their districts and pertaining to trade. Also, "the consuls are expected, once in three months at least, to write the department, if it be for no other purpose than that of apprising the department of their being at their respective posts."[16] Consuls were informed that their duties were to promote commerce and navigation. They were enjoined "not to enter into any contentions or disputes that can be avoided, either with their countrymen, or the authorities of the country in which they reside." They were also to stay out of local political concerns and to report on them only, and a particular caution was given to consuls in South America and the United Mexican States "to forbear intermeddling with their political or local affairs in the smallest degree whatevcr."[17] Thomas O. Larkin, the consul in Monterey, certainly had a set of these instructions on his bookshelf as he helped instigate his consular district's successful rebellion against Mexico.

Besides these hortatory platitudes, which were often honored in the breach, the instructions included a list of services consuls were expected to perform and the fees they should charge, which generally ranged from two dollars to twenty-five cents for authenticating documents, administering oaths, and certifying shipping documents. Consuls were allowed to charge the same rate as the notaries of their district for other services. Although incomplete, the list for the first time put a grip on the fee system that had been the source of so much contention. One flaw in the instructions was that consuls were not obliged to send a reckoning to the State Department on charges they had levied. This was probably an intentional omission, as there was not a sufficiently large staff in the department to carry out the audit, and only so much could be asked of the unsalaried consuls.

Despite the public statements of Secretaries Van Buren and Livingston on the deplorable state of the consular system, Congress continued to ignore any action toward reform. Some patchwork legislation was passed in the act of 20 July 1840, which spelled out consuls' duties regarding seamen and shipping, including the daunting provision that "if any consul or commercial agent shall neglect or omit to perform, seasonably, the duties hereby imposed, or shall be guilty of any malversation or abuse of power, he shall be liable to any injured person for all damage occasioned thereby;

and for all malversation and corrupt conduct in office, he shall be liable to indictment, and, on conviction by any court of competent jurisdiction, shall be fined not less than one nor more than ten thousand dollars, and shall be imprisoned not less than one nor more than five years."[18] This seemed a heavy burden for unpaid and untrained officials, but this law, apparently, was never enforced.

When James Buchanan was secretary of state, he responded to a request from the House of Representatives and sent his recommendations to Congress in 1846 for revising the U.S. consular system. Buchanan's report, in which he led off by complaining that "it has been impossible for me without neglecting the current and urgent business of the department, to devote the time necessary to comply in a satisfactory manner," called again for the payment of salaries to consuls. He pointed out, as had his predecessors, the dangers of having a merchant consul in a city abroad, which made the consulate "subsidiary to his private business; and the temptation is great to abuse his public trust, for the purpose of favoring his customers."[19] Buchanan repeated the Strobel report's recommendation that a fixed fee be levied on ships according to tonnage, which would do away with the different fees for different services regarding seamen and shipping papers. The monies collected would go to the Treasury, an indemnification, in part, for consular salaries.

Secretary Buchanan was concerned about the State Department's lack of adequate staff to supervise the far-flung consular system. The bill under consideration by Congress called for consular officers to furnish the department "at stated periods, such information as may be rendered useful to the country, and imposes on it the corresponding duty of communicating this information to Congress in a digested form."[20] The secretary believed that it would be:

> Indispensable that a competent person should be employed, as the bill proposes, to digest, arrange, and publish the information thus obtained, for the use of Congress and the people. It is impossible that the two consular clerks now in the department should, besides their present duty of corresponding with one hundred and sixty-eight consuls on the current business of their consulates, perform this additional service. Indeed, these clerks are not sufficient for the proper discharge of the present business of the branch on which they are employed.[21]

The two clerks dealing with consular affairs were a recent addition to the State Department, having been appointed in 1833 in a major reorganization. But two were obviously inadequate to handle such a large consular establishment.

While Congress considered consular reform but did nothing concrete, while the secretary of state was too occupied with other "current and urgent business" to tend to consular matters, and while the two clerks struggled to answer their mail, the American consuls abroad went about their business. A refreshing glimpse of how such a consul conducted business at an ordinary post in the 1840s is given in a book with the proprietary title of *My Consulship* by a young consul, Charles Edwards Lester.

Lester had some law training but abandoned the bar for the ministry when he became a Congregational clergyman in upstate New York. He gave up this vocation too and went abroad to improve his health. He was a delegate to an anti-slavery convention in England in 1840, but soon turned to literary work to earn his livelihood, writing books on nature, history, and the arts.[22] A Whig, Lester was appointed by President Tyler to Genoa at the age of twenty-seven. Not a typical merchant consul, Lester depended upon his consular fees and his pen to support his wife, and two small children during the five years he was in Genoa. He quickly threw himself enthusiastically into the work of his new post, learning Italian and enjoying local history, art, and the Italian way of life.

Lester describes an interview with a type of person frequently encountered by American consuls, the wandering religious fanatic. One morning there was a thunderous knocking at the consulate door and a young American from Worcester, Massachusetts, "tall, lean and most particularly lantern-jawed, and what the Yankees call bony," was ushered in. Dressed in homespun, the stranger asked Lester, "Be you the United States <u>Counsel</u>?" and when Lester allowed that he was, the Yankee replied, "Well I'm the Prophet of God." The Prophet said that he was on his way to Jerusalem to prepare the way for the second coming of Christ, and "if you wish to escape the last vial of wrath that is just a-going to be poured out, help me on my journey." He planned first to go to Rome to proclaim to the pope that the day of God's punishment had come and that in a few weeks Pius IX would be cast into the bottomless pit. Lester tried to dissuade the man but, of course, was unable to prevail over divine guidance; and so he issued him a passport, declining to take a fee for it, saying, "I don't charge Prophets anything for passports." Lester later heard that his client went to Rome, preached at St. Peter's, and was duly imprisoned as a maniac. Eventually, this Worcester man got to Jerusalem, where he died waiting for the Second Coming.[23]

Lester often found it hard to deal amicably with the masters and seamen of American merchant ships. When he was visited by a sailor who had swum ashore from his ship, complaining of having been shanghaied from Philadelphia, Lester recalled that he had received instructions from the State Department to be on the lookout for the young man. When he requested that the captain come to the consulate to explain the matter, the captain stoutly refused. Consul Lester then sent his guard to bring the ship's master to the office, but without success. Though somewhat unsure of his authority, Lester was convinced that the situation required harsh measures and arranged with the Genoese police to put the captain in the local dungeon overnight, which "taught him the art of good manners."[24] Lester then had the sailor discharged with three months' pay and sent him back to his parents as a passenger on another ship.

Appointments of U.S. diplomats and consuls had always lacked standardization and were therefore haphazard, resulting in a varying degree of competency among those appointed. There were no clear lines of authority between the consuls and the embassy or delegation. Often the consuls were more familiar with a country than were their diplomatic colleagues, as they generally served in a country longer than American diplomats. Business negotiations kept them much more in touch with events than were diplomats living in the exclusive nineteenth-century social world of courts. Consul Lester in Genoa, for instance, did not think highly of the American chargé d'affaires to the Kingdom of Sardinia in Turin: "He can speak nothing but English, and even that in a curious way. He was a doctor living somewhere in the Southern States, with a poor run of practice, and broken-down health."[25]

In 1848 the political situation in Italy demanded cool heads on the part of American consuls as an abortive revolution swept over the Italian states. Several consuls were caught up in the general enthusiasm of the time. The consul in Palermo, John M. Marston of Massachusetts, even recognized the brief insurgent government on behalf of the United States. Hearing of this audacious, though well-meant action, Secretary Buchanan sent an expeditious message to Palermo. "This act of high sovereign power certainly cannot, without instructions, be performed by a consul, whose functions are purely commercial; and he ought never, under any conceivable circumstances, to assume such a high responsibility."[26] During the early stages of the Sicilian revolt, Marston did more than assume unauthorized diplomatic powers. He acted as a consul should: protecting American lives at the risk of his own. Royalist forces bottled up in the citadel of Palermo were indiscriminately bombarding the city. Marston with several other foreign consuls went with a flag of truce, although under fire, to the royalist commander and arranged to have a twenty-four-hour cease-fire to give foreign residents and local civilians a chance to leave the city without being subject to attack.[27]

The consul in Palermo was not the only one to be caught up in the republican fervor in Italy. When Venice, which was then a part of the Austrian Empire, in March 1848 declared itself a republic, a large body of Venetians marched on the American consulate, shouting, "Long live the United States; long live our sister Republic!" As reported in the *New York Herald*, Consul William A. Sparks of South Carolina appeared in front of the consulate holding in one hand the American flag and in the other the new Venetian flag of the Italian tricolor with the lion of St. Mark's superimposed. He told the throng that all America would rejoice when it heard that the ancient queen of the Adriatic had thrown off the Austrian yoke. Later, Sparks called on the provisional government to assure them that his government would support the new republic.[28] In saying this, he was cautious enough to note, that he must await instructions from his government, but Venice was soon back in Austrian hands, and Sparks departed shortly thereafter.

American consuls were not uniformly on the side of the republican cause. The populace in Leghorn, Tuscany, which was also under Austrian rule, caught the fever of independence and in early 1849 demonstrated in front of the American consulate as had happened in Venice. Their reception was chilly. The consul, Joseph Binda, had been born in Italy and naturalized in South Carolina just prior to taking his post in 1841. He was not a supporter of the revolutionary movement and coldly informed the demonstrators that it was not the custom of the American government to interfere in internal affairs of other nations.[29] The revolt was short-lived, and Binda stayed on in Tuscany for another ten years. When eventually the Tuscans threw the Austrians out, Binda, a close friend of the reactionaries, was requested to leave, accused of offering a toast at a formal dinner to "the speedy return to power of the old regime." That put a cap on his consular career. [30]

The busiest consulate in the consular system was Liverpool, England, which was run by Nathaniel Hawthorne, the American novelist, from 1853 to 1857. Hawthorne was already a well-known author before his consular appointment. His major works, The Scarlet *Letter*, *The House of the Seven Gables*, and several other books, were widely known. The position as consul was not offered to support the arts but as a regular patronage gift.

When Hawthorne's college roommate at Bowdoin College and lifelong friend, Franklin Pierce, ran for the presidency, Hawthorne wrote his campaign biography. As newspapers were the only medium for journalistic campaigning in that era and, even with limited circulation, were extremely partisan in their choice of a candidate, a campaign biography was the only way to reach a broad audience. Pierce was able to call upon Hawthorne's powerful pen to help him. Thanks in good part to Hawthorne's persuasive talent, Franklin Pierce was elected as the Democratic candidate in 1852.[31]

Although Hawthorne was making some money from his books, his literary fame had not translated into wealth. He had a family to support. With Pierce safely elected and inaugurated by March 1853, Hawthorne wasted little time in traveling to Washington to secure a consular appointment. Hawthorne pressed his claim at the White House and received his reward, Liverpool.

Much to the regret of his literary admirers, once at his post Hawthorne was very much the working consul; the job would have been too much for a dilettante. Except for a journal he kept and later used for a travel book on England, *Our Old Home*, the period was unproductive for the writer. He had already reached his peak as a novelist before arriving in Liverpool at the age of forty-nine and was to write only one more novel, *The Marble Faun* (1860), based on a stay in Italy after leaving consular work.

Hawthorne was accustomed to putting in a full day of work and so was not daunted by his first weeks in the new office:

Every morning, I find the entry thronged with the most rascally set of sailors that were ever seen – dirty, desperate, and altogether pirate–like in aspect. What the devil they want here, is beyond my present knowledge, but probably they have been shipwrecked, or otherwise thrown at large upon the world, and wish for assistance in some shape. Daily, half a dozen or so of these rogues are distributed among the American vessels to be sent back to their native country; –

or rather to their adopted one; for no one in ten of them are really Americans, but outcasts of all the maritime nations on earth, in a uniform of dirty red-baize shirts.[32]

Hawthorne had a vice consul and a clerk who did most of the routine office business. It was the consul's responsibility to pay his staff out of the money taken in from consular fees. The new consul found that "the pleasantest incident of the day, is when Mr. Pierce (the vice-consul or head-clerk) makes his appearance with the account books, containing the receipts and expenditures of the preceding day, and deposits on my desk a little rouleau of the Queen's coin, wrapt in a piece of paper. This morning there were eight sovereigns, four half-crowns and a shilling – a pretty fair day's work, though not more than the average ought to be."[33]

Hawthorne was quickly immersed in his work. He arranged for funerals, attended inquests of dead seamen, and saw a never-ending stream of visitors to the consulate. Most visitors expected something from the consul, either financial help or merely the opportunity to pass the time with a famous author.

Because of his literary talent Hawthorne was lionized by English society, but he soon became tired of dining out. His wife Sophia, in a letter home, wrote that "Mr. Hawthorne has gone to West Derby to dine and stay all night. He left me with a powerful anathema against all dinner parties, declaring he did not believe anybody liked them, and therefore they were a malicious invention for destroying human comfort."[34] She wrote her father that her husband "goes from us at nine, and we do not see him again till five!!! With my husband's present constant devotion to the duties of his office, he could no more write a syllable than he could build a cathedral. He never writes by candlelight."[35]

The Consul's Prayer is "Oh Lord, not in my district, Amen," which translates to "Please, God, don't let any disaster, natural or man-made, such as the plague, an earthquake, or a ship or train wreck that involves my fellow countrymen happen in my consular district! Let it happen in some other consul's district!" Before he had been at his post six months, Hawthorne was not spared from having to deal with a major disaster, the sinking of an American troopship.

At Christmas time in 1853 the new steamship *San Francisco* was caught in a bad storm in the Atlantic and had to be abandoned by its almost 700 passengers, including members of an American artillery regiment bound from New York to California. Some 300 passengers and crew perished; ships in the area of the disaster picked up the survivors. Unfortunately for the consul in Liverpool, one of the rescuing ships was the *Antarctic*, which continued on its way to its homeport, Liverpool. Mrs. Hawthorne, in a letter home, gave her account of the situation:

> In the evening Mr. Hawthorne told me that there were suddenly thrown upon his care two hundred soldiers who had been shipwrecked in the San Francisco, and that he must clothe and board them and send them home to the United States. They were picked up somewhere on the sea and brought to Liverpool. Mr. Hawthorne has no official authority to take care of any but sailors in distress. He invited the lieutenants to come and stay here, and he must take care of the soldiers, even if the expense comes out of his own purse. Mr. Hawthorne sent to Mr. Buchanan [James Buchanan, then American minister to Great Britain] about the soldiers, and he would share no responsibility, though it was much more a matter pertaining to his powers than to a consul. Mr. Hawthorne has supplied them with clothes and lodgings, and has finally chartered for their passage home one of the Cunard steamers! such are his official reverses.[36]

Sophia exaggerated the differences between Hawthorne and Buchanan. There was a real problem, since it had never occurred to Congress in writing its laws that American soldiers would be stranded on foreign soil. Buchanan actually helped his consul open a line of credit with the banking house of Barings to sustain the soldiers and to charter a ship from the Cunard line, as American steamship lines were unwilling to assist.[37] Hawthorne, understandably, wanted to get the troops home as quickly as possible. He was concerned, among other matters, that the soldiers might be lured into the British army by recruiters who were beginning to beat their drums to raise men for the imminent hostilities with Russia, which turned into the Crimean War.

Recipients of lucrative political appointments had to expect partisan attacks even when least deserved. Hawthorne received a jolt when he learned of a story going around in the United States that the consul in Liverpool had been indifferent to the fate of the soldiers from the *San Francisco,* and Buchanan had taken matters in hand to arrange for their transport back home.[38] Hawthorne was well known as President Pierce's biographer, and Buchanan was an unannounced but acknowledged rival for the Democratic presidential nomination in 1856. The story appears to have been circulated to further the cause of Buchanan at the expense of a Pierce man, apparently without the candidate's approval or knowledge. The minister and consul got on fairly well together, but were caught up in the game of politics played at home.

Hawthorne had his moments of innocent fun. An American clergyman from New Orleans turned up at the consulate, destitute after having spent an entire week in an English brothel, seeking help to return to the United States and his congregation. In a letter to his publisher, William D. Ticknor in Boston, Hawthorne wrote, "Not knowing whether I should ever have another opportunity of reproving a Doctor of Divinity (an orthodox man too) I laid it on without mercy."[39] The consul then advanced the chastened clergyman funds out of his own pocket to go home.

The wind of reform, albeit only partial reform, finally swept over the consular system in the mid-1850s, leaving in its wake clear winners and losers. Hawthorne was a loser. Congress looked seriously at the problems of the consular system and passed remedial legislation. Among the provisions was one that brought benefits to consuls and agents at certain ports, who were to be paid a salary rather than to depend on fees. The salary for Liverpool was $7,500, at the top of the list, along with London, but still far below the money a lucky consul might make on fees at those busy ports. Mrs. Hawthorne wrote, as her husband prepared to leave his office, "That provoking Consular bill has been in force nearly two years, depriving us of our right to the amount now of about $35,000 because ever since it became law the times have been more prosperous. The year before that the business was miserable. I think it was unjust that the actual incumbents of the office should not have been allowed to fulfill their terms with the conditions upon which they commenced thcm."[40] Sophia Hawthorne was a true daughter of New England and would have enthusiastically supported political reform in any guise in the abstract, but $35,000 was a huge sum (she did exaggerate the potential earnings), and the loss of income was quite another matter. Anyway, her husband had had enough of consular life and, with his mentor Pierce out of office, decided to resign from his post, effective August 1857.

The Consular Reform Act was actually first passed by Congress in 1855, but because some of its provisions appeared to impinge on the authority of the president, the act was replaced by the Reform Act of 1856.[41] It had taken eighty years (1776–1856) to produce a comprehensive bill that would address some, but not all, of the problems that had been apparent for so long in the U.S. consular system. The act created two schedules of consular posts and commercial agencies, B and C (Schedule A was reserved for diplomatic posts since the Act also made an effort to reform the diplomatic system). Schedule B listed posts and agencies with more responsibilities than those in C, or so it was perceived, but the rationale for having the consul in Mexico City on Schedule C and Acapulco on B, and other such examples, is not clear. The salaries of the ninety-two posts on Schedule B ranged from $1,000 to $7,500, while the forty on C went from $500 to $1,000. Consuls and agents on B could not participate in trade and could not keep fees taken for consular services rendered. Those on C could be merchants but could not keep the fees, and the thirty or more not on either schedule could trade and keep fees. There must have been a good bit of horse-trading when congressmen and senators, most of whom had helped put men in one or more of the posts, drew up the schedules. There was also a provision in the 1855 act that allowed for "consular pupils" to number twenty-five, a unit that was expected to develop into a nucleus for a professional consular corps. Congress had second thoughts and repealed this promising provision the next year.

This reform legislation governed the consular service for the next fifty years, placing some men into consular posts who were expected to give their undivided attention to consular affairs and not to mix in trade. Fees were regulated, and reports were to be sent annually to Congress on the amounts collected by each post. This element of the reform was to end much of the acrimony between shipping interests and consuls. The act was also a serious attempt by Congress to bring more control and discipline over the consular system and to curb the possibilities for abuse and corruption. The tariff of fees was to be publicly posted in each consular office, and receipts were to be given for all fees collected. There was also some strengthening of the authority of consuls over the masters of American ships regarding ships' papers.

While the act of 1856 was a major step forward, it still did not provide for a professional, trained consular service, leaving appointment completely open to political influence. The merchant consul was not eliminated, and some 151 out of the 1858 level of 243 posts and agencies were open to men who could act as consuls or agents and merchants.

The other major weakness of the new system was that the salaries were scaled too low, a trap for the unwary office seeker. The salary paid to a consul or agent was expected to cover all his office expenses, including hiring a staff. Hawthorne pointed out the problem for such a well-paid (by 1850 standards) post as Liverpool in an 1855 letter to President Pierce. Using the then just-proposed $7,500 salary as a basis for calculation, Hawthorne said that a consul "cannot possibly live here with a family (unless he secludes himself from society and forgoes all the social advantages of a residence in England) at less expense than $5,000 per annum." Clerk hire, office rent, and expenses came to about $5,000, leaving only $2,500 for the consul's living expenses. "A man might be comfortable with this sum in a New England village, but not, I assure, you as the representative of America, in the greatest commercial city of England."[42]

An American looking for a political plum abroad might see that a post was open in Naples or Geneva at $1,500 and think that he could easily live on that salary, only to find that life in a foreign city was much dearer than at home, especially when he was obliged to maintain an office. At a post where legitimate consular fees were sparse, the temptation for corruption was increased as the American consul found that he was over his head in expenses.

Despite the obvious flaws in the system, consular work in Europe still took care of the tremendous increase in transatlantic shipping and the concomitant increase in merchant ships flying the American flag with American crews who needed special treatment. Consuls also had to deal with another increasingly familiar figure – the American traveler, including fallen doctors of divinity fresh from Liverpool brothels.

8

Consular Development in the Near East (1815–1860)

Consular expansion in the Near East and the northern coast of Africa, including the Barbary States, Egypt, the Levant (Palestine, Syria, and Lebanon), and Turkey, was limited to a few posts in the period between the War of 1812 and the election of Abraham Lincoln in 1860. There were no consulates in Mesopotamia or Persia, and on the Arabian Peninsula there was only a consular agency at Muscat and that was infrequently manned. American representation in the Near East, diplomatic and consular, was confined to ports on the Mediterranean and Constantinople.

Although the distribution of consular posts in the Near East, as in Europe, was in some regards haphazard, there were underlying dynamics – trade and politics. Because the attitude of the Department of State was passive in foreseeing where new consular posts might best be placed, Congress enthusiastically made political appointments in Europe, but not in the Near East.

American trade was at its apogee from 1815 to 1860. Although America ranked next to Great Britain as a cargo carrier, there was little incentive to seek markets in the non-European ports of the Mediterranean. The once-hostile Barbary States had been opened to peaceful trade, but their rulers, no longer collecting blackmail in the form of tribute, had nothing with which to pay for the gewgaws they had previously imported. The other lands of the Ottoman Empire were also poor, attracting only a few American traders and ships. The sending of American missionaries to the Levant and Turkey and the slow growth of trading opportunities after the United States and the Turks established diplomatic relations accounted for a modest demand for consular posts in the eastern Mediterranean. By 1860 the United States had a half-dozen consulates scattered from Egypt to Turkey.

Tangier, the first U.S. consular post in the Arab world, opened because of the friendly initiative of the emperor of Morocco shortly after the American colonies became independent. Notwithstanding a short and bloodless "war" with Morocco, part of an abortive attempt by the emperor to extract more tribute from the Americans in 1801–1802, relations between the two dissimilar nations remained extraordinarily amicable during the entire nineteenth century. Despite good relations between the United States and Morocco, Tangier was not a happy post for Americans assigned there in the first half of the nineteenth century. Consular discontent arose from the lack of money, isolation, and temperament. The men whom the various secretaries of state appointed and sometimes reappointed were often not suited for service in the Moslem world.

In 1796 James Simpson, the first consul in Tangier, had reluctantly moved across the straits from Gibraltar, where he had been consul. He stayed on as consul for twenty-four years, finally dying in harness in 1820. He served under six secretaries of state. To each he complained that the $2,000 salary was not enough to support himself and his family.[1] He was never reconciled to the fact that he had given up the lucrative and comfortable post of Gibraltar, where consular fees were substantial, for the less rewarding post of Tangier. His dissatisfaction increased when he learned in 1810 that Congress had kept the Tangier salary at $2,000 but had awarded the consul in Algiers $4,000, at the same time cutting off the Tangier rental allowance, leaving the Simpsons to fend for themselves.[2] An added insult to Simpson and his successors was the fact that most European consuls in Tangier were far better paid and housed than the Americans.

Simpson's successors almost invariably found themselves heavily in debt by the time they were replaced, becoming a burden to the new consul, for the Department of State did not pay for transportation to and from a post. The consul was paid only for his time at a post. A consul under the threat of being summarily removed by political or bureaucratic whim was left with appalling moving costs, not to mention an unhappy wife and children.

Consul Samuel A. Carr (1832–34), unable to raise enough money to return to South Carolina, was still in Tangier when his successor James R. Leib appeared, not a happy situation for the ex-consul or the consul. Shortly after his arrival Leib had to deal with the problems of Carr's debts because the American consul was the sole judicial authority for Americans in trouble in Morocco. Carr resented his successor's presence and, according to Leib, attempted to assassinate him. Leib had the ex-consul thrown into the consular jail, either for the debts or for the claimed assassination attempt. The British consul complained that Carr was being treated poorly, that his hands and feet were kept bound while in jail, and that conditions there were bad.[3] Carr was finally freed, and arrangements were made to settle the debt and get the Carr family back to the United States.

Leib was then able to attend to the business of keeping the emperor friendly toward America. He succeeded so well that the ruler presented him with a large lion and two fine horses as gifts for the president. The consul, with difficulty, persuaded his secretary of state that it behooved the American government to transport the lion and horses to the United States, where they could be sold away from the sight of the emperor. While waiting for the secretary's decision, Leib was obliged to keep the lion in the small consular residence.[4]

Toward the end of his three-year consular posting Leib, succumbed to the effects of drink. The Moroccan authorities confined Leib to the consulate building under the custody of the consular dragoman, the man who normally provided translation and acted as the main contact with the Moorish officials. The vice consul of Sweden and Norway filled in for Leib when he was suffering from an attack of delirium tremens.[5]

The next consul, Thomas N. Carr from New York, not related to Samuel Carr, found the consulate building falling apart, gifts destined for the emperor undelivered, archives scattered, and the prestige of the United States in shambles. Carr described Leib's condition:

> Wrapped up in the American flag, he would spend whole nights upon the terrace, making signals, by running lanterns up and down the flag staff, to the fleet which he had ordered from the Mediterranean for the purpose of battering the town; at the same time uttering the most discordant sounds, and alarming all the inhabitants. The Moors, like the other Mahotmetans, have great respect for an insane person, but the immediate causes of the insanity in this case are too well known [drink], and even by an insane person, it was not very agreeable to the Moorish authorities to have it demonstrated that there was an American line of battle

ship, the *Pennsylvania*, which could knock down all the walls and batteries of Tangier in fifteen minutes, and to be assured that she was coming in fifteen minutes to do so.[6]

Thomas Carr's departure from Tangier was also acrimonious, ending with a dispute over protocol procedures on leaving a post. Small matters, such as who presented what letter to whom, became major incidents affecting relations between countries. The enclosed, hothouse atmosphere of a small Western enclave on a foreign, unfriendly shore did not help the situation. Carr left in a rage, chopping down the consular flagstaff as he went, normally a sign that relations had been severed, as had been demonstrated during the Barbary Wars.[7] His successor tried to put matters back to normal but was replaced after only two years when the Democrats ousted the Whigs in the United States.

The new secretary of state, James Buchanan, showed deplorable lack of sensitivity in sending to Tangier as the next consul none other than the same Thomas N. Carr who had practically declared war on Morocco on his own initiative his previous time at the post. During his second tour Carr carried on a feud with the British consul, sparked by his contempt of that consul's greater appreciation of the Moslem world.[8] Carr was of the "gunboat and whiff of grapeshot" school of diplomacy with the benighted heathen. The Moors, unhappy with the reappearance of this truculent consul, declared him persona non grata, which resulted in his recall in 1848.

Succeeding American consuls usually reported on the peccadilloes or poor judgment of their predecessors. This regrettable disposition by consuls to make charges and countercharges was not characteristic in every post, but the accusations showed how an inadequate salary and a small community could have a pernicious effect on American consular operations, perhaps to the amusement or disgust of the local officials and other foreign consuls.

An effective consul in the Moslem world needed either to speak Arabic or Turkish or to have a competent interpreter. It was also necessary to have some understanding of how the Arab or Turkish minds worked and a knowledge of Islamic laws and customs. Such expert knowledge was a lot to expect from a U.S. political appointee. Other Western powers had the same problem in getting consular officers or diplomats with adequate language qualifications. Therefore, most diplomatic missions and consular posts in the Near East employed dragomen.

The position of dragoman arose in the earliest days of West–Near East relations. Dragomen not only were interpreters but served as officials in consular courts and acted as political advisors to ambassadors, ministers, and consuls. They usually came from local minority groups such as the Italians, Greeks, or Jews, straddling both the Eastern and the Western cultures but belonging to neither. By controlling the contact of the foreign representatives with the native officials, the dragomen could play their own game without diplomats or consuls being the wiser. Bribery and special privileges were a way of life in Ottoman circles, and the dragomen made sure that they got their share, not always to the advantage of their actual employers.

In its early contacts with the Barbary States the United States could take advantage of what was a harsh but effective school of diplomacy, the enslavement of Americans. By the time men like Richard O'Brien and James Cathcart had worked their way up through the slave bureaucracy of the dey of Algiers, they were well qualified to deal with the Barbary rulers as American representatives without the aid of dragomen.

John Quincy Adams, probably the most qualified man ever to hold the office of secretary of state, knew the importance of having American citizens proficient in what were termed "oriental languages," or Arabic, Turkish, and, later, Persian. Secretary Adams found no person in his department qualified to deal with matters of the Near East. When he became president in 1825, Adams was able to do something about this lack; he appointed young William Brown Hodgson, twenty-four, a native of the Washington suburb of Georgetown, to go to Algiers to serve as a language student, the first to be so designated.

Hodgson's term was for three years at a salary of $600 per year. He was already adept in the languages normally taught to American students, Greek and Latin, and had acquired a knowledge of French and Spanish.[9] As was necessary for a young man wanting to get ahead in the government, he had mentors, Francis Scott Key, a well-known attorney (and author of "The Star Spangled Banner"), and Adams's postmaster general, John McLean.

Adams brought to the presidency an unexcelled knowledge of the consular system (among other things, his wife's father had been the consul in London). He sent Hodgson to Algiers specifically because of William Shaler, consul general there. Shaler had been at that demanding post for ten years and was a scholar of the languages and customs of the area. He was the ideal person to oversee the training of the first U.S. language student. In a period and place where many relationships went sour, Shaler and Hodgson got on splendidly, and the young man bloomed in his study of Arabic, Turkish, and Berber.[10]

When Shaler was away from his post for health reasons, Hodgson was the acting consul and continued as such when Shaler was transferred to Havana in 1828. Hodgson was in charge in Algiers at a critical time, reporting on the worsening relations and then on hostilities between the dey and the French. Shortly after his departure, France took over Algiers as a colony. Hodgson was replaced by another language officer, George F. Brown of Virginia, sent by the new Jackson administration as consul to the now French colony of Algiers and to learn Arabic.

President Adams had intended that Hodgson, once he became adept in Arabic, Turkish, and Berber, should return to Washington to serve in the understaffed Department of State as the resident translator and expert on the Near East. The problem in trying to build a professional cadre of experts for the State Department or its diplomatic and consular branches abroad was that every job was open to political preferment; a change of administration could be devastating. Luckily for Adams's plan and for Hodgson himself, the assumption of power by Jackson and the Democratic party in 1829 did not hurt Hodgson's career.

The new secretary of state, Martin Van Buren, was a true "spoilsman," replacing eighteen of the twenty-six clerks in his department. But with a strong recommendation from William Shaler, now consul general in Havana, Van Buren offered Hodgson the newly created position of translator of foreign languages and oriental interpreter for the department at a salary of $1,000. Hodgson jumped at the chance, hoping that it would lead to an assignment later in the Near East.[11]

The young language student naturally wanted a posting where he could use his newly acquired skills rather than stay in Washington. Without political backing it was almost impossible to be nominated consul to one of the Barbary States or Constantinople. Most of these positions were salaried, attracting office seekers who wanted to serve abroad but did not realize that the salaries were often inadequate. The Washington assignment in the State Department, however, was an excellent opportunity for Hodgson to make the right associations for moving onwards.

Hodgson was fortunate in his timing. The year he started to work in the department, 1830, the United States successfully negotiated a treaty of amity and commerce with the sultan of Turkey. This treaty, long sought by successive administrations of the United States, had been frustrated, first by the Barbary Wars, then by the Napoleonic Wars and America's own war with Britain. Once peace had been restored in 1815, the United States found itself persistently blocked from direct contact with the Sublime Porte. None of the major powers with interests in the Ottoman Empire, France, Great Britain, or Russia, was eager to help the United States gain a commercial foothold in the empire, and they made every effort to keep the new Western power out of their spheres of influence.

The enthusiastic support by Americans of the Greek War for Independence against Ottoman rule in the 1820s delayed for some years chances for negotiations with the Turks. In 1827, after a joint British, French, and Russian fleet had sunk the Turkish fleet at Navarino in Greece, the Turks looked more favorably on the United States as a noninvolved naval power that could help them rebuild their fleet. A treaty was successfully negotiated, signed, and ratified that, among other matters, provided that American consuls might be stationed in the Ottoman territories, thus opening the Mediterranean coast of Turkey, Syria, the Holy Land, and Egypt to consular expansion. Egypt, although quasi-independent of the Sublime Porte, was governed in certain matters by rules agreed upon by Constantinople, and consular acceptance was one of these.[12]

Of major importance to Americans who would trade, visit, or live in the Ottoman domains was the fact that the treaty allowed the United States to participate in the benefits of the capitulatory system, which provided that Americans getting into trouble, like the citizens of European nations with treaty rights, be tried by their own consuls or ministers rather than by Ottoman authorities. Americans found guilty would be "punished according to their offence; following in this respect, the usage observed towards other Franks [i.e. Westerners].[13] These capitulations and powers given American consuls were to remain in force until after the end of World War I.

In 1831 Hodgson was sent to Constantinople to help the newly appointed American chargé d'affaires, Commodore David Porter, late of the United States Navy, with the initial establishment of diplomatic relations between the United States and the Ottomans, after which Hodgson was to return to Washington. In the War of 1812 Porter, as a naval officer, on his own initiative had seized in the name of the United States an island in the Pacific Marquesas group. After the war, when on antipiracy patrol in the West Indies, he sent a strong landing force ashore and seized a Spanish fort on Puerto Rico to elicit an apology for the ill treatment of one of his officers. When he was reprimanded for this action against a "friendly power," Porter indignantly resigned and took an appointment as commander-in-chief of the Mexican navy, which he held for several years.[14] When Andrew Jackson became president, he wanted to do something for his like-minded naval colleague who cared as little as he did for diplomatic niceties. Porter was first named to be consul general in Algiers, but when the French took over, thus diminishing the importance of the position, the president offered him the more sensitive assignment of opening relations with the Ottoman sultan. Porter accepted.

Porter was to be the American chargé (later raised to minister) in Constantinople for the next twelve years. This tough sailor, a most unlikely candidate for a difficult diplomatic assignment, was actually to prove a creditable representative of the United States. Hodgson got on well with Porter in their initial association, and the language specialist returned to Washington with Porter's strong recommendation that he replace the post's dragoman. The president, acting on Porter's wishes as well as on other political endorsements that Hodgson had picked up while working in Washington, granted Hodgson what he had long sought. In April 1832 Hodgson was on his way back to Constantinople with his appointment as dragoman in his pocket.[15]

Unfortunately for the new dragoman, working with Commodore Porter did not meet his expectations. Porter had discovered that a diplomatic mission was an ideal place to advance the interests of his large family. Hodgson found that Porter had secured the services of his two nephews, George Porter and John Porter Brown, to act as the commodore's assistants. Nineteen-year-old John Brown had a flair for languages and was put to studying Turkish and Arabic with the obvious goal of training to supersede Hodgson. The other nephew, George Porter, who had been in charge of the consulate in Tangier for a short time before coming to help his uncle, was given the task of doing the writing for the post since he wrote with a clear hand, an important skill in the days before typewriters.

Porter had never been easy to deal with. Soon Hodgson and he were at loggerheads as Hodgson realized that the nephews were replacing him. Relations turned sour as Porter and Hodgson complained to the department, each one about the other. Seeing little future in Constantinople under the commodore, Hodgson tried to change places with George Brown, consul in Algiers.[16] Unfortunately, he too was a nephew of Porter. There was no place for a nonrelative in the commodore's universe.

The secretary of state took heed of the storm signals coming from Constantinople and in 1833 detailed Hodgson to Egypt as a confidential agent to examine "how far it may be desirable and practicable to form commercial relations with the Pacha [sic] of that country, distinct from those of the porte."[17] The pasha of Egypt, Muhammad Ali, was waging a successful revolt against his nominal overlord, the sultan in Constantinople, and the United States wanted to open up commercial and consular ties with Egypt without upsetting its new relationship with the Sublime Porte. America raised its commercial agent in Alexandria to consul, a decision based on Hodgson's report, but did not make a formal treaty with Egypt. Both Muhammad All and the sultan were willing to accept this move.

When he returned to the United States in 1835, Hodgson found no regular position in the State Department waiting for him. He was sent on a short mission to Tangier to help the consul there renew the treaty between the United States and Morocco but then was back, unemployed, in Washington. Again the secretary of state found use for Hodgson by having him deliver a ratified treaty to Peru, a poor way to utilize one of the few specialists in Oriental languages in the entire United States.

Hodgson applied for but failed to get the consulate in Tangier. There was not even an opening for him as a clerk in the State Department. He had another treaty-delivering assignment, this time to Berlin, again returning to unemployment in Washington. It was now 1840; Hodgson had been without a steady job for six years. In 1841, when William Henry Harrison, a Whig, replaced Democrat Martin Van Buren as president, Hodgson turned to his mentor, former Postmaster General McLean, who helped him obtain appointment to a position that was suited to his talents, that of consul in Tunis. Hodgson was to replace Consul Samuel Heap, who was being transferred to Constantinople as the dragoman. Not surprisingly, Heap was Commodore Porter's brother-in-law. So, after a sixteen-year odyssey, the once-young language student that Secretary of State John Quincy Adams had envisaged as the forerunner of a professional corps of Near Eastern experts was given his own post, although it was the least significant American consular post in the region.

By the time Hodgson achieved his consulship, the fire that had burned in him to serve in the Turkish/Arabic-speaking world had been dampened by the long series of disappointments received at the hands of the State Department and the trivial assignments as a treaty deliverer. His interests had turned elsewhere. En route to Tunis he met and fell in love with a young American woman of some wealth. She did not want to live in the Near East. Following his heart and common sense, he saw little future in a system that had treated him so shabbily. He resigned shortly after assuming his duties in Tunis, returned to Savannah with his bride, and there administered her large estate. He found time to correspond with other scholars interested in the study of languages, not only Arabic and Turkish, but those of black Africa[18]

The story of William Hodgson has been related in some detail because it highlights the obstacles that might be encountered by a secretary of state or president in trying to create a body of professional men to represent the United States abroad. Frequent changes of administration in Washington, patronage, nepotism, and an insensitive attitude toward the qualifications necessary for American diplomats and consuls effectively obstructed even the most elementary attempts to bring some logical order to the system. The moral of Hodgson's unfortunate career would seem to be that a man wanting to make a career of representing the United States abroad would have been well advised to look for a wealthy heiress, settle down on her estate, and forget about the lures overseas.

Despite the disappointing history of William Hodgson, a respectably professional body of Near East experts developed. The patron saint of this corps was not the quintessential diplomat, John Quincy Adams, but that crusty old salt himself, Commodore David Porter. Long after his death in 1843 his relatives and their descendants, the Porters, Browns, and Heaps, were serving the United States in Constantinople, Tunis, Tangier, and Tripoli, moving in and out of consular and diplomatic positions. Their knowledge of the languages, their contacts in the region, and their desire to work in what was always to be a set of relatively undesirable posts were valuable assets to their country. For example, Commodore Porter's nephew John Porter Brown was set to language studies by his uncle in 1832 and died in Constantinople in 1872 after almost forty years of service as dragoman, consul, consul general, and secretary of legation. Nine times Brown was called upon to act as the chargé when the various American ministers were away from their mission, often for extended periods. His knowledge of Ottoman affairs was an immeasurable asset to several generations of American diplomats and consuls who were to serve in the area.[19]

The State Department's records also show that a David Porter Heap and a G. Harris Heap served in Constantinople, each as consul general. The former served in the 1860s; the latter died in office there in 1887. Commodore Porter's son, Admiral David Dixon Porter, and his adopted son, Admiral David Glasgow Farragut, were major figures in the Civil War. The Porters were quite a breed.

While influential friends in the various administrations helped establish the Porter consular dynasty, a man of initiative could establish such a dynasty on his own. Such a consular entrepreneur was David Offley of a Philadelphia Quaker family, who arrived in Smyrna, Turkey, a major port of the eastern Mediterranean, in 1811 as the supercargo on a merchant ship representing the Philadelphia trading firm of Woodmas and Offley. He settled in Smyrna to take care of the firm's business and was to remain there for the next twenty-seven years until his death.[20]

Offley was no lover of the British, and his aversions were strengthened by his convictions that the Levant Company, a British-chartered merchants' monopoly, was doing everything to keep American merchants at a disadvantage. As there was no commercial treaty between the United States and the Ottoman government, American traders had to depend on the British for consular protection (for which they paid a fee); they were also charged customs fees of 6 percent by the Turks instead of the 2 percent charged to Europeans.[21]

Offley went to Constantinople determined to do something about the high, discriminatory rates charged American goods. After being put off by Turkish officials, he threatened to exert the traditional right of public redress by intercepting Sultan Muhmed on his way to Friday mosque. Such a threat had never been carried out by a Frank, that is, a Westerner. The officials wanted no public confrontation, which might have unpredictable consequences for all involved. Therefore, they gave American goods the most-favored-nation treatment despite the lack of a treaty. But Offley got no support from the American traders in Smyrna, reluctant to give up British support despite its expense. The subject almost immediately became moot when the War of 1812 cut off American trade from the Mediterranean until 1815.

At the end of the war Offley was able to persuade the rest of the American traders to join him in remaining independent from the British. He worked out an arrangement with the local pasha whereby American traders were to be treated as "guests of the Sultan" and were to receive in practice the rights they might have had had there been a treaty.[22] With the judicious use of modest gifts in the right places, Offley was able to keep the "guest" status for his countrymen even after his friend the pasha was executed for treason. Without a treaty or official support by the U.S. government, Offley was accorded treatment equal to that of other foreign consuls. Despite the opposition of the entrenched European mercantile establishment in the Mediterranean, this Quaker trader alone accomplished what every administration from that of Washington to that of John Quincy Adams had sought but failed to do, without the support of his fellow American merchants, bombardment by the United States Navy, or lavish tribute to the ruler.

In 1823 Offley was officially appointed consular agent, which helped his standing in the foreign community. Firmly convinced that a regular treaty was essential to protect American rights throughout the empire, he willingly accepted appointment as one of the negotiators who hammered out the 1830 treaty with the Turks. He was rewarded for this important contribution by being named the consul in Smyrna in 1832. On his death in 1838, his son David W. Offley was made consul. When that son died in 1846, still another son, Edward S. Offley, became the consul until 1861.

Smyrna, aside from its importance as a Mediterranean port and site of the Offley consular fiefdom, was also the center for American missionary activities in the Near East. The Protestant missionary movement in foreign lands was born early in the nineteenth century in New England. After Europe had settled down following the end of the Napoleonic Wars and the Barbary pirates had been subdued in the Mediterranean, the first missionaries, mostly Congregational, began their first tentative essays into Ottoman lands. The Turkish rule was relatively tolerant of missionary activity, secure in the knowledge that Christians would make little progress in converting Muslims; what minorities (mostly other Christian sects and Jews) wanted to do about their own religious beliefs was of little concern to the Sublime Porte, providing no unrest developed.

Josiah Brewer, one of the first of these American missionaries, sent in 1826 to Jerusalem by the Female Society of Boston and Vicinity for Promoting Christianity among the Jews, did not get to

Jerusalem, as there had been a revolt against the pasha there and the countryside was in a state of anarchy.[23] Instead Brewer settled in Smyrna, where he was joined by other American missionaries supporting the work of their brethren in Constantinople, Beirut, Bursa, Trebizond, Erzurum, and northern Persia.

The missionaries quite quickly developed a wider Near Eastern network than did the American consular service, which was tied to the port cities where American trade was concentrated. This pattern emerged at about the same time in the Far East, most particularly in China, where missionaries went farther afield (which usually meant farther up the rivers) than did the American consuls, who remained in the port cities.

Relationships between American consuls and American missionaries were generally uneasy. Jesus said, "Render therefore unto Caesar the things which are Caesar's; and unto God the things that are God's" (Matt. 22:21). In the Holy Land and elsewhere in the eastern Mediterranean some 1,800 years later, this commandment was no easier to carry out than when first given. By nature of their zeal, missionaries were destined to run head on against religious leaders, Greek Orthodox, Jewish, and Muslim. Unrest in religious communities caused difficulties for local officials.

American consuls and their consular colleagues, the British and French especially, did not like their missionaries to stir up the natives and make the Ottoman officials unhappy. Such agitation was bad for trade and might damage relations carefully nurtured with the local bureaucracy. Although most consular officers were active members of various Christian churches, few could sympathize with missionaries of more fervent persuasion who attempted to proselytize for their particular brand of Christianity oblivious of the indigenous culture. One consul in the Far East, when called upon to help a missionary who had run into trouble because of his stupidity and narrow mindedness, remarked that he had gained a much greater sympathy for Pontius Pilate after dealing with the matter.[24]

Despite growing interest of Americans in the Near East and the religious impetus behind many of the early contacts with that area, it was a long time before a U.S. consulate was established in Jerusalem, the center of the Holy Land, as it was inland, difficult to get to, and served by an indifferent port at Joppa. Because there was little commerce with Palestine, no American traders called for a consulate there. The post in Beirut, established in 1835, served the whole region, with Jasper Chasseaud, a native of the Levant, its consular officer.

In 1844 President Tyler commissioned Warder Cresson, of a well-known Quaker merchant family in Philadelphia, as consul in Jerusalem, but within a month Secretary of State John C. Calhoun wrote Cresson in Philadelphia, cancelling the appointment, a revocation probably sparked by information Calhoun received that Cresson "had been laboring under an aberration for many years: his mania is that of the religious species, he was born a Quaker, wanted to be a preacher but they would not [let him]. He has gone around the compass from one job to another, sometimes preaching about the church door & in the streets, his passion is for religious controversy & no doubt he expects to convert Jews and Mohamedans in the East. But in truth he is withall a very weak minded man."[25]

Weak-minded or not, Cresson left his family, got himself to Jerusalem – no mean feat in the 1840s – and there called himself the American consul. He had even procured a false consular seal, which he confidently used to provide protection to noncitizens of the United States by documenting them as "consular protegees."[26] The puzzled Ottoman authorities, becoming aware of this strange apparition in the Holy City, questioned the American minister in Constantinople about Cresson. Because of his irregular status, now revealed, Cresson was repudiated, but he stayed on and later converted to Judaism. After the Cresson experience the State Department decided against sending a consul into the Holy Land, depending on the consulate in Beirut to cover the area until 1856, when a legitimate consul was appointed.

Consular appointments to Near Eastern posts did not always fall to relatives of Commodore Porter or to men like those in the Offley family. An atypical assignment was that to Tunis. When Hodgson married his heiress and retired to Savannah, he was replaced by John Howard Payne.

Payne, a New Yorker, had been an overnight sensation in both New York and Boston as an actor while still in his teens.[27] When his fame faded, he moved to London, hoping to make a comeback as an actor. Failing, he turned to dramatic hackwork, barely keeping alive as he drifted to Paris and back to London, fleeing his creditors. One of his plays, which he made into an opera, *Clari, or the Maid of Milan* (1823), brought him a certain amount of fame because of the lyrics to one song, "Home, Sweet Home." For well into the next century this remained one of the most beloved songs in the English-speaking world.

Collaborating with Washington Irving, who was himself a part-time diplomat, Payne produced several plays in London with varying success, but he never made enough money to support himself. At last, in 1832 he returned to the United States a poor man. With a greater reputation than in England, due largely to "Home, Sweet Home," he was still unable to translate his fame into making a living. When John Tyler became president after the election of 1840, his secretary of state, Daniel Webster, appointed Payne in 1842 to be the consul in Tunis, replacing Hodgson. The position paid $2,000, the first assured income the writer had ever had. Payne, a Whig, was recalled after the 1844 election and was replaced by Samuel Heap, a Democrat and one of the Porter clan. In 1851 Payne was called back but he died in Tunis in 1852.

As consul in Tunis, Payne left no memorable contributions to the consular system. He had, however, made his mark in the legacy of "Home, Sweet Home." The closing lines:

Home, home, sweet, sweet home!
There's no place like home,
Oh, There's no place like home!

could well have been the consular service hymn. For the next hundred years there must have been many a consular family who gathered around a piano or guitar in the evening to sing this nostalgic song. For those who remembered Payne's death, this must have been especially poignant, for Payne died far from home, a bachelor, at a remote consulate. He was one of the many consuls whose epitaph in the records of the Department of State was "Died at post."

9

Consular Operations in Africa, Asia, and the Pacific (1790–860)

The scarcity of American consular posts in Africa, excepting those bordering the Mediterranean, reflected the United States' lack of interest in that continent This lack of interest in what would later be termed 'black' Africa was to last until the early 1960s. The main African commercial product to America had been black slaves; a trade legally abolished in 1808, although there was still some clandestine export by slavers.

Occasionally American merchant ships, usually the ubiquitous Yankee whalers sailing out of Marblehead, Nantucket, and other New England ports on cruises lasting several years, called at obscure African ports, where they landed to restock supplies. In only buying food and taking in water, they needed little consular support.

There were no consulates on the western coast of Africa and only one on the eastern coast in Zanzibar. Cape Town, however, in the extreme south was an important and pleasant port of call for ships rounding the Cape of Good Hope, far preferable to the dreaded voyage rounding Cape Horn of South America. The American consulate in Cape Town was established in 1799. The first American consul there, John Elmslie, traveled to his post on the U.S. frigate *Essex* while convoying American ships in the East Indies trade during the Napoleonic Wars. Elmslie, having no official approval or *exequatur* from the British government, was accepted at the sufferance of the British governors. The undocumented consul's situation became even more uncertain when Britain returned the colony to the Dutch in 1801 as part of the Peace of Amines. The Dutch governor, while tolerating the American consul, also refused to give him official status. Changing alliances during the war in Europe enabled a British expedition to conquer the territory again in 1806. The new British governor finally gave official recognition to the American consul, but Elmslie left soon after the British reoccupation.[1]

British and French interference with American trade during the Napoleonic Wars and the East India Company's strict monopoly in all trading activities with India limited the need for consular services en route to the East Indies, what with the lack of American commerce. The Cape Town consulate remained vacant until 1834, when the Jackson administration appointed a consul to that post.

The other main consular post in the African region was on the island of Zanzibar. The Jackson administration, showing more interest than previous administrations in opening commercial relations outside the European–Latin American orbit, designated Edmund Roberts, an American sea captain and merchant, as agent to obtain commercial treaties with various countries. His mission was unceremonious; he was forced to sleep on the gun deck with the crew of the U.S. naval ship that carried him. Roberts's first call at Cochin, China (present day Vietnam) was unsuccessful, but he established commercial relations with Siam and Muscat.[2]

The spice island of Zanzibar off the east coast of Africa was conquered by the sultan of Muscat and made his seat of government. An American consular station, only intermittently manned, was founded in Muscat in 1838, although an American consul had hoisted his flag on Zanzibar as early as 1836. Zanzibar was a busy port, not only for the spice trade but for whalers hunting in the Indian Ocean.

The first consul in Zanzibar, Richard P. Waters, was soon reporting on murders and mutinies on American ships.[3] Seamen cruising to distant seas had more difficult lives than those in transatlantic or coastal trade. Yankee skippers and their bucko mates were notoriously hard: driving crews to the edge for commercial advantage over rival traders.

The consul often found himself unable to help a seaman who legitimately signed on a ship but discovered once at sea that conditions were intolerable. One such man was John Ross Browne, a well-educated man who had signed on a whaling ship as a lark in 1842. By the time the ship reached Zanzibar, he found life unbearable under a captain he described as a "man apparently about thirty-five years of age, with a hooked nose, dark crop hair, large black whiskers, round shoulders, cold blue eyes, and a shrewd, repulsive expression of countenance. Altogether he had a sneaking, hangdog look that was not very encouraging to those destined to be subject to his will during a year's cruise, or perhaps longer."[4]

Browne went to Consul Waters for help to get him off the ship. Waters told him: "I am willing to aid you so far as I have the power, but have no authority to demand your discharge from the vessel. If you can procure a hand to take your place, it is probable that the captain will consent to an exchange." Browne, thinking that this was impossible, threatened to desert. Waters warned him: "That would be unwise. We have no alternative here than to put deserters in the fort, and there you would soon take the fever." Browne was fortunate in finding a black sailor from South Carolina willing to sign on for ten dollars and Browne's sea chest and clothes. Browne was off the ship he had not so affectionately dubbed in his account the *Barque Styx*. Later, the consul helped Browne sign on to a more congenial ship bound for Salem.

During much of the first half of the nineteenth century the United States had not been able to establish viable consular posts in India. Beginning in 1792, sporadic attempts to keep consuls in Calcutta, and later Bombay, were forestalled by British colonial authorities working hand in glove with the East India Company. The British kept tight control over trade to India, charging American ships four times the duty on goods charged to British carriers. Despite adverse conditions, a consulate was permitted at Bombay in 1838 under Philemon S. Parker, who stayed less than two years, finding no profit or need for a post where the British dominated American trade. The post in Bombay was vacant until 1849. Samuel Simpson from South Carolina was appointed, but when on arrival he found that there was not enough trade to sustain him, he defected to the enemy, the East India Company, by becoming their superintendent in cotton cultivation, residing several hundred miles from Bombay. Instead of resigning, he wrote the Department of State that he was willing to continue as consul if he were paid the salary he received from the East India Company, $5,800 a year. He was fired as soon as the mail could go from and to the post.[5]

The consular system gradually expanded to include more ports of Southeast Asia, such as Singapore, Melbourne (Australia), Hobart (Tasmania), Manila, and Batavia. The last two posts had first been established prior to the War of 1812, but records of their first years have not survived. The Spanish realized that it was imprudent to keep the Philippines sealed from foreign trade, since the islands were too far from the mother country to be kept as a Spanish trading preserve; they opened Manila to foreign consuls, in contrast to their most of Spanish Latin America, where American consuls had to take advantage of the revolutionary movements to establish their posts.

Establishing a working consulate in Singapore was an example of the difficulty for American traders to gain entry into a market. By 1819 the British had set themselves up in Singapore to challenge the longtime commercial ascendancy of the Dutch in the East Indies, where there were products highly valued around the world: camphor, pepper, rice, sugar, tea, coffee, and tin. In the treaty between the United States and Great Britain ending the War of 1812, American trade with the British East India was to be limited to four ports; Singapore, not in existence as a trading port in 1815, was not included. The British East India Company had powerful friends in London who pressured the British navy to keep American ships from trading with Singapore, which had developed into a major port for the region.

In 1833 the Jackson administration wanted a consul in Singapore to foster American commerce with that important trading center. Faced with British obstruction, the secretary of state sent Joseph Balestier of Massachusetts to the port of Rhio on the island of Bentang, a small Dutch settlement with little trade forty miles across the straits from Singapore. Balestier was expected to reside in Singapore and work to remove trade restrictions. The British governor of Singapore accepted Balestier in his somewhat circuitous role and allowed him to function as a commercial agent.[6]

In 1837 the East India Company relaxed its opposition to a Yankee consul in Singapore when it became apparent that it made commercial sense to have Americans as buyers of their products. Although Balestier was relieved of his ambiguous role and issued an *exequatur*, there were still restrictions on American ships trading along the Asian coast, which lasted until 1849. These early restrictions had already caused great damage. Singapore did not develop into the major port of call that it should have been for American traders. The consuls suffered accordingly, as consular fees were sparse.[7]

In the years after the war with Britain, the Pacific Ocean and neighboring seas were busy with enterprising Yankee captains probing to find markets for their goods and profitable cargoes to bring back to Boston or New York for an increasingly affluent American society. New England whalers ranged wherever there were whales, including the Indian Ocean and among the islands of the Pacific.

The sailing trade was fraught with the danger of typhoons, uncharted reefs, lee shores, and unfriendly natives. Pirates prowled the China Sea and East Indian waters. Every prudent skipper sailed a well-armed merchant ship and was prepared to fight any threatening Malay or Chinese junk. Despite precautions, ships were caught off guard. The *Friendship* out of Salem, in the pepper trade between America and Sumatra, was overwhelmed by Malay natives in 1830 suffering the loss of the crew and the ship.[8] Merchant captains were undaunted by threat of peril. They took greater precautions and raised their prices. One dangerous but profitable trade item was *bêche-de-mer*, or sea cucumber. Some Salem men approached several cannibal tribes in the Fiji Islands, encouraging them in exchange trinkets for diving to the ocean floor to collect the *bêche-de-mer*, which were then boiled and cured before being taken to Canton or Manila as banquet delicacies eagerly bought by wealthy Chinese.[9]

The Department of State oversaw a gradual increase in consular posts in the vast region of the Pacific basin, most of which, even after the consular reform of 1856, were given to men who were principally traders but could act as consuls or consular agents. By 1860 there were consulates or consular agencies in the Pacific and adjacent waters at Batavia, Dutch East Indies, and Manila (established 1801), Honolulu (1820), Tahiti (1835), Bay of Islands, New Zealand (1838), Hobart (1842), Apia, Samoa (1844), Laulhala, Fiji Islands (1844), Lahuna, Hawaii (1850), Hilo, Hawaii and Melbourne (1852), and Guam (1854).

The Pacific consular presence, made up of unpaid American merchants acting as agents, made sense. Had only professional, salaried consular officers been sent out, posts would have been limited and American interests, especially those of the merchant marine, would have been less well served when help was needed. Distances were too great to expect a professional consul, out of Hawaii, for example, to service ships and crews for such an enormous area.

The first American consul to Tahiti was Jacques Antoine Moerenhout. Although he was Belgian, a veteran of Napoleon's army and a trader in the Pacific Islands for some years, by 1835 he had arranged for an appointment as U.S. consul to the Society Islands because no one else competed for that unpaid position.

These islands, including Tahiti and its main town of Papeete, were under rule of a queen; the French were not to make them into a protectorate until 1842.

The consul's main problem in Tahiti was dealing with deserters from whaling ships. Papeete, a favorite port while the ships were being resupplied, offered the sailors the free and easy morals of feminine companionship, a delightful contrast to life on board whaling ships and New England Puritan upbringing. Tempted not to let this paradise pass by, many deserted. Authorities made little effort to round them up.[10]

Moerenhout was unable to control the problem of the deserters. There was no jail to hold them; there were no visiting American warships to exercise naval authority. A crisis arose when two deserters broke into his house, killing his wife and wounding him. While convalescing, Moerenhout received by long-delayed mail word from Washington that he was going to be replaced by an American. At the same time he was offered the appointment as French consul in Papeete, which he accepted, but from 1838 to39 he served concurrently as both French and American consul. Later he was transferred to Monterey, California, as French consul, after California became part of the United States.[11]

Although the French protectorate of Tahiti was an important port for American whalers, finding qualified men to serve as consuls was difficult, because there was little American commerce and almost no opportunity for an American to develop a business for a livelihood. Papeete's last consul prior to the Civil War was Vicisimus Turner, appointed in 1858 with recommendations as to trustworthiness and party affiliation (Democratic). After Turner left in 1860 because of broken health, he was discovered to have been a semiprofessional gambler from San Francisco, who apparently had been submitting inflated bills to the United States Treasury for the "relief" of seamen in order to help sustain himself in Tahiti.[12]

In Honolulu, established as a post in 1820, some consuls emulated American missionaries there, of whom it was said, "They went to the islands to do good, and did well," a reference in later years to the missionary antecedents of some of the wealthiest families on the islands. One of the first consuls to Hawaii, Peter A. Brinsmade of Maine (1838–49), was also a prominent land developer who made a special trip to Washington to urge Secretary of State Daniel Webster to have the United States recognize the islands as independent (their status was uncertain at the time) in exchange for land concessions from the Hawaiians.[13] Brinsmade's successor, Elisha H. Allen of Massachusetts (1849–54), resigned his consular commission to become a principal advisor to King Kamehameha III and in later years served as envoy to the United States for the Hawaiian rulers.

Hawaii was an even greater rest and recreation center than Tahiti for the whaling industry, giving consuls much concern for keeping order among their unruly charges. The consuls had another problem, that of whaling captains who put American sailors ashore under any pretext in order to hire Hawaiians at a considerably lower rate. This only added to the unemployed and troublesome American population on the islands. The United States Navy interceded from time to time to bring order out of the chaos that had been developing with so many unemployed sailors. In 1826 the U.S. ship *Peacock*, commanded by Captain Thomas ap Catesby Jones (the same who years later was to "invade" California without a declaration of war with Mexico), set up a committee with the first American consul John Coffin Jones, Jr., the British consul, the governor of Oahu, and a Spaniard resident in Honolulu. Any seaman not vouched for by these responsible community members must choose between shipping on the *Peacock* or one of the whalers in port. This edict cleared up the port for a time, but the improved situation deteriorated once the warship left.[14]

The relief of seamen was an aspect of consular work that was to prove a source of corruption. While whaling, seamen were often injured or became ill aboard ships. Hawaii was not only a place for rest but also where sick and injured seamen were left to recover. While in most matters involving public relief the U.S. government had a laissez faire attitude, the care of seamen abroad was a major exception. The United States must look after its own men overseas.

The U.S. method for relief payments was not satisfactory. Consuls were expected to pay expenses incurred for the care of seamen and send the bills to the Treasury Department for reimbursement, a transaction requiring months for payments and even then uncertain, since the Treasury did not always approve vouchers. A consul was likely to be out of pocket for a considerable time. To help defray relief expenses, ships' captains were obliged by law to deposit three months' wages with the consul for every seaman discharged; of this a certain amount went into a relief fund. It was up to the consul to put recovered seamen on ships and provide for the available hospitalization of the sick.

Many seamen were laid up for long periods with broken limbs, a common injury in rough seas. The seamen's' relief fund was insufficient. Consuls were still obliged to support the sick without certainty of reimbursement. They were also responsible for boarding and lodging until seamen found berths. Since shipwreck was common, the consul could be swamped with destitute charges. To alleviate this burden consuls sold drafts on the United States Treasury to local businessmen, who bought them at a suitable discount in hope that the Treasury would eventually honor them.[15] Some consuls struggling in this unhealthy situation were tempted to inflate charges to cover future expenses, a practice that often turned into out-and-out swindling.

Lahaina on the island of Maui was of particular concern to auditors of the Treasury. At first a consular agency under the consul in Honolulu, Lahaina was later raised to a full-fledged consulate in 1850. Harvard graduate Charles Bunker of Nantucket, consul at Lahaina, evidently saw a chance to make a profit from seamen's' relief by submitting bills almost twice those of Honolulu for the care of a comparable number of seamen. In 1852 the cost for a quarter year for Lahaina was $20,566.00 for the care of 187 seamen, compared to $11,913.90 in Honolulu for the care of 191.[16] When the Treasury became concerned about the bills from Lahaina, Bunker left the islands without notice and presumably was never charged with what seems to have been malfeasance.

CHINA

In China, and later in Japan, the American consular system was to have some of its greatest responsibilities and challenges in the nineteenth century. Both were magnets for mercantile, missionary, and even consular penetration by the aggressive Western powers. Long before the United States became a nation, China and Japan had individually and at widely separate times acted to seal their countries from foreign contamination and restrict their countrymen from trading abroad. Their laws confined sailing ships to coastal trade, and shipbuilding was limited to vessels that could be used only on the rivers and short-haul coastal voyages, edicts strictly enforced.

The potential for a huge market in China and for China's goods, such as tea, silk, china, and lacquerware, which had a ready market in the West at a substantial profit was irresistible to Western traders. If the Chinese would not come to the West, the West would come to China. In 1760 the Chinese met the barbarian menace, as they termed it, by establishing a sealed-off area in the southern port city of Canton, where Western merchants were restricted to business during the trading season only. Traders from the West might not bring their wives or make any effort to settle permanently in the city. Between trading seasons they were to go to Macao, a Portuguese territory, or India. There was no direct contact with the imperial Chinese government.

All transactions went through government-appointed Chinese merchants known as the *co-hong*. Thus no foreigner need be recognized by the imperial government. As long as trade was profitable to Western merchants and to certain Chinese, ranging from the *co-hong* to provincial officials to the Imperial Palace in Peking, the system worked.[17]Samuel Shaw, the first U.S. consul appointed under the new constitution (he earlier had held a commission from the Congress of the Confederation), never presented his commission to an imperial Chinese official or received an exequatur from that government, although he was expected as the American *taipan* or chief trader to be responsible for his compatriots.[18] He was in effect the consul, as were his immediate successors, and the *taipans* working under the Chinese *co-hung* system.

From 1790 to 1835 the consulate was to function without a single American who could read, write, speak, or understand Chinese. Neither John Quincy Adams, nor other secretaries of state, showed concern in having U.S. consuls develop skills in the language of one of the United States' most lucrative trading markets.

In 1821, when Benjamin Wilcocks was the consul at Canton, a most unfortunate episode occurred. A sailor of the American merchant ship *Emily* threw a jar off his ship at some Chinese in bumboats, small vessels the Chinese used to bring items for sale to the shipside. The Chinese, it was later asserted, had been pestering the crew to buy their goods. Unhappily for the sailor, Joseph Terranova, the Chinese declared that the jar had hit and killed a Chinese bumboat woman. The Americans claimed that the woman had accidentally fallen overboard and drowned.

The Chinese officials insisted that Terranova be turned over to them to come under their law of a life for a life. At first the Americans refused, but when the Chinese threatened to stop all trade with the American community, the merchants gave in. The decision was not left to Consul Wilcocks, as would have seemed proper, but to an American committee of five sea captains, five supercargoes, and five resident merchants. The committee allowed Terranova to be tried on board the *Emily*, where the Chinese immediately found him guilty. He was taken to Canton and strangled to death by the local executioner.[19]

The *Emily* case demonstrated the U.S. consuls' lack of authority in Canton. Although they were responsible for ship and cargo documentation, a matter of life or death (or a threat to trade) was best put in the hands of captains, supercargoes, and other merchants. In the *Emily* case, the consul must have welcomed the insistence that an almost inevitable decision be handled by a committee, rather than to be personally responsible for the surrender of an American to the Chinese and a preordained execution.

After 1815 the American merchant community in Canton grew substantially as American ships came to rival the British as cargo carriers. When foreigners were permitted to settle in the city, several large American trading houses, such as Russell & Company and Olyphant & Company, absorbed most of the smaller traders, replacing the supercargoes with resident agents handling matters at port.

American Protestant missionaries made their first appearance in 1829 as the U.S. missionary movement gathered momentum. China, not too restrictive of missionary activities, offered splendid opportunities for conversions, in great contrast to the Near East. The major trading houses and the missionaries would be the two major forces driving the policy of the United States toward China, with the American consuls merely supporting their activities.

As demonstrated by the unfortunate *Emily* case, the U.S. consul in Canton was not an important figure in the early years of the China trade. There were long gaps from 1790 to 1840 when no one held the office. American traders in China carried on without any particular difficulties, generally because they were intent on quiet and profitable relations with the Chinese.

While the American merchants confined their efforts to trade, the British were aggressive in annexing territory in India, Burma, and the Malay Peninsula. The Chinese became concerned for their authority because of opium, a major trade commodity despite its illegality in China. Almost everyone seemed to gain from smuggling opium into Canton – merchants, mainly British and American from the so-called most respectable trading houses; Chinese officials, handsomely paid to turn a blind eye to the trade; and Chinese traders who distributed the "foreign mud," as it was called. Only the Chinese addict suffered.

Confronted with the fact that the opium trade was draining too much specie (gold and silver) from their country and with the disastrous effect of opium smoking on a large and increasing segment of the population, the Chinese government decided to stop the trade in late 1818.[20] To assert their authority they began executing native opium dealers in front of the foreign quarter. The superintendent of British trade, Charles Elliot, and the French and Dutch consuls were outraged, proclaiming it "a direct and positive insult," which it was intended to be.[12] The Chinese insisted that foreign merchants desist from the opium trade and threatened to punish all violators. Moreover, if foreigners refused to follow the law, the port would be closed to all commerce.

Peter W. Snow of Rhode Island, American consul at this time, was unsympathetic to the general European and American indignation over the Chinese attempt to stop the opium trade. On the contrary, he reported that the Chinese demands were "just."[22] Snow also tried to distance himself from the British and to downplay the American participation in the opium trade, which was considerable.

To force foreign merchants to stop the illegal drug flow into the Canton area, the Chinese closed the port for a while to all foreign trade. Snow had already informed the State Department that the Chinese were "satisfied, I think, that no opium is grown in our country; that Americans in the future will not, under any circumstances, engage in the trade."[23]

When the port was reopened, the British merchants, encouraged by their consul, moved to Macao to reprimand the Chinese for interfering with a profitable trade and trying to cut off Canton from foreign goods. American and other Western traders were urged to join in the boycott but did not. Instead, they stayed on to take over for a time much of the British legal trade or act as agents for British merchants, who were developing their own trading center on the small and previously sparsely populated island of Hong Kong.

American merchants resident in Canton had taken a pledge not to engage in the opium trade after the Chinese reopened the port in 1839, but in the absence of the British the American flag was soon being used as a cover for the illicit trade, with fast, heavily armed ships under U.S. registry smuggling the valuable cargo. A small U.S. East Indies naval squadron attempted to keep the flag off ships dealing in opium, but with minimal success because there was little cooperation from the Americans in the area. Lawrence Kearny, commodore of the squadron, reported to the secretary of the navy

(19 May 1843) his seizure of an American-registered ship, the *Ariel*, the forced discharge of its cargo of opium, and the confiscation of the ship's papers.[24]

The commodore was contemptuous of American merchants and consuls in Canton and elsewhere in the region. "The owners, as well as the consular establishment of the United States, seem to have been clearly regardless in making transfers [of ships' registries to the American flag] that are illegal. These sham sales are well known, by which our national character is daily losing ground, and will so continue to do while the public consular duties are confined to merchants whose interests are so deeply involved in the transactions."[25] Kearny found that a vice consul in Canton was involved in the drug trade while his superior, Consul Snow, was reporting to Washington that American hands were clean.

The British refused to accept the loss of their opium market. In 1840 they blockaded the Pearl River leading to Canton and began active hostilities against the weak Chinese Empire, the so-called Opium War (1839–42). The result of this "drug war," which the dealers (the British) won, was beneficial to the growth of the U.S. consular system in the Far East. The British-Chinese Treaty of Nanking (1842) ending the Opium War and the supplementary treaty of 1843 were essentially commercial, opening the ports of Canton, Foochow, Ningpo, Amoy, and Shanghai. The treaty also abolished the *co-hung* system, set Chinese tariffs at a low rate, established Hong Kong as a free port, and opened the way for other Western powers to obtain the same privileges through the most-favored-nation provision included in the supplementary treaty. Of course, these treaties tacitly permitted the opium trade, although it was not made legal.[26]

The United States benefited to opportunities won from the Chinese by the British. Unlike the negotiations leading to the treaties with Morocco and Turkey, which moved with exasperating slowness, negotiations with China moved swiftly, backed by an active pro-China lobby in Boston, Salem, and New York. Merchants of these cities, influential in political as well as financial circles, did not want their flourishing trade inhibited by the deleterious diplomatic inaction of Secretary of State Daniel Webster. Webster, a Massachusetts native and a good politician, promptly sent a negotiating team to Macao led by Massachusetts congressman Caleb Cushing, which arrived in February 1844.

Cushing was indirectly responsible for an incident at the American consulate in Canton that might have harmed negotiations. He had brought an impressively large flagstaff, but considering it unwise to raise it in Macao, Portuguese territory, where he would be working, he sent the pole up the Pearl River to Canton for the use of Consul Paul S. Forbes. Forbes had the flagstaff raised in front of his consular office with a weather vane in the form of an arrow set on its tip, an innovation that frightened the Cantonese, to whom a foreign flag was always threatening. Another warlike symbol, an arrow pointing to different sectors of the city where there were likely to be deaths or fires apparently aroused fears in the Cantonese, who suspected the introduction of barbaric magic in their midst. A mob broke into the consulate compound and tried to take down the flagstaff, but was repulsed by armed Americans. Forbes quickly had the arrow removed.[27]

The Cantonese were still unhappy about foreigners in their city. In another mob attack upon some Americans, a Chinese man was killed. The Chinese governor and Cushing agreed to let his countryman who fired the fatal shot be tried by an American jury under American law, the first such occasion with Americans in China. The man was acquitted by his peers on the grounds of self-defense, an important precedent for establishing extraterritorial jurisdiction of Americans over Americans in China. [28]

Although American trade interests in the Orient were almost as great as those of England, the United States played second fiddle to the British in China throughout the nineteenth century. The American consuls were not as well equipped to administer the new responsibilities given by the Chinese as the British. Under the British-Chinese treaty provisions consuls had important functions. At each treaty port the British consul was the equivalent of a Chinese magistrate, a high official in the Chinese hierarchy. He settled pilot fees, took in a ship's papers, notified customs of its arrival and departure, examined cargoes, heard appeals over duties, cooperated in setting standards of coinage, kept standard sets of weights and measures, controlled seamen, heard grievances against both Chinese and British subjects, punished British offenders, and ran the consular jail. He also kept track of British warships in the region, was responsible for the security of British trading ships, acted as a type of landlord over the British property in the British concession, and tried to prevent smuggling.[29] When the China treaty ports opened, the American consular system still depended on the merchant consul appointee, who was ill equipped to deal with the problems of extraterritoriality, his business was paramount. The roles of judge and policeman were not compatible with the interests of a man whose guiding principle was not to annoy potential customers. Until 1848 the American consuls in the five Chinese ports, besides not having the time or temperament to serve as judicial authorities; they did not have the right to pass judgment on fellow Americans because Congress had not yet enacted the necessary legislation to give them such authority.

In the Near East the lack of this legislation seemed not to have been a serious problem. Few Americans except traders and missionaries, not generally the type to get into trouble resulting in a judicial trial, were active in the Near East. The real troublemakers were seamen and those engaged in smuggling or quasi-legal ventures, to whom the Near East was inhospitable. Seamen wanted girls and whisky. The Muslim world, especially in the nineteenth century, did not provide these.

The Far East was different. When the five Chinese treaty ports were opened and Hong Kong established as a free port, contact with the Chinese was no longer limited to members of the merchants' organization, the *co-hung*, or bumboat people. Hong Kong and Shanghai were especially attractive to the foreigner, with sing-song girls, rice whisky, and good food – a smuggler's delight. Both were new cities that grew quickly as centers for Western trade, with none of the conservative traditions or society that had distinguished Canton for centuries. Chinese and Westerners went to Hong Kong and Shanghai primarily to make money from each other.

The atmosphere in these cities was that of a boom town where quick profits could be made and the pleasures of the flesh were available and cheap. Life ashore was a seaman's paradise and a consul's hell. His job was to haul the seaman out of the dens of iniquity, settle with bar owners and madams, and get his unwilling charge on an outward-bound ship. Since legal authority was not well established, the American consuls in these new posts were frustrated in fulfilling their judicial and punitive obligations under the Chinese-American treaty of 1844.

To give their consuls proper authority to enforce the American side of the 1844 Chinese treaty and the 1830 treaty with Turkey, Congress passed a judicial bill on 11 August 1848 granting impressive powers to men who were still only part-time functionaries of the United States.[30] Consuls were authorized to arraign American citizens charged with offenses against the law in China or in the Turkish domains, to try offenders, and, if called for, to punish them. The consuls could themselves try simple cases where the fine was not more than $100 or imprisonment was less than sixty days, without the right of appeal, a power that would enable consuls to deal with most obstreperous seamen. Cases calling for fines of up to $500 or ninety days in jail could be appealed to the American minister to China). The consul could assemble an advisory group of approximately four other American citizens to help in a complex legal case or if a severe punishment, including the death penalty, were contemplated. The consul decided the case, but if any citizen advisor disagreed, the judgment would be referred to the commissioner.

The U.S. law of 1848 stated under Section 15 "that murder and insurrection, or rebellion against the Chinese government, with intent to subvert the same, shall be capital offenses, punishable with death."[31] Such a judgment would require the concurrence of the commissioner, and capital offenses could be referred to the president for possible pardon. Although this was tremendous power to entrust to persons not required to have judicial training, it did not become an instrument of oppression. Keeping order was the consul's primary consideration. As at first there were no American jails, imprisonment depended on the willingness of the British or French to accommodate prisoners.

There were questions about the constitutionality of the law that allowed the trying, convicting, and executing of Americans for rebelling against China, but it appears that no Americans were tried for offenses against the sovereign rule of China. There would have been opportunity for a vindictive American consul to become a hanging judge during the Taiping Rebellion (1850–64), a major insurrectionary movement to which some Americans, mostly sailors and ex-soldiers, sold their services.

The consuls were given a thousand dollars a year for time spent on judicial cases in the treaty ports of China and in Turkish domains, a sum expected to cover costs of a police force, court expenses, jails, and jailers. One thousand dollars, even in the 1850s, was not enough. In 1860 Congress, in amending the judicial law to make it more responsive in some respects, withdrew the thousand dollars for judicial expenses, perhaps because consuls in most port cities had been given small salaries in the consular reforms of 1855–56.

Even if handled by experienced judges, the judicial process

would have been a major challenge. For example, oaths were pre-scribed in different forms for Christians, Jews, Mohammedans, Parsecs, and Chinese since one of any of these sects might appear before a consular court.[32] The problem of interpreting suits by a Parsee or Arab trader against an American must have caused con-sternation to both consul and litigant.

The Judicial Act of 1848 called for the use of "common law," but what was common law when litigants came from different states? Common law in New York had English law as a basis; Louisiana's law was a version of the Code Napoleon. Such difficulties would have provided fertile fields for modern lawyers to fight the system by appeals, but acting in much the same spirit that later inspired Judge Roy Bean to be "the law west of the Pecos," U.S. consuls dis-pensed their rough-hewn frontier justice only when forced to.

The situation in the China posts resembled that of the American Far West during its early years, when places such as Dodge City and Deadwood Gulch were at their most violent, with no sheriff or U.S. marshal to bring order. Humphrey Marshall, the American commissioner to China, reported in 1853:

> There are now in this port [Shanghai] at least one hundred and fifty sailors ashore, men of all nations who go into the Chinese city and drink and riot and brawl, daily and night-ly. The United States having assumed jurisdiction over their own citizens in China, are expressly bound to compel them to keep the peace, and this cannot be done as long as there is no place to confine the delinquents in, except a loathsome hole inhabited by the foulest lepers, and in itself so weak that a man of American energies can kick his way out in a few minutes.[33]

Not all alien troublemakers were Americans, but many miscre-ants claimed American citizenship, knowing that it was difficult to prove them otherwise. Thus they often avoided the more certain justice of the better-supported consuls from other nations.

In 1854 the next U.S. commissioner to China reported to Washington on the state of the poorly paid American consuls. The new consul at Ningpo had to live on the thousand dollars paid him for judicial services and almost nonexistent consular fees; he did not speak Chinese and could not afford to hire an interpreter. Being forced to live at almost the poverty level had a poor effect on relations with the status-conscious Chinese, who saw how shabbily

America treated its officials. In Foochow the post was in the hands of a temporary consul appointed by another acting consul. In Shanghai the new consul, with not enough money to hire an office, was forced to live and work in a seamen's boarding house. He was also dependent on the British consulate or merchants to lend him an interpreter.[34]

The U.S. consul in Hong Kong between 1853 and 1861 was James Keenan. He had been an army private at the start of the Mexican War and took part in the battles of Vera Cruz and the march to Mexico City. He ended the war as a second lieutenant and returned to Greensburg, Pennsylvania, to enter county politics as a Democrat, where he attracted the notice of James Buchanan, then about to go to London as the American minister. Wanting to help a fellow Pennsylvanian, Buchanan spoke to President Pierce about Keenan, mentioning that it was regrettable that few men from Pennsylvania had consular positions. Pierce appointed Keenan as the new consul for Hong Kong.[35]

Although Keenan had originally applied for the post at Glasgow, he readily accepted the appointment and set out for the Far East, arriving at his post in 1854 to find a small city with great potential. According to a census taken about that time, Hong Kong had 2,416 Chinese and 491 Europeans, plus a large population of unregistered Chinese living on boats.[36] Hong Kong has always been an anomaly among U.S. consular posts. Although next to the Chinese mainland, the consul looked to the American minister in London rather than to the American commissioner in Canton as his immediate superior. Keenan was to exploit this peculiar and distant chain of command whenever his temper or impulsiveness got him into trouble.

Keenan was not content to remain office bound. When China-based pirates captured and looted the *Calder*, an American ship, the British, at a point where they could no longer tolerate sea crimes, organized a joint British-Chinese expedition against the pirate stronghold. Keenan somehow arranged to accompany the expedition. He landed at the stronghold with the attacking force, which burnt several pirate villages and junks. Perhaps reliving his days at Vera Cruz with the American army, Keenan returned to his consulate with the pirate chief's banner as a souvenir of his adventure.[37]

Back at his post, he became involved in a serious altercation with the Hong Kong police force as to who had jurisdiction over American ships, the Americans or the British. The clash was reminiscent of the issue that led up to the War of 1812. Keenan insisted that the British could not board American ships and take men off against the will of the captain. The British navy, it was evident, was still not respectful of other nations' rights where foreign ships were concerned. There had been many protests about naval boarding parties looking for smugglers and illegal trade.

A case that aroused Keenan's ire concerned the American ship *Reindeer* in Hong Kong harbor. A sailor on the ship had originally signed on board in the United States as an American citizen, but wanting to leave the ship and join the Hong Kong police force, he told the police that he was actually a British subject. At that time it was difficult to prove or disprove nationality; almost anyone could be what one claimed to be if he were far enough away from home and birth records. When he returned to the *Reindeer* to collect his gear, the sailor was put in irons by the ship's captain. The Hong Kong police then boarded the ship and freed their would-be recruit. When the captain resisted the police, he was taken to jail and charged with assault and battery. The captain called for his consul; James Keenan appeared.[38]

Keenan, unable to get the captain released and the charges dropped, arranged for him to slip away from the court just after he was tried and convicted. Outside the court building Keenan had him quickly spirited away to the U.S.S. *Powhatan*, part of the China Squadron, whose captain would not give the American up. Frustrated, the British then charged Keenan with aiding in the American captain's escape, a charge not without basis. After Keenan ignored a summons, he was arrested and taken to court, where he was freed on bail. The charges against the consul were eventually dropped, but the British authorities in Hong Kong, understandably displeased with Mr. Keenan, complained to London about his actions. The State Department gave its consul a gentle slap on the wrist, noting his "zeal and attention to the interests of American commerce and his protection of American citizens" but saying that he had gone too far in his assistance of the American captain.[39]

Keenan was not one to stay out of trouble. When his own consular post was relatively peaceful, he visited a neighboring district when action was brewing. On 8 October 1856 a small Chinese-owned vessel, the *Arrow*, sailing under the British flag with a British master and Chinese crew, was seized by the imperial forces, which took off the crew. The British protested to the Chinese. When there was no immediate satisfactory reply, the British used the chance to chastise the Chinese for a long series of slights and restrictions by storming and taking Canton. Keenan, the old warhorse, accompanied the British marines who took the city by breaching its walls.

Keenan's actions once he was inside the city are somewhat hazy. He claimed that he strolled into the city after the attack and came upon an American sailor with a furled American flag. Together they left the combat zone after a short time. Other accounts describe Keenan waving the Stars and Stripes while leading the British marines as they went through the breach. The story then became more embellished with an account of the thoroughly drunk U.S. consul the first over the walls of Canton and planting the American flag in the city.[40]

As some of this account was given by a man purported to be seeking Keenan's consular position, it is suspect. When the tale appeared in a British newspaper and was read in Washington, Keenan was in hot water. The angry Secretary of State William Marcy asked Peter Parker, the American commissioner to China, to investigate the incident and to see about Keenan's removal. Keenan claimed that Parker had no jurisdiction over him because he was responsible to the American minister in London. Nothing came of the investigation, not only because of the jurisdictional dispute, but because Marcy was soon out of office. Keenan left his post in 1861 when the Republicans replaced the Democrats. He died on his way back to the United States in 1862.

A major problem that Keenan and his fellow consuls along the China coast had to deal with was the coolie traffic. With the discovery of gold in Australia and California, the shutting down of the slave trade from Africa, and the continuing need for labor in the Philippines, West Indies, and Latin America, China's poor millions were a natural source. Unscrupulous suppliers, Chinese and Westerners, worked to provide contract laborers to willing employers around the globe. Often the Chinese found themselves duped, cheated, or "shanghaied" by being lured onto a ship and imprisoned in its hold until this human cargo was delivered to a labor camp in a foreign country, a camp that was nothing more than another prison. Prevailing conditions on ships engaged in the coolie trade were often almost as bad as those on slave ships.[41]

The British government passed the Passengers Act in 1855 aimed at preventing the greatest abuses of the labor trade, but it only resulted in the removal of the traffic from Hong Kong to Macao and the China ports. Early U.S. laws regarding passenger conditions on

American ships applied only to passengers leaving from American ports. U.S. consuls had no control over American ships engaged in what amounted to traffic in slavery. Ironically, many such ships were owned by Northerners, often from abolitionist Boston. A consul's attempts at moral persuasion made little impression on the masters of these vessels. The Chinese government, however, tried to stop some of the worst abuses.

A notorious American ship in the coolie trade was the *Wandering Jew* out of Maine, which Chinese authorities had under surveillance while it was taking on "passengers" near Shanghai, intercepting some 300 coolies on their way to the ship. Albert L. Freeman, temporary consul in Shanghai, attempted to ward off serious trouble for the captain of the ship. He boarded the *Wandering Jew* accompanied by an interpreter and a Chinese official to talk to the passengers. The captain maintained that he had only picked up a few passengers to take down the coast to Fukien Province.

The ship was actually on the way to Cuba with laborers for the sugar plantations. On board, Freeman through his interpreter talked to all the passengers and reported to the Department of State:

> Many of them stated that a Chinaman in the employ of Mr. Connolly the Consignee had promised to give them three dollars provided they would go on board the foreign ship to work for a few days, others stated that they were to receive three hundred cash per day to come to Shanghai to serve as soldiers, others were to form part of a mandarin's retinue. Nearly every one was questioned and not one was found that came on board with any idea of going to a foreign country. Many of the coolies upon being informed that they were to be taken to a foreign country begged to be allowed to go on shore as they had wives and families dependent upon them. Out of two hundred and thirty-six (236) coolies on board, one hundred and seventeen (117) were found to be there against their own free will and consent. [42]

Those Chinese not wanting to go to Cuba were allowed to disembark; the others, mainly beggars with no real choice, stayed on. After another call at Amoy for further passengers the *Wandering Jew* left for Cuba. Few ships like the *Wandering Jew* were visited by an American consul to remove unwilling coolies; countless others slipped away with their unwitting cargoes.

During the Taiping Rebellion in 1853, the rebels briefly captured part of Shanghai, leaving the Chinese civil government in disarray. The Western consuls stepped in to run what was to them the most essential service, the customs house. When the tide of the Taiping Rebellion receded, a compromise was reached between the American, British, and French consuls over the collection of duty. The old imperial system of collection had collapsed because of its corruption; neither imperial Chinese nor Western merchants wanted to revive it, since the government got little revenue by the time corrupt officials had taken their large cut. The merchants wanted a fair, known system that would save them from being "squeezed" by the Chinese customs collectors.

An agreement was reached with the Chinese whereby American, British, and French consuls would help administer the customs service, making their own appointments to its Board of Inspectors. Thus foreigners took over the Shanghai customs. [43] Arrangements were made for a special customs court under the consuls to settle disputes. Although the United States had made a commitment to help in the running of a vital service in China, in practice there was minimal influence over the operation because there was too little concern for the appointment of competent men. Congress was unwilling to provide the necessary staff for the consulate, including a corps of student interpreters, to ensure America's efficient contribution. While the U.S. consular system did serve Americans in trouble if an energetic consul were available, the system was not organized and lacked trained staff to deal with the complex extraterritorial challenges developing in China. The United States had to give way in authority to the superior British and French systems.

JAPAN

In the entire history of the consular service, no appointment was more crucial than that of consul to Shimoda, Japan, in 1855. Commodore Matthew Perry "opened" Japan when, backed by a powerful fleet, he secured the Treaty of Kanagawa in 1854 from the unwilling but weak Japanese government, which had wished to keep Japan sealed from the rest of the world. That treaty opened two ports to commerce (Shimoda and Hakodate in the remote northern island of Japan), provided for better treatment of American castaways, permitted controlled trade, and allowed a consul to reside at Shimoda, but did not spell out details or give extraterritoriality. With this promising but vague agreement Perry sailed away. Further difficult negotiations would be required with the extremely reluctant Japanese to reach agreement on a commercial treaty that would in truth open Japan to American trade. Obviously, such negotiations called for the United States to send a skilled and proven diplomat backed by another impressive show of strength to work out a favorable agreement.

The choice of a consul for the critical assignment to Shimoda fell upon an unlikely candidate, Townsend Harris, a man without diplomatic or consular experience. A once-successful businessman and civic leader, Harris had come upon bad times in New York City and had gone to Asia to restore his fortunes, but there he also failed. Turning to the bottle for solace after the death of his mother was apparently the reason for Harris's downfall. In Asia he made many friends in the business community. Living mainly in Hong Kong, he traveled all over the region on minor business errands to India, Burma, Siam, Java, the Malay ports, and China.[44] Harris probably saw Japan as presenting the opportunity to redeem himself in the eyes of his family, especially his brother, a New York merchant who was paying him a remittance to stay in the Far East.

Harris overcame his drinking problem and looked to a position with the American government to make a new beginning. He had tried to go with Commodore Perry on his expedition to Japan in 1853. Although he had been rejected as having no particular qualifications, he had impressed the commodore, an asset that would be useful later. Harris had not been to Japan and did not speak Dutch, the one Western language spoken by Japanese in contact with foreigners. Unable to make himself useful to the United States Navy, he applied for a consular appointment at one of the treaty ports in China, using his Democratic Party connections in New York City to strengthen his application. He had hoped to be given Canton or Shanghai, but when the unimportant post of Ningpo was offered, he accepted it despite the fact that it paid no salary and had little American trade. His only compensation would be the one thousand dollars paid for judicial services.[45] This newly appointed consul to Ningpo never assumed his duties at his post. There was a bigger fish to be caught, the consul generalship to Japan. Harris had kept his ties to influential friends in New York City who assured him that there was not much competition for the Japanese appointment, for the Japanese had stipulated that they wanted no foreign women in Shimoda. The candidate had to be a bachelor. Pierce, a Democrat, was in power in Washington. Harris was both a bachelor and a Democrat.[46]

Not wanting to let the opportunity for a Japanese post slip away, Harris raced back to New York in a little more than two months, where he heard that Pierce had offered the consul general's position to John Romeyn Broadhead, who had some familiarity with Dutch and had served at one point as secretary of legation in London. Fortunately for Harris, Broadhead turned down the appointment, leaving the position open to Harris if he could persuade the president and secretary of state.

Even before Harris had returned to the United States, Secretary of State Marcy had been assured that Harris no longer had a drinking problem, a matter of concern to both the secretary and the president. To clinch the appointment Harris went to Washington to have several conferences with Pierce, which went well. Harris had excellent support for the position from influential Americans, including Commodore Perry, who remembered him from the Far East, Senator William Seward of New York, and John Broadhead, who had declined the appointment.

While waiting for the president's decision, Harris wrote Pierce on 4 August 1855:

I have told Your Excellency that I have long had a strong desire to visit Japan; and so deep has this feeling become that, if I were offered the choice between Commissioner to China or Consul to Japan, I should instantly take the latter. I have a perfect knowledge of the social banishment I must endure while in Japan, and the mental isolation in which I must live, and am prepared to meet it. I am a single man, without any ties to cause me to look anxiously to my old home, or to become impatient in my new one: – You may rely, Sir, that I will not ask for leave to visit my friends, or resign the place for any reasons of dislike of the country, but will devote myself, zealously, to the faithful discharge of my duties. I have only to add, that I shall be much obliged by your early decision on my application."[47]

The letter apparently cleared up any doubts Pierce may have had about Harris's appointment, for he signed the commission. Not only was Harris, still an unproven diplomat, given the crucial Japanese appointment, but he was also given another task on his way to his new post, to negotiate a commercial treaty with Siam. Such was the manner in which diplomatic duties were parceled out by the United States in its seventy-ninth year of independence.

Harris hired a Dutch-born American citizen, Henry Heusken, to act as both interpreter and secretary. Heusken, a lively twenty-three-year-old, added some lightness and balance to the solidity of Harris, who tended to be pompous. In fact, Harris's pomposity nearly cost him his assignment.

Harris had overplayed his importance while passing through Paris. Secretary Marcy wrote one of Harris's political sponsors, a General Wetmore: "I am overwhelmed by an avalanche of the most scandalous reports of our friend Harris. It is said that his conduct was shameful on his way out, and is attributed to drunkenness. At Paris he has behaved, so reports say, like a fool. Has been strutting about in a gorgeous court dress, distributing cards of an Envoy Extraordinary and Minister Plenipotentiary, etc. Can these things be so? I tell you I have serious apprehensions on the subject."[48]

Oblivious to the poor impression he had made in Paris, Harris went on to Siam, where he successfully arranged for a treaty, not too difficult a task as the British had just finished their negotiations and the United States benefited from advantages won by the British. In Japan the situation would be reversed, with Harris leading the way through a far more difficult negotiation process and other nations benefiting from his efforts.

In 1854 Commodore Perry appeared in Tokyo Bay on his final visit to Japan escorted by ten warships and two thousand sailors and marines. In contrast, the new Consul General Townsend Harris arrived at Shimoda on 21 August 1856 on the U.S.S. *San Jacinto*, with little of the power Perry had demonstrated with his fleet. Harris would have to impress the Japanese with the importance of himself and that of his mission alone. Luckily for the United States, Harris could himself display sufficient pomp without needing a supporting cast.

The Japanese wanted no foreign consul setting up residence in their country, claiming that the matter of a consul would be a subject of discussion rather than an issue already settled by Perry's treaty. When asked to leave, Harris refused, insisting that a proper residence be set aside for his use. While the Japanese officials sent from the capital Edo (now Tokyo) were interested in keeping Harris out, they were under instructions not to order him away peremptorily because of a distinct possibility that such an insult would bring back a vengeful American fleet. A more sensitive man might have been deterred by such a frigid reception, but Harris ignored the requests and insisted on help in establishing his consulate, which he received. For the consulate he was given a disused temple outside Shimoda.

His first days were concerned with arranging for his quarters and the all-important matter of having a proper flagstaff erected in front of the ex-temple, now the first consulate in Japan. These simple wooden objects, flagstaffs, were given inordinately large importance in nineteenth-century consular accounts. As the overt symbol of a foreign presence they were often resented. The Japanese, for all their unhappiness about the Americans now in their midst to stay, were not as perturbed by the presence of foreign flags as were the Chinese or Arabs.

To make sure that his flag would sufficiently reflect his dignity, the new consul general arranged for carpenters off the *San Jacinto* to erect an eighty-foot staff to fly the Stars and Stripes. On 4 September 1856 Harris wrote in his journal, "Flagstaff erected; men [from the warship] form a ring around it, and, at two and a half P.M. of this day, I hoist the `First Consular Flag' ever seen in this Empire. Grim reflections – ominous of change – undoubted beginning of the end. Query – if for the real good of Japan? The *San Jacinto* left at five dclock."[49]

While Harris was to prove a tough negotiator not afraid of running roughshod over Japanese sensitivities and customs that got in his way, his journal and later career show that he was well aware of what he was doing and the impact that he would have on a society and people whom he admired. Although Commodore Armstrong had promised Harris that the San Jacinto would return the next spring, the consul general and his assistant Heusken were left stranded on an unfriendly shore by the United States for the next eighteen months with no visits by American warships or communications from the State Department. This absurd show of indifference was unhappily characteristic of the United States, notorious for leaving its representatives abroad to their own devices. In the case of Harris, the isolation worked out well.

The Japanese had a purpose in choosing Shimoda as a port for American vessels. At the end of a mountainous peninsula, removed from major trading and governmental centers, this was a place where Western contamination would have the least effect. While the isolation frustrated Harris, who spent much of his negotiating skills on getting permission to go to Edo, it has been of great benefit to historians. The Japanese sent a group of officials to deal with the consul general, who were required to send detailed reports to the capital on the course of negotiations. These reports, together with Harris's journal, give a fascinating glimpse of East and West negotiating, revealing that the ruling Japanese class, despite the nation's self-imposed isolation, was very much aware of recent events in China, which also had tried to contain the foreign menace only to have the British smash open the doors to the country by force in the Opium War.

The Japanese were under no illusion that their feudal levies could hold off a determined Western assault; the more enlightened members of the shogun's government saw Harris's arrival as an opportunity rather than a threat. A moderate, controlled treaty with the United States would set a precedent for treating with the European powers, especially Britain, France, and Russia. These countries were likely to be more demanding than the Americans if they were to dictate their terms from the cannon's mouth.

On the other side were hard-line conservatives opposing any concessions to the world outside Japan. Townsend Harris did not fully understand the division within the Japanese ruling class; he did not appreciate a real concern on the part of the men who were negotiating with him of a possible assassination attempt by the xenophobic feudal lords or their followers, who saw their way of life threatened by the Western presence.

Much of Harris's early negotiations revolved around housekeeping details such as quarters, servants, the ability to walk about the country, and the purchase of supplies. An integral part of the negotiations concerned establishing the consul general's dignity; Harris, in effect, dictated whom he would see and whom he would not and where and when. He insisted that no matter what the urgency, he would do no business on Sunday and that only officials of sufficient rank could deal with him.[50] On most of these matters the Japanese reluctantly gave way to his stubbornness, aware that every concession to the American would be setting a precedent that could be used by other Westerners.

The Dutch, working out of a small enclave in Nagasaki, who had been trading with the Japanese for two centuries, had already negotiated a preliminary commercial treaty that provided for some extraterritoriality and even allowed the traders to bring their wives and children. The Japanese had not yet ratified this treaty.

The Russians had also just obtained a somewhat similar treaty. But Harris, the first consul in residence, was breaking new ground with every demand.

He used his journal to vent his frustrations over the delays and difficulties of his negotiations. In his 12 September 1856 entry he described a call by the Japanese negotiating team:

> The object of the visit was my demand for two boys as house servants. It was a rare scene of Japanese deceit, falsehood, flattery and politeness. I at last got them cornered and they were compelled to promise me to supply my wants by the 16th. They fought hard to have the boys leave at sunset and return at daylight, but I was firm and carried my point. I may here remark that at all these visits they readily drink all I offer them, – wine, cordials, brandy, whiskey, etc., etc., and many of them drink more than enough. Spirits of all kinds they drink raw.[51]

Harris may have been drinking with his guests, but his effectiveness was apparently not impaired, although his health may have been, for during his time in Shimoda he had several bouts of illness. He was convinced that all Japanese were liars, but the record shows that they were actually trying to explain matters as they saw them and that they had not the easy control over servants and others that he assumed.

Although Harris felt himself surrounded by consummate liars, he liked the Japanese. He wrote a friend in Hong Kong:

> The Japanese are a fine race of men; genial in their temper, and cleanly in their persons & houses – They are possessed of so much graceful, natural politeness, that they might be called the French of Asia – I am living on cordial terms with the authorities here, and no restraint is placed on me, or on my movements [he was putting a good face on his situation]. – This friendly intercourse has been increasing from the time they had recovered from the agitation caused by my arrival, and from what I observed, I am sure the masses of the Japanese would gladly see the country opened to Foreigners.[52]

One item of negotiation not indicated in Harris's letters, his journal, or reports to the Department of State concerned the acquiring of female companionship. The fifty-two-year-old consul general and Heusken, his young assistant and interpreter, were both kept in strict isolation by the Japanese authorities, who were concerned over the safety of their unwelcome guests and wanted to avoid unpredictable consequences from their having too much contact with the populace. The Japanese officials did not want the Americans to settle in and made sure that every attempt to do so was resisted. Everything, including obtaining food, procuring servants, and walking outside the consulate area, was the subject of obstinate negotiations. These two lonely men tired of their enforced companionship. A new item appeared in the negotiating agenda. After they had been in Shimoda ten months, the Japanese negotiators reported to Edo:

> For some time the Consul General has been asking us to find two girls to serve him and his interpreter, basing this request on the grounds that there is no one to attend them if they become ill. We have politely refused and tried to avoid discussing the issue. A few days ago he very forcefully repeated his request and asked for an immediate reply. Since this is a private concern and we are in the midst of official negotiations, we said we would continue the matter when our negotiations were concluded. At this he became very angry.[53]

To offer Japanese girls to foreigners could establish a precedent, but the negotiators had put themselves in a corner by their rigid control over the environment in which Harris and Heusken were confined. The officials continued in their report that because they had been

> specifically instructed in Edo to show good will in negotiating with the American official we have sent a girl to the Consul General under the title of nurse, with the approval of those concerned. The girl was formerly employed to attend seamen when they drank. Similar arrangements will be made for the interpreter. Since it would be most troublesome if such accommodations are requested each time a foreign ship makes port here, we have made it clear that this arrangement is for the Consul General and his interpreter only. The American official has assured us that he would

keep it secret, because it would embarrass him if it became public.[54]

In Japan a legend grew about Okichi, a poor girl plucked from the bosom of her family to sacrifice honor and herself to satisfy the lust of a foreign barbarian for Japanese national interests. In fact, meticulous records were kept; Okichi was on call as a "nurse" only three times. She had been a quasi-prostitute prior to her assignment. Heusken and his assigned "nurse," Ofuku, had a longer and presumably more pleasurable relationship than that of Harris and Okichi.[55]

The Japanese willingness to allow the Americans female companionship coincided with a major breakthrough by the negotiators, not an unconnected occurrence. On 8 June 1857 Harris wrote:

I have at last carried every point triumphantly with the Japanese, and have got everything conceded that I have been negotiating since last September. Am I elated by this success? Not a whit. I know my dear countrymen but too well to expect any praise for what I have done, and I shall esteem myself lucky if I am not removed from office, not for what I have done, but because I have not made a commercial treaty that would open Japan as freely as England is open to us. Besides it is easy to criticize, and so agreeable to write imbecile, ass or fool, than to say able, discreet and competent.[56]

Harris's pessimistic view of the American system of rewarding or condemning its public officials was justifiable, but in this instance he was indeed rewarded by eventually being made the first U.S. minister to Edo. The entire course of his negotiations with the Japanese had been perilous. He had certainly exceeded the instructions given him in September 1855. These read in part:

A principal motive of the President in selecting you as Consul General for Japan was the hope that, by your knowledge of eastern character, and your general intelligence and experience in business, you would make such an impression upon the Japanese as would in time induce them to enter into a commercial treaty with us. As it is possible that a juncture for this purpose might arise before you could communicate with the Department, upon the subjects, after your arrival at Shimoda, you are now furnished with a full power to negotiate and conclude such a Treaty."[57]

This rather superficial language dear to the heart of a government clerk allowed Harris plenty of latitude. But if things went wrong, if he antagonized the Japanese to the point of expelling him, the Department of State could easily disavow him for "exceeding instructions." Had Harris been a different person, unwilling to take chances or apply pressure, his successors might still be sitting in Shimoda waiting for a juncture favorable for making an overture.

Harris's first and foremost goal had been to sign a commercial treaty in Edo, the capital, and to have that the seat of American representation in Japan, not the third-rate port town of Shimoda. His knowledge of the Western experience in China had bolstered his resolve that the United States would not be excluded from representing itself to the center of the Japanese government. In China the efforts of the imperial court to keep itself aloof in Peking, while leaving all contact with foreigners to distant officials, had had a negative effect on both Chinese and Westerners, a situation Harris was determined to avoid. It took several British and French major military campaigns, the last being in 1860, which included the infamous sacking and destruction of the Summer Palace in Peking, before Western diplomats could reside there. Harris, with the assistance of Heusken laboriously translating from Dutch to English and English to Dutch, carried on a similar and successful campaign in Japan against almost the same stiff opposition, but by bluff.

Harris had a letter from the president to the emperor of Japan, a conventional letter showing the consul general to have the power to make a treaty and asking the emperor to "receive Mr. Harris with kindness, and place entire confidence in all the representations which he may make to Your Majesty in my behalf."[58] The consul general refused to show this letter to the officials in Shimoda, insisted that he deliver it in person to the shogun, and threatened an intervention by the American fleet if denied his mission, an unrealistic threat because America was domestically preoccupied over the slave issue in the late 1850s. But, further, he made it clear that the United States would be far less demanding than the British or French if they were to dictate a treaty after using their military power. He did not then know that the British threat, quite real when he had left for Japan, had receded. Her Majesty's forces were occupied with the Sepoy mutiny in India and with opening the way to Peking in China. The Japanese understood what Harris was hinting. As in all successful negotiations, his points were well taken.

Within the crumbling Japanese feudal system there was considerable opposition by diehards to any concession to the West. But the same forces that were to restore the Meiji Dynasty to power over the long rule of the shogunate were pushing for an opening to the West. Harris and a benign, commercially oriented United States seemed to be a better initial partner than the territorially acquisitive military powers of Great Britain, France, and Russia. The more liberal circles in the Japanese capital eventually won out, and Harris was able to proceed to Edo with the pomp he so enjoyed to deliver his letter from the president and to sign a commercial treaty on 29 July 1858.

Harris served as the minister to Japan until 1862, when, having had enough of a still-isolated life, he returned to New York City, now thoroughly redeemed in the eyes of his family, and lived the life of an elderly, respected clubman, known as "the old Tycoon," the name the shogun had been known by in the West. Heusken did not live to enjoy a comfortable retirement. He was assassinated in 1861 in Edo, as the Japanese officials had so often feared, by xenophobic *ronin*, unemployed samurai.[59]

The contrast between the poor, second-rate consular system in China and the splendid work of Townsend Harris in Japan clearly emphasized the importance of the individual in the system and the care the government should have taken but did not to select and support its consuls abroad. The appointment of Harris and his having independent resources were fortunate for the United States. The entire Japanese negotiation effort might have resulted in a disaster had an impoverished consul general been desperately searching the horizon for a naval ship that did not come, while the amused Japanese watched. The government of the United States had learned nothing, however, from its Far Eastern experience, and as North and South separated, what was left of the Union would have to depend on a widespread but indifferently staffed and supported consular system to deal with the worldwide problems created by the Civil War.

10

Consuls and the Civil War
(1861–1865)

The Lincoln administration, assuming power in the spring of 1861, faced the daunting task of preserving the Union. Almost equally important and urgent was the filling of federal patronage positions. The new Republican Party had many political debts, and, consular posts made good payments. The men in consular positions prior to 1860 reflected the sectional tilt of the Democrats, in power since 1851 and strong in the South.

With a civil war approaching, the new secretary of state, William Seward, must have viewed with concern some of the consuls at strategic points in the U.S. consular system. Robert Campbell, a former South Carolina congressman, was now the consul in London, supported by the Virginian, Beverly Tucker, in Liverpool, a post of dire importance in any war. Tucker became an active Confederate agent in Britain during the Civil War. After Liverpool, the most crucial post was Havana, where Charles Helm of Kentucky presided as consul. The consul in Marseilles, France's main entry to the Mediterranean, was from Louisiana; Edwin DeLeon of South Carolina was in Alexandria, Egypt, a busy cotton port. At Mexico's main port of Vera Cruz was Kentuckian, John T. Pickett; a Virginian was the consul at the major shipping center of Rio de Janeiro. Other Southerners were scattered about the consular system, some of whom, including Tucker, DeLeon, Pickett, and Helm, became Confederate agents when the split came between North and South.

During the hectic opening days of his administration, Lincoln was as busy in the appointment process as he was in trying to hold the Union together. On the same day (7 March 1861) that the new president sent a note to Secretary of State Seward regarding the wisdom of provisioning Fort Sumter in Charleston, South Carolina (the act that precipitated the war), he also sent his approval of the appointment of Mark H. Dunnell of Maine to replace the Kentuckian, Pickett, as consul to Vera Cruz.[1] One of Lincoln's first appointments was the replacement of the aging Southern firebrand Campbell in London with a former Maine congressman, Freeman H. Morse, who was to run an effective counterintelligence operation in London while tending to that typically busy consular office.

In his appointments, consular and otherwise, Lincoln made sure that states that supported him were getting their fair share of the patronage plums; he also kept an eye on the cost, as indicated in two of his messages to Seward:

April 29, 1861

Dear Sir
    If you have no objection to Timothy C. Smith having one of the $2000 consulships remaining open in Russia, I have none. Yours truly, A. Lincoln [Smith went to Odessa.][2]

July 11, 1861

Hon. John P. Veree of Pa. wishes George Hogg to be appointed Consul to Trinidad; as this place has fees only, suppose we end our responsibility to him by giving it to him at this time. [Hogg did go to Trinidad.][3]

The United States was facing the gravest challenge since the founding of the Republic. In view of the seriousness of the threat to the Union, an administration should have made sure its best people were in positions of responsibility. But loyalty and political balance were principal criteria for consular appointments, rather than potential competence in protecting American interests abroad.

There was not, however, an overhaul of all consuls; Horatio Jones Sprague, for example, was kept on in Gibraltar. He had succeeded his father, who had been consul from the War of 1812 to 1848. Lincoln's confidence in Sprague was fully rewarded by the yeoman work of the veteran consul at that chokepoint. Because of his standing in the local commercial community, Sprague was able to dissuade merchants in Gibraltar from supplying the rebel raider *Sumter* with coal; he kept close tab on all Confederate naval activity in and out of the Mediterranean and reported this information to the United States Navy. He was to remain in Gibraltar until 1901, a total of fifty-three years, a record for the consular service.

One of Lincoln's consular appointments went to William Dean Howells, a self-educated young man beginning to make a name for himself as a poet. A reporter and editor of the *Ohio State Journal,* Howells had followed in the footsteps of his illustrious consular predecessor, Nathaniel Hawthorne. In 1860 he put together a campaign biography of the Republican candidate for president. Lincoln rewarded Howells with the consulate in Venice, where for the next four years he avoided military service with little to do except view the charms of Venetian life, which fueled his later book, *Venetian Days.* Howells became one of America's most well known literary figures in the post–Civil War period.[4]

There was a serious flaw in the appointment procedure during this period. The State Department failed, not only to make a thorough examination of the qualifications of men given consular appointments, but to prepare appointees for the unfamiliar work they would be doing. Consuls sent to protect U.S. interests during the Civil War had no real instruction for new complexities of the job. By the 1860s, there were several books of regulations and a series of laws to guide consuls in routine matters, but there were no established operating procedures for thwarting Confederate agents, inhibiting rebel cruisers, or preventing shipment of supplies to the South. The consuls had to make their own rules with little help from the State Department. Although the Confederacy had no consular system, there were agents abroad who worked on its behalf, as did the precursors of the U.S. consular service in France and elsewhere during the American Revolutionary War. These rebel agents purchased and arranged shipment for military supplies on blockade runners, supported Confederate raiders in foreign ports, passed on military intelligence, and worked to persuade foreign governments to support the South.

Several former U.S. consuls became Confederate agents abroad. As soon as he was replaced by a Lincoln appointee, Charles Helm in Havana set up a separate office in the city to further Southern interests in Cuba, drawing on his already-excellent relations with the Spanish captain-general and the British consul general. Edwin DeLeon, consul in Alexandria in 1861, left his post to serve the Confederacy in Europe. A personal friend of Jefferson Davis, DeLeon was entrusted with $25,000 (a large sum for the time) to pay the venal press in France to report favorably on the Confederacy. A feud with the Confederate commissioners to Europe, especially with John Slidell, soon dissipated his usefulness. After several of DeLeon's official and private dispatches, critical of the French and Slidell, fell into the wrong hands and were published in the Northern press, he was blacklisted.[5]

John T. Pickett of Kentucky, the consul Lincoln had dismissed from Vera Cruz, became the main Confederate agent to Mexico. After his discharge in 1861, Pickett was returned to Mexico to represent the South to the Juarez government. At heart Pickett was a filibuster, not a diplomat. The ex-consul was not warmly received in Mexico City, as local public opinion favored the North, with the South regarded as the predominant aggressor against Mexico in previous years and a potentially dangerous threat. Pickett had a difficult cause to sell. He also conducted himself in an undiplomatic manner, eventually getting into a barroom fight with a Yankee merchant, causing his arrest and incarceration for thirty days. After buying his way out of jail, he found it prudent to leave Mexico, his short diplomatic venture a complete failure.[6]

Beverly Tucker of Virginia became a rebel agent in Britain as soon as he was replaced at Liverpool as consul. Another early Confederate representative in Europe seeking recognition for the South was A. Dudley Mann, who had been the U.S. consul in Bremen in the 1840s. One of the more successful ex-consuls who acted as a Confederate agent was Duncan McRae of North Carolina, who had been the U.S. consul in Paris from 1853 to 1857. At the start of the war he fought as a colonel with great bravery in the Army of Northern Virginia. Wounded at the battle of Antietam, McRae left the military and was sent to Europe to purchase supplies for North Carolina troops, where he made sure that the regiments from his state were the best equipped in the Confederate army. The prewar consular system of the United States had unintentionally been the training ground for the embryonic foreign service of the Confederacy. The wartime split of men with consular experience into Northern and Southern branches was somewhat parallel to that experienced in the officer corps of the United States Army, but the ex-consuls used by the Confederate States of America were not nearly as successful as were their military counterparts.

When war started in earnest and the need for new troops became apparent to Lincoln's cabinet, the U.S. consuls in Europe were instructed to encourage emigration to the North from their consular districts. In a circular (no. 19) sent to all posts, consular and diplomatic, in August 1862, Secretary of State Seward asked that the attention of potential emigrants be directed to the agricultural and manufacturing opportunities in the United States, or what was left of those states.[7] Anything, however, that smacked of recruiting in foreign countries was a sensitive matter, since their rulers might be rightfully outraged by attempts to recruit soldiers. Consul General John Bigelow in Paris suggested that the United States might pay the passage of soldiers-to-be, but this unwise proposal from a usually very capable consul was not put into practice, thus saving consuls in Europe from a barrage of protests by their host governments.[8]

Nevertheless, emigration flourished. Toward the end of the war many Union recruits spoke with decidedly foreign accents, mainly Irish and German. The consuls' role in promoting emigration from Europe was only one factor in the continued exodus. Lack of opportunities in the Old World inspired most Europeans to look for new options in the New World. Articles placed by consuls in local newspapers about the possibilities in the United States and their encouragement of the emigration process helped prime the pump.

Another concern of the North was preventing Southern agents from going to Europe. Two important Southern agents, James M. Mason and John Slidell, were sent by the Confederacy to garner official recognition and support abroad. A consular officer who was to play a role in trying to stop the Confederate envoys was Robert Wilson Shufeldt of Connecticut, who had been appointed to Havana in 1861 to replace Charles Helm, now a rebel agent. Shufeldt was an ex-naval officer who had resigned from the navy in 1853 to become a captain of merchant ships and a promoter of an American development in Central America. As a naval officer and merchant captain, Shufeldt had served in Caribbean waters and dabbled in Central American affairs. He had experience with the Spanish authorities in Cuba and belonged to the "old-boy network" of American naval and ex-naval officers, a qualification that would prove useful in cooperating with the Union naval blockaders who would use Havana as a port of call and intelligence center.

Shufeldt was established in Havana within a short time after the firing on Fort Sumter and the start of the war. Once at his post the new American consul general quickly locked horns with his British counterpart, Consul General Joseph Crawford, who had been in Havana nineteen years. Crawford was pro-Confederate, as were many of the British upper class; he saw it as his duty to make sure that trade was unimpeded between the United Kingdom and the South especially ensuring that British manufacturers got all the cotton they needed for their mills. Shufeldt's job was precisely the opposite. Matters were not helped by the mass change of American-registered ships to the British flag in order to avoid involvement in the war, a process the British consul general happily assisted.[9] Furthering the divide between United States and British consuls general was the seizure of the British mail packet *Trent*. The Confederate States had appointed their two commissioners, Mason and Slidell, to go to Europe to obtain recognition for the Confederacy. Their departure from Charleston, South Carolina, was widely known, but attempts to stop them by the United States Navy on the first leg of their journey to Cuba, were unsuccessful..

When Mason and Slidell landed in Cuba, none other than the British consul general introduced them to the Spanish captain-general, although only as private citizens of the Confederate States of America, not as officials. This was a blatant act on the part of Consul General Crawford; he had some explaining to do to the British minister in Washington. Shufeldt immediately responded by assembling the captain and officers of the USS *San Jacinto* and presenting them, decked out in full dress, to the captain-general to offset the impression made by Mason and Slidell.[10] Back in his office, Shufeldt and Captain Charles Wilkes of the *San Jacinto* considered their next move. They knew that Mason and Slidell were leaving for England on the *Trent,* which could be intercepted by the *San Jacinto.* In consulting legal books on international law at the consulate, these two found the subject unclear as to whether enemy officials could be taken off a neutral vessel, but they knew what they wanted. Since there was a lack of a clear precedent, they came to the conclusion that Mason and Slidell were not "innocent travelers upon the ocean," but enemies of the U.S. government going as envoys of the Confederate States of America and that the *Trent* was not an official vessel of the British government, although it was carrying mail, but a private vessel chartered by the British. Hence it was fair game.[11] Shufeldt and Wilkes were amateur sea lawyers. At best they had made a weak case, but as in most international incidents of the time, the final settlement would rest on political realities, not legal quibbling.

Captain Wilkes stopped the *Trent* on the high seas on 8 November 1861 and took Mason and Slidell to bring them as prisoners to the North. The action was popular in the North, and Captain Wilkes was lionized. Shufeldt's role got little attention, which was just as well for him, as the *Trent* affair soon ballooned into a major crisis between the United States and Great Britain with the threat of war between these two powers. Lincoln and Seward were able to mollify the British by allowing Mason and Slidell to go to Europe, but the *Trent* matter strained relations with the British during the critical early years of the Civil War. Shufeldt was neither reprehended nor questioned about his role in bringing the United States to the brink of conflict in the *Trent* affair. He continued as the consul general, feuding with his British counterpart and doing his best to see that the Spanish authorities were not too friendly to the Confederate cause.

Eventually Shufeldt tired of his consular office and sought reassignment to the navy. By May of 1863 the ex–consul general was in action off the South Carolina coast as the commanding officer of a gunboat. He stayed on in the navy after the war and rose to the rank of rear admiral. In later years he was given semi-diplomatic assignments and had more dealings with the U.S. consular service.[12]

Although consular posts such as Havana were important, the major burden in the Union's efforts to isolate the Confederacy fell on Charles Francis Adams, the American minister to Great Britain, and his consuls in the British Isles. To a somewhat lesser extent, the American minister and consuls in France were duplicating the work of their counterparts in Great Britain with the added concern of keeping an eye upon Napoleon III's adventure in Mexico while the United States was busy with the Civil War. The most important consuls in Britain and France were Freeman Morse, ex-congressman from Maine, in London, Thomas H. Dudley in Liverpool, and John Bigelow, a former editor of the *New York Evening Post* and consul general in Paris.

Liverpool had always been considered the premier consular post in Europe because of fees generated from the busy shipping point. With the advent of the consular reform of 1856, it was made one of the two top-paying posts in the worldwide consular system; London held the other high, for which the pay was also $7,500 per year. When the Civil War started, Liverpool's reputation as a lucrative post was quickly overshadowed by its importance as a center for Confederate intrigue and Union countermeasures. Near London and facing the Atlantic, Liverpool was the closest port in England for ships bound to and from America and the West Indies.

This was the most convenient port for the shipment of supplies to the North and, via blockade-runners, to the South. Couriers and spies working for both sides came and went. Liverpool and its environs comprised a major shipbuilding center, with the Laird shipyards specializing in ships destined to be Confederate raiders or warships.

Thomas H. Dudley of Camden, New Jersey, was chosen for the crucial position of U.S. consul in Liverpool. At forty-two he had earned his political reward by helping Lincoln get the Republican nomination at the 1860 party convention in Chicago. A lawyer, he showed a flair for the dramatic and clandestine life in his first case. A black woman and her three children had been kidnapped from New Jersey and taken south as slaves. Dudley disguised himself as a slave trader with whip, pistols, and broad-brimmed hat. Under the noses of hostile Southern officials he found and brought his charges back to freedom.[13]

Although he did not have to resort to disguise in Liverpool, Dudley had secret informers. Originally he had been considered as the replacement for Townsend Harris, the American minister to Japan, but after being in a steamboat fire in 1856, which left him in poor health, he begged off the Far Eastern assignment as too strenuous and went instead to the most active post in the consular service, the one with the greatest pressure on the incumbent. [14]

The first major challenge to the Northern diplomatic and consular attempts to keep the South from acquiring a navy built in England came in early 1862 with the construction and outfitting of a war vessel initially called the *Oreto*, supposedly destined for Italy. Dudley had brought the work on this ship to the attention of his minister, Adams, who protested to the British that it was being built in violation of the Foreign Enlistment Act. The protest came too late. By the time the Foreign Office had ascertained that the *Oreto* was not in fact ordered by the Italians, the ship had left port, unarmed but ready to be fully equipped once it rendezvoused with a British supply ship at Nassau in the West Indies. Despite attempts by the U.S. consul in the Bahamas to prevent the conversion, the *Oreto* became the CSS *Florida* and won renown as a successful raider until its capture in 1864.[15]

Dudley intended not to be caught a second time on the construction of rebel raiders by the Laird shipyards and others. He recruited spies, mainly sailors and shipyard workers, to keep him supplied with information on ship construction throughout Britain.

It became obvious that the Laird yards were building a sister ship to the *Florida*, called No. 290 because it was their 290th ship. The British authorities, friendly to the Southern cause, were reluctant to take action, claiming that there was not sufficient evidence to stop the construction. Dudley tried to convince the collector of the port, Price Edwards, that if No. 290 was being built like a Confederate raider, was financed like a Confederate raider, and was known by everyone in Liverpool to be a Confederate raider, then it was a Confederate raider. But the collector, an ardent Southern supporter, would take no action.[16]

Dudley took the depositions gathered from his agents, shipyard workers, equipment suppliers, and others and went to London to consult with Adams, having failed to settle the matter at the local level. Adams in turn went to Earl Russell, the foreign minister, but there too was unable to prod the British government into taking steps to keep the now nearly completed ship from leaving port. Discouraged, Dudley expressed to his friend Benjamin Moran at the London legation his opinion "as to the undisguised hostility of all England towards the Union in this great struggle" and his feeling that "the entire British people with but few exceptions are heart and soul in favor of slavery and rebellion."[17] This was an exaggeration, as there was wide support for the Union cause, which was to grow stronger as the war progressed, but still in the ranks of the British upper class there was little sympathy for the Yankees, who were getting what was felt to be their just deserts.

After some delay, Consul Dudley prepared his case against No. 290/ Adams had instructed him to turn it over to the Board of Customs after ensuring that everything was done in its proper legal form. The legal technicalities caused some extra delay. Then the lawyers on the Board of Customs quibbled over the meaning of the Foreign Enlistment Act, eventually turning the whole matter over to the Foreign Office for a decision. It was a long-drawn-out affair. To compound the situation, the Foreign Office gave the papers over to the queen's advocate, Sir John Harding, who had just suffered a nervous breakdown and was shortly thereafter certified as a lunatic; so no action was taken by the poor man, merely the addition of yet another delay to the proceedings. Meanwhile Lairds, spurred by the Confederate naval agent James D. Bullock, was working hard to bring No. 290 to readiness. Before the lethargic British authorities could take measures to stop the ship, the future CSS *Alabama* had slipped out of the Laird shipyards and was on the high seas.

The *Alabama* turned to the Indian Ocean and the Far East for a profitable cruise, picking up a number of Northern merchant ships and forcing others quickly to change their registry to British. The U.S. consuls in the area not only reported on the number of ships the *Alabama* captured and burnt, but had to deal with the aftermath, the misfortunes of American seamen suddenly unemployed, dumped by a raider at the nearest port and left to seek out the American consulate for help. It was a repetition of consular work during the War of 1812. There were many jobless American sailors, but safe ships were few and far between because of the threat of the *Alabama* and its sister raiders.

As the war continued, the Confederates became more ambitious. Instead of limiting their resources to commerce raiders, they ordered, in June 1862, a pair of ironclad warships from the Laird yards, ships that became known as the "Laird rams." With enough secret-service money to support an effective spy net, Dudley knew as much about the construction of the rams as did the Confederate agent in charge of the project. Despite growing evidence of the ultimate destination of the ships, the British government still took no firm steps to stop the ships' construction, leaving the matter to the builder as a function of free enterprise until absolute proof could be presented that the rams would indeed go into Confederate hands. Understandably, Lairds and the Southern purchasing agent did everything to obscure the destination of the ships, as they had in the cases of the *Florida* and *Alabama*. The rams were supposedly bound for Egypt, but no one was fooled.[18]

Slowly, the attitude of the British government began to change. Lincoln's Emancipation Proclamation in September 1862 put the North squarely on the side of freedom for slaves and left the South as the slave power, a position the British could hardly support. Charles Adams was also receiving reports from Yankee consuls all over the world on the destruction carried out by the *Alabama*, the *Florida*, and other raiders, almost all of which were British built. As these reports were given to the Foreign Office, bills for damages were mounting. The British were having second thoughts about setting the precedent, as a neutral government, of allowing a belligerent state to construct warships in their yards, no matter what legal fig leaf covered this hostile act. Great Britain was the preeminent seafaring nation and often at war. If the United States, which now seemed more likely to emerge the winner of the Civil War, were to take seriously the *Florida* and *Alabama* examples, the Yankees in the future could build commerce raiders to be used by France, Russia, Turkey, Japan, China, or whomever the British might be at war with at the moment. Benjamin Moran, a consular officer at the U.S. legation in London, noted the weakness of the British case regarding the *Alabama:* "This buccaneer has never been in a rebel port, her crews, her armament, and her entire equipment are English, and half the time she flies the English flag."[19] He was not exaggerating. Although the officers of the *Alabama* and other raiders were mainly Southern, the crews were almost entirely from Britain, as were the guns and ammunition. The ships used British ports around the world as convenient stopovers, where they received sympathetic assistance. It would have been difficult for an objective observer to allow the British to separate themselves from the results of their inattention to enforcing their own laws of neutrality. And the U.S. representatives were doing their best to make everyone aware that there would be a reckoning.

Tension built up in August and September 1863 as the Foreign Office began to look more closely at the title to the Laird rams. The British consul general in Egypt checked on the supposed order from the Egyptian government and found it false.[20] Here were two undoubted warships unclaimed by any government. The foreign minister likened it to finding a person in the early hours of the morning carrying a bag of burglar's tools near an uninhabited house.[21]

While the foreign minister had made up his mind to have the rams held as a case was built against them, Dudley saw that one of the ships was nearing completion and taking on coal. It was ready for engine trials, which would be an opportunity for the ship to slip away before authorities could prevent the departure. The U.S. consul in Cardiff, Wales, reported groups of men landing from a French ship that had come from Brest, where the CSS *Florida* was docked. They were going to Liverpool as a crew for a ram. Obviously the South, with the support of sympathizers at Lairds, with or without permission, was going to attempt to take the ship to sea.

The Foreign Office had legal problems with detaining the ship despite its obvious destination: the threat of a suit by Lairds over the illegal detention of one of its products was inhibiting. The British government, however, forced Lairds to keep the ships at its yard and eventually ended the controversial matter by purchasing the ships. In the midst of the disputes over the ships prior to their detention, Adams, tired and discouraged, wrote to the foreign minister, "It would be superfluous in me to point out to your Lordship that this is war."[22] This sentence has often been quoted as decisive in causing the British government to take action against the rams, but matters had been moving in that direction as a result of the good work of Dudley and other consuls who had been collecting evidence against Lairds and the Confederates.

While Dudley was watching the shipyards in Liverpool, Freeman Morse in London was doing the same in his consular district, having considerable success in counterintelligence activities. As Benjamin Moran noted, "By some means or other Mr. Morse our consul here has obtained an original dispatch from the rebels to Lt. North."[23] The "some means or other" was a result of Morse's intelligence operation. The nature of Northern and Southern operations in Europe, which were often dependent upon foreigners as couriers, purchasing agents, spies, or interpreters, made it relatively easy to penetrate each other's organization by well-placed payments. Not every Southern man by virtue of his origin was loyal to the Confederacy, nor every Northerner to the Union.

In this promising environment of easy access to funds and direct communications with Washington, Consul Morse and his colleagues throughout Europe flourished, for they could operate out of legitimately established consular offices with some immunity. The Confederate agents, however, had limited funds and problems getting information to and from Richmond. All ship ordering by the Confederacy must be in secret, with the British or French doing all the construction. Foreign workmen were usually not committed to the Confederate cause and could be paid to talk.

Morse was an imaginative consular officer. When the danger of the Laird rams became apparent, he wrote to Washington proposing that the Northern government in effect outbid the Confederacy for whatever ships were being ordered, as the cost would be slight compared to what damage even one of those ships could cause if it were let loose.[24] The proposal made sense. A mission led by two wealthy Northern shipowners, John Murray Forbes and William H. Aspinwell, was sent to England to see what money could do.

This mission, although not successful in purchasing the ships, indirectly helped Morse and Dudley, because Forbes, on his return to Washington, urged Seward to give the two consuls more money for their espionage activities.[25] As an example of this illustrious counterintelligence mission, Morse recruited a French sailor off the *Agrippina*, which was alleged a supply ship for the *Alabama*, to help pass on information to the Union navy as to where any rendezvous with the Confederate cruiser would take place.[26] Unfortunately for all its potential, this plan was unsuccessful.

When not occupied in frustrating the Confederates, Morse, Dudley, and other consuls were preparing the U.S. government's case for the future by taking affidavits from discharged British seamen who had served on rebel cruisers or their supply ships. These men had no particular allegiance to the Confederacy and had signed on to the *Alabama*, the *Florida*, and other ships for prize money and adventure. When the USS *Kearsarge sank the Alabama off the coast of France* in 1864, some of the crew came back to England, where Morse took their voluntary statements, which the U.S. government later used in the *Alabama* claims.

In France, the Northern consuls, headed by Consul General John Bigelow in Paris, worked to prevent the Confederates from using the Southern sympathies of Napoleon III to build and equip a navy. Bigelow, a former newspaper owner, writer, and editor, made sure that the case of the Union was favorably presented in the French press. Although those newspapers on the side of Napoleon III and his government normally favored the South (with some help from ex-consul DeLeon's Confederate funds), Bigelow found the liberal press in France receptive to the Union cause.[27]

When Confederate agents saw challenges arise in 1863 with their plans for a British-built navy, they transferred some of their activities to France, which had a stricter neutrality law, but where almost anything could be done if the emperor smiled on the project. Because much of the Southern shipbuilding effort had initially been concentrated in Britain, by 1863 Bigelow had become bored in France and asked for release from his consular duty, but Seward would not consider his request. Bigelow stayed in Paris and thus was on hand when the South turned to France for its navy. He took full advantage of a stroke of luck. The confidential clerk of a French shipyard owner with whom the Confederates had placed orders for several armored vessels and wooden corvettes offered to sell information regarding the contracts to the consul general. Bigelow had not realized the state of Southern ship orders, considering stories he had heard rumors and believing that French law would prohibit such bold construction. After dickering over the price for proof regarding the contracts, Confederate payments, and the involvement of the French Ministry of the Marine, Bigelow bought the documents for 15,000 francs.[28]

It took time for the U.S. legation in Paris to prepare a legal brief to protest the work on the Confederate ships. Because Napoleon III's government was implicated, the matter would have been hushed up while the ships were rushed to completion. Bigelow, as a good propagandist, arranged for private publication of a brochure by a French opponent of the government giving the details of the illegal construction at shipyards in Bordeaux and Nantes. The broadcast of this activity to the French public and the official protests of William L. Dayton, the American minister, were instrumental in stopping the collusion between the Confederacy and Louis Napoleon.

The French emperor and his supporters were following the military progress of the war in America, which was becoming more favorable to the North. The Confederate cause gradually lost its appeal. With a major overseas expedition in Mexico, Napoleon III wanted no angry and dangerous Union navy threatening his vulnerable lines of communication between the French channel ports and Vera Cruz. French efforts to equip the Confederate navy ceased. Bigelow succeeded Dayton as minister to France in 1865 following Dayton's death, supposedly of overeating, in the Parisian apartment of an American lady whose loyalty to the Union cause was suspect.

After the sinking of the *Alabama* off Cherbourg in June 1864 and the thwarting of the scheme to have the French build Southern ironclads, the naval threat to the North was considerably lessened. U.S. consuls were under less pressure to ferret out the schemes of Confederate agents. However, a major hole in the Union consular net appeared in the fall of 1864. Rather than rely on ships built to order as commerce raiders, James D. Bullock (an uncle of the young Theodore Roosevelt), the chief Southern naval agent in Britain, bought a steamer, the *Sea King*, well suited for the business but initially unarmed. This new British-built ship that had been designed for the Far Eastern trade was able to cruise long distances without refueling.

Without the need to make protracted arrangements with British shipyards, which by this time the Northern consuls had amply stocked with spies, Bulloch had an English friend buy the ship in his name. The ship was then transferred to Confederate ownership outside British territorial waters. A supply ship, the *Laurel*, took the crew, armament, and supplies from England and rendezvoused with the *Sea King* at a barren island in Spain's Madeira group off Morocco. There the transformation from merchant steamer *Sea King* to the raider CSS *Shenandoah* took place out of sight of prying American consular eyes or those of Spanish authorities on the main island.[2]

A week after the *Sea King* left England, Dudley and men at the U.S. legation in London realized that they had missed the creation of a new rebel cruiser. Luckily for the Union cause, the Confederacy had not concentrated at an earlier stage on making British and French merchant ships into commerce raiders, since these were far easier to acquire and made evasion of neutrality laws quite simple.

The *Shenandoah* went to the Far East, where it almost wiped out the New England whaling fleet during the spring and summer of 1865, which was after Lee had surrendered but before the ship's captain had heard and verified the news. Eventually convinced that the Confederacy had actually collapsed, the *Shenandoah* with guns dismounted returned with its crew, many being British, to Liverpool, where Consul Dudley still presided.

The British sold the *Shenandoah*, while Dudley had the satisfaction of arranging sales for other ex-Confederate raiders, the *Tallahassee*, the *Rappahannock*, and the *Sumter*, the money going to the United States Treasury. Dudley was kept on at Liverpool until well after the end of the war to help with the *Alabama* claims against the British government, as he had the greatest experience in that matter.

During the war life was difficult for American consuls in the small but important island colonies of the Bahamas and Bermuda, supply centers for Southern blockade- runners. Because there was great profit to be made by British merchants, the sympathies of the white islanders were almost all on the side of the South. Historian Bruce Jenkins described the life of one consul appointed to Nassau, capitol of the Bahamas:

> The United States consul had a miserable time. Ostracized severely and convinced, not without reason, that everyone in the colony was a friend of the rebels, the unhappy Samuel Whiting sought solace in drink. Once under the influence he physically assaulted a group of tormentors in a local hotel and on another occasion launched into a violent tirade against the governor. Dismayed and disgusted, he resigned [1863] before the British could request his recall. His successor [Seth Hawley] met with the same hostility, as did their colleague in Bermuda, where the local bloods cut down the consul's flagstaff.[30]

The U.S. consuls on these island colonies launched a series of complaints to British authorities against favoritism shown the Confederates. Rebel naval ships were welcomed with open arms, while the United States Navy was met with discourtesies and delays. The American consuls lost even more popularity within the merchant community when they were instructed by Washington to certify whether goods coming from Northern ports were for local consumption or destined for blockade-runners. Unfavorable reports could cause restrictions and hurt local trade and profits.

A consul in the Brazilian port of Bahia found himself in a similarly difficult situation. Brazil had always been friendly to the Southern cause; it was a slaveholding state itself and had an aristocracy more comfortable with their Southern counterparts than with Yankee traders. In October 1864 the CSS *Florida* put into Bahia for supplies and repairs. After anchoring, the captain of the *Florida* made the unpleasant discovery that another warship was in harbor, the USS *Wachussett*, larger and better armed.

According to international law, the Confederate ship could not be attacked in the port and the Union ship could not clear the port until the rebel ship had been given a twenty-four-hour head start.[31] Thomas F. Wilson, the consul in Bahia, had been transferred there in 1862 from Montreal. The governor of Bahia informed him that he should make sure that there was no breach of Brazilian neutrality, but the commander of the *Wachussett* would have no diplomatic interference. The *Wachussett* attacked and took the *Florida* under the noses of the Brazilian authorities. Consul Wilson, forewarned, was prudently onboard the *Wachussett* when it captured the *Florida*, and sailed away on it. Hearing this news, a mob attacked the consulate building in Bahia, and the Brazilian government withdrew Wilson's exequatur, but he was already gone. Although apologies were made to Brazil by the U.S. government and the captain of the *Wachussett* was court-martialed (he was eventually exonerated), the deed had eliminated one more raider. Wilson did not suffer from his part in the Bahia episode; he later returned to Montreal as consul general.

In Canada Confederate agents were exceptionally active, but not in acquiring warships, for Canada had no suitable shipyards. It was, however, an excellent place to arrange for shipment of supplies to the Confederacy through the Northern blockade, using Bermuda and the Bahamas as way stations. Canada was also a good place to meet Southern agents working in the North, to help escaped Confederate prisoners of war return home, and to arrange minor raids against Northern towns. Confederate agents worked to keep the Canadians and their British officials friendly to the South and unfriendly to the North.

The ranking U.S. consular officer in Canada was Consul General Joshua Giddings in Montreal, not the ideal man for the job. He was in his late sixties and not in good health (he died in 1864). As a leading abolitionist in and out of Congress from the 1830s, he had little understanding of the often pro-Southern bias of British officials and the ruling circles in Canada. The unofficial recruiting of susceptible young Canadians for the Union army made British officialdom and the parents of the young men angry. In the Canadian provinces there was also unease because of talk in the American Senate and rumors in Northern newspapers about taking over Canada with the powerful Union army once the Confederates were defeated.

Giddings became the target for collective anger, as he was considered the master recruiter as well as master spy for the North. Although he was neither, the impression was one that Confederate agents could help foster.[32] Confederate agents set up a snare to implicate, or to appear to implicate, Giddings for complicity in the kidnapping and false arrest of a British subject who was taken across the border from Canada to the United States. Giddings was arrested and detained for a short time until bond could be made. The case was eventually dropped, but the mutual dislike between Giddings and the Canadians was reinforced.

In Tangier the consul James DeLong arranged with Moroccan authorities to arrest two Confederates, Lt. Henry Meyers, a naval officer off the CSS *Sumter*, and one of the ubiquitous ex-U.S. consuls who had joined with the South, Thomas T. Tunstall of Alabama, who had been the consul to Cadiz until Lincoln's election. While the *Sumter* was docked in Gibraltar awaiting new boilers, Meyers and Tunstall were sent to Cadiz to purchase coal on board a French ship that stopped in Tangier. Consul DeLong had the two Southerners arrested while they were strolling on the shore and kept them prisoners in his office to await a warship that DeLong had requested from the U.S. naval squadron off Gibraltar.

Bringing the war to their consular district angered the European consuls in Tangier. They especially disliked seeing Southerners arrested, since the Confederacy was popular at the time. These consuls did nothing to prevent several hundred English, Spanish,

French, and Italian subjects from demonstrating in front of the U.S. consulate. DeLong called upon the Moroccan authorities to bring order, threatening – in the grand tradition of his Barbary consular predecessors – that if they did not, he would chop down his flag-staff and leave the country. The Moroccan governor sent troops. The two Southern officers were carried protesting through the mob to the USS *Ino* and were eventually taken to the United States and a Boston prison.[33]

When peace came in 1865 and the last Confederate raider had surrendered, the U.S. consular service could take stock of how it had done during the war for which it had been totally unprepared. The service could come away with considerable satisfaction over its performance. The efforts of Dudley, Morse, and Bigelow, not one of whom had previous consular or diplomatic experience, did as much to inhibit the Confederate naval effort as a fleet of Union war-ships. U.S. consuls in posts around the world were isolated and often ostracized because they were representatives of an initially unpopular cause. Despite hostility and isolation, the majority of consular officers served to the best of their ability under difficult conditions, with low or no pay and with little recognition or sup-port from home. The South could not match the consular presence of the North. Since Confederate consuls went unrecognized and the Confederacy was unable to afford to keep many offices in foreign cities, the Southern effort abroad suffered badly in comparison. Re-lying heavily on former U.S. consuls, the South chose its represen-tatives unwisely. Some were adventurers, not serious envoys, with more improbable schemes than diplomatic ability; others were sim-ply ineffective.

By the end of the Civil War the U.S. consular service included 644 consular posts, of which 296 were consular agencies, about 100 having been added during the war. Agencies were often headed by foreigners engaged in other business but willing, for reasons of prestige, to serve as agents. Many agencies were short-lived and replaced by others at the whim of the U.S. consuls in cities abroad, who had the approval of the State Department to appoint agents. Although consular appointments were limited to males during this period, there was a remarkable exception. When Ebenezer S. Egg-leston, consul in Cadiz, left his post for an extended period in 1863, his wife informed the department that she was taking charge. She was never reprimanded for her audacious assumption of this male prerogative. It is very probable that other wives had done the same thing without bothering to inform the State Department, since the family's income was dependent on the consulate being kept open.

Weakness in the consular system during the Civil War can be ascribed to the lack of adequate salaries and support from the Department of State. There were too few clerks in Washington available to keep American consular officers abreast of developments affecting their work or give advice on difficult consular problems or political situations. Consuls were sent out with no training in consular work, without knowing the local language or how to survive in a foreign environment.

The U.S. consular system worked at a critical time despite problems, corruption, mistakes, and some foolish appointments. Northern interests were served amazingly well. The relative success of the consular system throughout most of the nineteenth century and especially in the Civil War period, despite the handicaps given it by a cost-conscious Congress and understaffed Department of State, could be attributed to the American temperament. In general, Americans respond to challenges, new experiences, and problem solving in difficult situations. Consular work required all these attributes and more. It is entirely possible that a more structured service with Washington sending instructions and advice to men working under conditions undreamed of by clerks would have functioned no better than the one existing until early in the twentieth century. The old consular service was all head and no tail, an ideal sought but never achieved by modern bureaucracies.

11

Post–Civil War Consular Activities
(1865–1900)

The return of peace to the United States in 1865 brought a return to the status quo antebellum for the American diplomatic and consular services. From this point until the turn of the century there would be a few minor adjustments regarding salaries and instructions; real reform was not to come until 1906. The consuls in China, Latin America, and the Middle East were often faced with natural disasters, civil unrest, wars, and hostile governments, the demands of which challenged them to show initiative, firmness, and often bravery, but it was the more humdrum business of American consular officers in northern Europe that gives the best view of the consular service at work.

The biggest market for American goods was in Europe, and Europe, especially northern Europe, was the major exporter to the United States during the period when the consular service existed as a separate body (1776–1924). The man stationed in Hamburg in the 1870s serves as a good representative of an average consul at work. Hamburg and Bremen were the major ports of Bismarck's new German Empire. The two ports faced the North Sea, and most shipping to and from the United States went across their wharves. Both consulates had been in existence for some time and were part of the large American presence in Germany (there were twenty consular posts in 1876 plus many consular agencies). The consuls of Hamburg and Bremen were paid $2,000 per annum and were not allowed to have business outside their official functions.[1] The consul in Hamburg in 1875, one hundred years after the first American commercial agent, Silas Deane, went to Europe, was Edward Robinson of New York. A lawyer, he had been a major in the Union army, serving under General Carl Schurz.[2] His father had been a biblical scholar of some note, and when his mother, residing in Germany, became ill, he resigned from the army and went abroad to take care of her. He spoke excellent German and lobbied for a post either in the legation in Berlin or as a consul elsewhere in Germany. He eventually was rewarded and became the U.S. consul in Hamburg in 1869, where he remained until 1876.

One of the tasks of consuls was, and still is, to act as a notary public, with prime attention to authenticating foreign documents so that they can be used in American courts and in business. The consul certifies that the seals of a foreign court or notary are legitimate. Both Robinson and his fellow consul in Bremen were busy authenticating legal documents for immigrants on their way to the United States. Upwards of 20,000 men, women, and children each year passed through these two ports during the 1870s. They had birth, marriage, death, and property documents that needed to be in order to be presented in the United States, and the consuls made them official. This was tedious but necessary work. Americans did not need passports in the nineteenth century, but if requested, the consul could produce one upon proof of citizenship. Robinson was not much bothered with this function, issuing only four in 1875, for example.[3]

Besides dealing with personal documents, a major consular function was certifying various shipping certificates. In 1875 Robinson had a long-range dispute with the Department of the Treasury over what appears to have been the sharp practice of the shipping firm of F. Aleandre and Sons. They would ship goods to a variety of consignees in Germany but file a landing certificate for only one, who would in turn send the goods to their ultimate destination. There was a $5.00 fee for each certificate, so the shipping firm was obviously circumventing the law. Robinson told the Treasury Department, "I cannot and will not certify to the truth of a certificate which I *know* to be false."[4] He was concerned that Aleandre and Sons had received some sort of assurance from the Treasury that this was all right. This became a long-running quarrel with the Treasury people and may have reflected the lax public standards prevalent during the Grant administration by which certain companies could get special privileges, but the consul in Hamburg would have nothing of this.

As with officials in any bureaucracy at any time and in any place in the world, Robinson spent an inordinate amount of time protecting his territory from the inroads of his immediate superior, the consul general in Berlin, and attempts by the State Department to cut off his consular agencies in Kiel and Lubeck. Regarding the latter, Robinson justified his need for these agencies on the grounds that Kiel was a major naval base of the growing German navy and that ships of the United States Navy often called there and needed assistance. The consular agent also authenticated many documents of emigrants from Schleswig-Holstein. When the Elbe (the river serving Hamburg) froze, American vessels had to discharge their cargoes at Kiel, and, as the saying goes, "an idle crew and the rewards of the land makes trouble," which required the service of a consular agent to get the sailors out of the local jail. Lubeck, on the Baltic, was a growing port with more American ships calling at it, and they also needed consular assistance.[5]

Regarding his quarrel with the consul general, Robinson was annoyed that he had been instructed to refer all problems regarding infractions of treaties to Berlin. Robinson protested that his fellow consuls in Austria, Belgium, France, and Italy could settle most of these problems on the spot and that "I believe them [American consuls in Germany] as intelligent and capable as their colleagues."[6] The consul was correct; most consular problems are best settled close at hand without going first to the central government, which usually will create more problems than it will resolve.

Robinson was diligent in protecting Americans in his district from unjust punishment by the local German authorities. In one case the first officer of the American bark *Chalntette* was arrested and imprisoned for assaulting a messenger from one of the shipping firms who had come on the ship under false pretenses. The first officer was jailed, but the consul had him released on bail. At the trial the American was given a fourteen-day sentence but was released again on the complaint by Robinson that the court had not followed the correct procedure in dealing with a crew matter.[7] Problems of this nature required a diligent consul with a good network of informants to let him know if an American was in trouble, and a diplomatic but firm manner to settle cases at the source without embarrassing local officials by calling the attention of the central government, in this case Berlin, to the case. And, of course, Robinson always had to keep in mind that he would be going back to the same officials on other matters and needed to keep their goodwill.

One of the consul's main duties was to point out what American goods were in demand. Consular reports from Germany in the

1870s noted that most American-made tools, such as wrenches, augers, auger-bits, saws, and agricultural implements were well received, as were "mouse and rat traps of all kinds." On the other hand, American coopers' tools found no sale at all, not being in conformity with the forms and shapes of German barrels and casks.[8] A good consul had to be notary public, public defender, bureaucratic infighter, and trade promoter as well as a diplomat representing his country's interests in his consular district. The Department of State recognized the multifaceted role of a consul and in its consular manual published in the 1850s and kept in print in the decades following. The document spelled out what was expected from a man given a consular appointment, but it seemed a futile exercise:

> Many of the consular duties arise from peculiar circumstances: such as the character and habits of the nation in which the consul resides, its laws and customs, and the nature of its intercourse with the United States. In the most restricted sense, they are important and multifarious duties which are quite different from those of other officers employed in foreign affairs and require for their proper performance an amount of practical information for which the consular officer needs a special training. Consuls are often so situated as to exercise towards their countrymen within their consular jurisdiction the duties of judges, arbiters, and peacemakers; they are the registers of marriages, births, and deaths; they act as notaries, and sometimes as revenue officers; they watch over and verify the sanitary conditions of their consulates; and, through their social and official relations, they are able to obtain a full and accurate knowledge of the commerce, navigation and industry peculiar to the country of their residence.[9]

A consul's duties also included commercial responsibilities, but no provision was made even for brief training, much less for competitive examinations to choose the most qualified. Appointments continued to be made by political influence and chance, a cheap and easy way to settle political debts, but a system that attracted adventure-seeking, yet ill-qualified men impressed by the prestige of foreign appointments. There seems to have been a deterioration in the types of men who received appointments following the Civil War. The great adventure of the war had fostered wanderlust. For many young men consular appointments were ideal ways to escape life at home. There were no standards except that an applicant be male, a citizen, and not a felon. Also, most positions paid at least a small amount. The United States was lucky to have men such as Edward Robinson in important posts like Hamburg, but consular appointments were still hit or miss.

Congress had upgraded professionalism in the consular service slightly in 1855 by authorizing the appointment of up to twenty-five consular pupils at salaries not to exceed $1,000. These men were to be examined for their qualifications prior to appointment and assignment to consulates abroad. They were expected to work their way into the service, which would in time provide a corps of experienced consuls. This worthy provision was repealed the next year when the 1855 act had to be rewritten to take care of constitutional conflicts.

In 1864 Congress again authorized the appointment of consular pupils, but reduced the number from twenty-five to thirteen.[10] Men destined to be consular clerks were to take a qualifying examination before appointment; a salary of $1,000 was again provided. This experiment did not work. Of the sixty-four consular clerks appointed between 1864 and 1896, only eight were promoted to be consuls.[11] The obstacle was that a consular clerk moving up to a consul's position could be quickly removed by a more politically deserving applicant. By staying a clerk one had at least the assurance of a $1,000 salary.

The United States most needed professionals in China. Reliance on interpreters meant that consuls were cut off from a real understanding of the Chinese. It would be 1902 before a language program was established to give American diplomats and consuls the needed training in Chinese. Moreover, the consuls in China were expected to play expanded roles in the large American community there, and this demanded of them skills and knowledge not required elsewhere in the consular system. The congressional act of 1862 prohibiting the coolie trade by American citizens required consuls to be alert to American ships taking involuntary labor out of China, a problem unique to their area.[12] In addition, consuls in the China ports were required by treaty to exercise judicial functions, many of which would have tried the competence of skilled jurists. No provision was made to assure that the men appointed were trained in the law.

The American treaties with China and the congressional acts of 1848 and 1860 set forth the powers of U.S. consuls in China, extensive powers that included the right to inflict the death penalty on Americans with the concurrence of the commissioner (this title, equivalent to minister, was used in China until 1856). The U.S. consuls in the Ottoman domains had much the same powers, but in China the large foreign settlements, especially the main American settlement in Shanghai, required the full exercise of these responsibilities. Instead of sending a trained lawyer as the consul to that important and demanding position in 1861, the Lincoln administration sent a lawyer's nephew. William H. Seward, the secretary of state, not only made his son Frederick the number two man in the State Department, but also arranged for his young nephew George F. Seward to go to Shanghai as consul.

George Seward was only twenty-one. He had not received a degree from Union College, having withdrawn before graduation, and had not studied law.[13] This unpromising appointment, however, did not work out as badly as one might think. For almost fifteen years Seward performed creditably as consul, then as consul general when the post was raised to that rank in 1863. Appointed to be the American minister to China in 1876, a position he held until 1880 when he had to resign under fire because of financial "irregularities" in his consular accounts and in his dealings with business schemes in China. Despite these financial manipulations that were to bring him down almost twenty years later, Seward at least had time to grow into his job and develop an understanding and appreciation for the Chinese.

Early in his consular career George Seward had the difficult task of presiding over a series of murder trials, with Americans as the defendants. In 1863 an American, David Williams, leader of a band of pirates attacking Chinese ships in the Yangtze River, was tried in Seward's court for piracy and murder. After the killing of three Chinese on one boat he was caught and turned over to his consul for trial and punishment according to the Chinese-American treaties. Williams was found guilty and sentenced to death. After reviewing the records of the trial, the U.S. commissioner to China, Anson Burlingame, instructed Seward to go ahead with the execution by hanging. Williams had been kept in the British jail in Shanghai, presumably because it was more secure than the American consulate. A few hours before the time of his execution, Williams obtained a small knife and cut his own throat, thus avoiding being the first American to be executed by a consular court.[14]

At about the same time another American came before Consul Seward. This was James White, accused of murdering Samuel Webster in a Shanghai boardinghouse. White pleaded guilty, but claimed that he was drunk at the time of the shooting. The court, consisting of Seward and four associates drawn from the American community, found White guilty and sentenced him to death by hanging, not allowing drunkenness as a mitigating circumstance. But there was to be no execution, since White escaped before the sentence was carried out.[15]

In April 1864 an American found guilty of murder by a consular court was hanged. John D. Buckley, siding with the South, had got into a heated discussion with John McKennon, captain of an American merchant ship, about the Civil War. Buckley left the bar where the argument took place, got his pistol from his boardinghouse room, returned, and shot McKennon. The court found Buckley guilty and sentenced him to death by hanging. The first execution by a consular court was described in the official report as follows:

At the hour of 10 a.m., the 1st day of April, A.D. 1864, the prisoner was brought from a low room of the jail buildings of the United States consulate general at Shanghai, up a flight of stairs to a veranda, and thence to the scaffold, which was constructed in front of the same, and the floor upon the same level. He was placed upon the drop and asked by Mr. Lewis, the deputy consul, whether he had anything to say. He remarked, in reply, that he was innocent of the crime of murder, he having shot McKennon in self-defence; that he was of Irish birth, and had never denied his nationality, but he could forgive those who had perjured themselves upon his trial, and those who had informed upon him, but that he could not forgive Mr. Seward, who had caused the publication of alleged remarks of his at the time when his sentence was read to him, which was false. He then said he had nothing more to say, and after repeating a few words of prayer after the attending clergyman, Pere de Jacques, forgiving his enemies and committing his soul to God, the fatal noose and death-cap were adjusted, and at a signal, the support of the drop was instantaneously removed. He fell nearly ten feet, and hardly made a struggle. Upon subsequent examination it was shown that the vertebrae of the neck was [sic] dislocated by the fall, and it is probable that he suffered no more than a momentary pain.[16]

Seward closed his report on the execution by writing, "I have only to say, in conclusion, that I trust no similar duty will be imposed me again so long as I remain in this office." [17]

The series of death penalties and the one actual execution appeared to have some effect on the turbulent American community in China, which prior to the trials of Williams, White, and Buckley had been contemptuous of the authority of their countrymen. Commissioner Burlingame in Peking wrote Washington: "The United States authority was laughed at, and our flag made the cover for all the villains in China. I felt that any relaxation of our purpose to punish the guilty would only aggravate the evils of our situation, that the lawless would find fresh inspiration in the uncertainty of punishment. The result has shown the wisdom of the course taken. There has been a regular exodus of foreigners from China since." Burlingame noted that the British vice consul in Chin-Kiang told his minister that "the steps taken by the United States consul general of Shanghai will have the best effect. I do not hear of many acts of violence now." [18]

In contrast to the American system of justice in China, the British referred major cases to Hong Kong, where a resident attorney general ruled on legal questions. The American system provided only for the referral of such complicated matters to the minister in Peking, who might or might not be able to give a satisfactory decision.

Despite its inadequacies, the U.S. consular court system brought some law and order to the Yangtze River basin, at least as far as American rowdies were concerned. Seward was able to continue his consular career without the threat of being labeled the "hanging consul general."

After the Civil War American consuls reflected a new confidence in the destiny of the United States and, especially, in the benefits they expected their country could bring to the rest of the world. Nowhere was this confidence illustrated better than during the 1865–80 period by American consuls in lands that were, or had been, under the Ottoman rulers – Crete, Bulgaria, Romania, Palestine, and elsewhere in the region. The United States, in contrast to the major European powers, had no political and almost no commercial interests in the Near East or Eastern Europe. These countries were intensely concerned with the fate of the Ottoman Empire, which seemed to be disintegrating. The fact that the United States had no political stake in the affairs of the Turks and their subject peoples allowed U.S. consuls to engage in what would later be considered human-rights activities. European diplomats and consuls were so tied to their countries' pro-Turkish or anti-Turkish policies that they could not effectively prevent many of the abuses they witnessed in the Balkans and the Near East. American consuls were relatively unrestrained in helping the oppressed and publicizing the worst acts of the oppressors.

An American who devoted himself to the cause of an oppressed people was William J. Stillman, U.S. consul to Crete, an Ottoman possession, during the 1866–68 insurrection on that island. Stillman, an artist and journalist, well-known landscape painter, and founder of *Crayon,* a literary and graphic arts magazine, had studied and traveled throughout Europe but had returned to the United States at the start of the Civil War to enlist in the Union army.[19] He was rejected due to poor health. Although he was not active in American politics, a friend secured him the consular appointment by the new Lincoln administration in Rome.

Before leaving for his post in 1861, Stillman met consul-to-be William Dean Howells. "We could, each of us, offer condolence for the other's disappointment; for Howells had asked for Dresden and was appointed to Venice, while I had asked for Venice, intending to write the history of Venetian art. But Rome had always been given to an artist, and, though there was no salary, but fees only, it seemed to have been a much-sought-for position, and I accepted."[20] Rome at this time was still a papal domain and not the capital of Italy. The consul's work was not taxing. Stillman noted: "Before leaving Washington, I had received a hint from a friend in the Department of State that the fewer despatches I troubled them with the higher would be my favor in the department."[21]

In Rome Stillman was able to observe American representation abroad and was not highly impressed. With the exception of Charles Francis Adams in London and George P. Marsh, minister in Florence and later in Rome (1861–82), Stillman found that "political huckstering" had caused

the standing disrepute of our diplomacy. My predecessors at Rome, and the ministers before my time, had left a bad odor behind them. One of them was notorious for his devotion to a form of dissipation much and scandalously known at Naples during the reign of the Bourbons as a springtime sport [possibly homosexuality]. [There was] a minister of the United States of America found drunk in the streets of Berlin by the police, and a charge' d'affaires who, in an outbreak at Constantinople hoisted the flag over a brothel he frequented. Our representation abroad was a disgrace to America.[22]

Finding Secretary of State Seward indisposed to do anything about apparent diplomatic scandals, Stillman gave up the consulate and devoted himself to painting but found trouble supporting his family. Some friends in Congress, aware of Stillman's difficulties, arranged for him to be posted to Crete, which afforded a small salary. Stillman accepted with the understanding that there was "nothing to do but make my quarterly report."[23]

The new consul found the situation in Crete totally different from sketching landscapes in the Roman Campagna. Greece, already free of Ottoman rulers, was helping the Cretans, who were on the verge of revolt against the Ottomans, by creating a climate for insurrection and union with their fellow Greeks. Stillman's sympathies were with the Cretans and their fight for independence that broke out soon after his arrival. He had little regard for the pasha governing the island, whose policy was "to provoke a conflict with any new consul, and either break him or buy him over."[24] He obviously enjoyed carrying on a feud with the pasha, using his position as consul to complain to the pasha's rulers in Constantinople whenever matters got too oppressive.

At first Stillman had little to do but carry on archaeological research and develop a new interest in photography. He spent much of his time pursuing these activities in the interior of the island, to the pasha's discomfort, as that official did not like to have the foreign infidel out of his sight. After settling in at the consulate, Stillman brought his wife and two young children over from Rome. They were to find themselves under a virtual state of siege for the next two years. Political events in Crete came to a head in 1866 with Greek agents from the mainland fanning the islanders' hostilities toward their Turkish rulers and the Turks sending in more troops. Soon there was full-scale fighting, with thousands of Cretans, mainly women and children, fleeing to Greece while the men took to the mountains to wage guerrilla war.

During the insurrection, which lasted for two years, the U.S. consul was the prime source of news for Europe and America on the developments there. The Cretan cause was popular in the

United States, with Congress making its support of the islanders a matter of public record. Stillman was also writing for major American journals, the *Nation* and the *Atlantic*, both widely read in the United States and England. He reported on the atrocities of the Turkish troops as they tried to end the war by destroying villages and slaughtering the men, women, and children caught there. Stillman, afraid that his family's lives and his own were at risk from the Turkish rulers, tried to persuade his wife to go with the children to the Greek mainland until the fighting was over, but she refused, saying that "the women gathered around the friendly consulate, seeing her yielding to the panic, would lose all courage and fly to the mountains."[25] Stillman himself always traveled outside the consulate well armed and made sure that the Turks knew that he was skilled in the use of his revolver.

The Turkish troops and Egyptian reinforcements found suppression of the insurrection difficult because of the mountainous terrain with few roads. The Cretans were natural mountaineers and guerrilla fighters, defeating attack after attack by Turkish and Egyptian troops, who vented their frustration on the Christian villagers.

Stillman described his position thus: "By this time I had become the recognized official protector of the Cretans. Around me had spontaneously formed an efficient service for information, the runners of the various sections coming to me at Kaleka with the earliest information on every event of importance, and I communicated with the legations at Athens and our own minister at Constantinople."[26] Stillman relied on his instincts in opposing the Ottoman authorities on the island and helping the Cretans. Unlike other American consuls who had put themselves into a somewhat similar position during the 1848 revolts in Italy, Stillman was supported, for the time being, by Washington. He received the following dispatch:

W.J Stillman, Esq. U.S. Consul Canea:

Sir,—Your dispatch, No. 32, with regard to the Cretan insurrection and the attitude you have assumed in the matter, has been received.

Your action and proposed course of conduct, as set forth in said dispatch, are approved. Mr. Morris, our minister resident at Constantinople, will be informed of the particulars set forth in your dispatch and of the approval of your proceedings.

Rear Admiral Goldsborough has been instructed to
send a ship-of-war to your port.—I am, sir, your most obe-
dient servant, W.H. Seward[27]

But Stillman's situation on Crete had become uncomfortable.
His role as a strong patron of the Cretans, a source of intelligence
to the outside world on the Turkish excesses in its pacification attempts, and a giver of refuge to a number of Cretan women and
children at the consulate during times of trouble in the town of Canea did not please his Ottoman hosts. Toward the end of his stay
on Crete, Stillman and the pasha were not on speaking terms. His
family suffered even more, not daring to go beyond the threshold
of the consulate. His wife had even been shot at during a walk early
in their stay on Crete.[28] Relations also were not good between Stillman and his minister in Constantinople, who, understandably, was
uncomfortable in trying to represent American interests in the seat
of Ottoman power while a subordinate was publicly supporting
insurrectionaries in an important area of the Sublime Porte's territory.

In time, Secretary Seward lost his interest in the Cretan cause
and would have liked to recall Stillman, but the Russians, anti-
Turkish and supporting the Greek Orthodox Cretans, wanted the
American consul to remain. Stillman had become a symbol for
those who were pro-Cretan. Since Secretary Seward was at that
time bargaining with the Russians for the purchase of Alaska, he
saw no point in making an issue over the staffing of a minor consular post. So the U.S. consul and his wife and children, though
wanting a transfer to a less taxing consulate, were caught in a game
of international politics.

Stillman's salary of $1,000 was not enough. He wrote, "I had, in
the second year of the war [1867] determined to resign on account
of the pecuniary difficulties of my position. We were living in a
besieged town, with all the necessaries of life at famine prices, and,
since my brother's death, I had no fund to draw on for my excessive
expenses."[29] He was rescued for a time by the Cretan Committee
of Boston, which did not want to see the American friend of the
insurrection leave. The committee, whose members included Samuel Gridley Howe, Edward Everett Hale, Oliver Wendell Holmes,
Wendell Phillips, and other Bostonian philhellenes, arranged for a
wealthy American banker to meet the consul's expenses over the
$1,000 salary.[30] This was a startling subsidy of a government posi-

tion by an interested party, the friends of Crete in the United States. It was apparently accepted by the State Department without question as to the propriety of the arrangement. Later the American Jewish community would make a similar arrangement to keep a U.S. consul in Romania.

Stillman's partisanship for the insurrectionary cause eventually began to act counter to his goals. The State Department had arranged for a ship of the United States Navy's Mediterranean squadron, the USS *Canandaigua,* to call at Crete. If the Turkish authorities agreed, the ship was to transport Cretan refugees to the mainland as an act of humanity.[31] Had Stillman maintained a more neutral or more restrained position, he might have been able to persuade the Turks to let the U.S. ship take a number of women, children, and elderly men off the island to Greece, but relations were so poor between the consul and the pasha that this mission of mercy was impossible. The *Canandaigua* sailed away without the refugees.

The Stillman family faced a crisis. Laura Stillman had given birth to Bella, their third child during the conflict. Her Polish doctor, attached to a hospital in Canea, told the consul that "he would not guarantee the life of one of us if we remained in the island two weeks longer."[32] Living in a state of siege for over two years had taken its toll on the Stillmans, especially Laura, who had become mentally depressed over the failing Cretan cause and Turkish reprisals against the civilian population. The insurrection had run its course with Turkish and Egyptian armies finally gaining the upper hand. Stillman realized that he was no longer benefiting the Cretan cause, so he moved his family to Athens in September 1868, leaving the consulate in the hands of his vice consul, an Englishman who had long been a resident of the island.

By the time Stillman left Crete, enthusiasm in the United States for the Cretan cause had passed, as had the support from the Boston committee for the consul. In Athens Stillman had to scrape for a living by taking photographs of the ruins, which he had sold in Europe and the United States. Crete's plight, the recent birth of her child, and the privations the family was suffering in Greece were too much for Laura. Soon after moving to Athens, Laura Stillman committed suicide. The Greek government honored her with a public funeral because of her heroic work in Crete.

Laura Stillman is one of the unrecognized heroines of the U.S. consular service. She could have stayed in Rome or Athens with her children while her husband carried on his dangerous work, but

she willingly joined him and threw herself into the work of trying to ease the suffering of the Cretan women and children. She
was in constant danger, maintaining her family while under siege
and watching her children suffer from the diseases then prevalent
on the island. Her husband wrote years later in his autobiography,
"The Cretan women looked upon her as their best friend, and always spoke of her after her death as `the Beloved' – their form of
canonization."[33] After Laura's death Stillman attempted to obtain
another consular post, but he no longer had influential friends in
Washington. He eventually settled in London, devoting himself to
journalism and writing.

The consulate on Crete had become a center for humanitarian
help to oppressed peoples at the outbreak of the insurrection. While
the efforts in Crete had occurred somewhat spontaneously, the establishment of a consulate in Bucharest, Romania, was a deliberate
move on the part of the United States to help the Jewish minority
in that country.

Romania in 1870 was technically still under the rule of Constantinople, although the Ottomans had long before removed their
troops as their empire shrank and the Russians became dominant.
Britain and the other major European nations, including Austria-
Hungary and France, kept watch on the Russians, concerned over
their possible expansion at the expense of the Romanians. Romania
existed in a peculiar state, neither independent nor dependent, but
sustained by the rivalry of the great powers.[34]

A large Jewish community existed in Romania, yet it was de-
prived of citizenship, as under that country's new constitution only
Christians were eligible. Anti-Semitism was strong. Facts concerning the growing persecution of the Romanian Jews, which worsened by 1870, became widely publicized. Concerned American
Jews appealed to President Grant to intervene. Grant's response
was forthright and prompt despite the nation's lack of influence in
an area far removed from its borders or navy. Grant asked Secretary of State Hamilton Fish to instruct the American ministers to the
courts in London, Vienna, Paris, St. Petersburg, and Constantinople
to bring the president's concern to the attention of these major powers.

Since Romania was not yet fully independent, holding somewhat the same status as Egypt at that time, Grant could not send
a minister, but a consul could be as effective in Bucharest as a U.S.
consul had been in Alexandria. There was no need for a regular

American consul in Bucharest because trade was minimal, few Americans lived there, and it was not a seaport. The president opposed establishing a post requiring a congressional appropriation to pay a consul's salary and instead appointed an American to assume the title and prestige of the office, but called upon him to look elsewhere for financial support.

Benjamin Franklin Peixotto, a Sephardic Jew and New York lawyer, was chosen for the position. He had been president of B'nai B'rith, a national Jewish fraternal organization, had served in the Union army, and at the time of his consular appointment was practicing law in San Francisco.[35] An American lawyer could not earn a living in Romania, and as he had no independent income, Peixotto had to be supported. A group of wealthy American Jews, together with some prominent Jews in England and France, agreed to underwrite the consulship, an unusual arrangement including not only financial support but also political influence in Washington, London, and Paris.

At his departure Peixotto was given his personal instructions from President Grant, which concluded: "Mr. Peixotto has undertaken the duties of his present office more as a missionary work for the benefit of the people he represents, than for any benefit to accrue to himself. The United States, knowing no distinction of her own citizens on account of religion or nativity, naturally believes in a civilization the world over which will secure the same universal laws."[36] This most unusual assignment might well be termed the first deliberate step of the United States toward a policy of promoting human rights outside its sphere of influence.

Peixotto's mission was not a quixotic gesture on the part of Grant, for it had an impact where other methods had failed. The American diplomatic appeal to the various European courts for the protection of the Romanian Jews received lip service rather than support, for the English, French, Austrian, Russian, and Turkish diplomats were far too involved in making sure that no one country gained too much influence in Romania to extend protections to individuals.

John Jay, the American minister in Vienna, reported that "the question of foreign intervention was one of extreme delicacy; and so far from accomplishing the desired object, an intervention might result in diminishing the ability of the [Romanian] government and in subjecting the Israelites to increased prejudice and further persecution."[37] In other words, nothing should be done, a refrain that

would often be repeated in the next century. Diplomats of all nationalities, including Americans, had little sympathy for, or understanding of, the position of Jews in Eastern Europe.

Consul Peixotto in Bucharest was well received by Prince
Charles, the ruler of Romania, a member of the Hohenzollern family, who promised to do what he could to prevent any outrages
against the "Israelites" by his unruly subjects.[38] The promise was
well meant, but it took the constant prodding of the American consul to help ameliorate conditions for the Jews in Romania.

After a series of anti-Jewish riots following an alleged theft and
profanation of the cathedral, supposedly by a Jew in Ismail, Peixotto reported: "A deputation sent by the Jewish inhabitants of Ismail
waited upon me this morning, and, presenting a very detailed and
circumstantial account of the recent violence perpetrated in that
town, besought my intercession in behalf of their still suffering and
imperiled condition." Peixotto explained to the delegation that he
"could not officially interfere in the internal affairs of the country,
unless the rights of an American citizen herein had been invaded,"
but "the good relations which I had the honor to hold with the government of the Prince might permit me to speak in their behalf."[39]
Peixotto saw the appropriate minister the same day and arranged
for the members of the Jewish deputation to present their case to
the government, which resulted in an official inquiry that cleared
up the matter of the alleged theft and profanation and for a time
calmed the Christian population.

Peixotto was not alone in his protest over the persecution of
the Romanian Jews. Consuls from the Western European countries
sometimes joined him in approaching the Romanian government,
but he was the catalyst for this collective action. As occasions war-
ranted, he was willing to go on his own to the prince or to a cabinet
minister.

During his six years as consul in Bucharest, Peixotto did not
limit himself to protesting against persecutions. He helped found
Jewish schools and cultural societies and tried to bring the backward community into the modern world. His well-publicized presence worked well to inhibit anti-Semitic legislation in Romania and
probably deterred pogroms. He was not able, although he tried, to
advance the cause of giving Jews full Romanian citizenship; they
remained strangers in their native land.[40]

Consul Peixotto got into trouble with his Jewish backers in the
United States when he explored the possibility of having the Ro-

manian Jews emigrate to America. At that time and continuing into the twentieth century, the American Jewish community, mainly of German and Spanish origin, felt obliged to help its coreligionists in Eastern Europe, but it definitely opposed any mass migration that would bring these extremely orthodox and quite backward people to the United States. Such a migration would be sure to arouse latent prejudices in the American Christian community and likely threaten the American Jews' own hard-won social position, a fear well founded and actually experienced by the turn of the century when the great Jewish migration from Russia began.

Dropping his public espousal of emigration, Peixotto concentrated on helping the Jews within Romania until he left the post in 1876. Shortly thereafter he was appointed to the consular position in Lyons, James Fenimore Cooper's old post, where he served as a working consul for eight years before returning to New York to engage in law, Republican politics, and Jewish affairs.

In 1876, the same year that Peixotto left Romania, a series of massacres involving thousands of Orthodox Christians took place in Bulgaria, south of Bucharest. There had been a short-lived attempt at an insurrection by Bulgarians against the Turks, who responded with ferocity, turning irregular bands of troops called *bashi-bazoieks* loose upon the Christian villagers. By most accounts the repression was completely disproportionate to the cause. The United States had no consular or diplomatic representatives in Bulgaria, which was still completely under Turkish control.

Reports of the "Bulgarian horrors" began to trickle out through American missionaries and other Westerners who had only limited access to that remote area of the Balkans. The British vice consuls in Bulgaria showed little initiative in investigating the uprising and reporting to their government, a grave lack of concern, especially for Great Britain, whose public was not likely to accept its government's pro-Turkish policy if its ally was the butcher of innocent women and children, as was alleged by the first unofficial reports from Bulgaria. The British ambassador to the Sublime Porte tried to minimize the incidents to his government while at the same time strongly protesting to the Turks about their actions in Bulgaria.[41]

As in Crete during its insurrection (1866–68), Russia, France, and Britain had conflicting interests that affected their help or abstaining from giving help in a local matter within the turbulent Turkish domains. At stake in Bulgaria in 1876 was the continuing support of Britain for the integrity of the decaying Ottoman Empire, a policy designed to keep Russia from becoming too powerful, which had been maintained for the past fifty years.

The United States had no particular interest in either the integrity of the Ottoman Empire or the plight of the Bulgarians. Despite general American indifference, at the instigation of concerned American missionaries at Robert College in Turkey, the U.S. minister in Constantinople sent an investigator to Bulgaria, Eugene Schuyler, the newly arrived consul general to Constantinople.[42]

Schuyler was to prove himself a jewel in the tarnished crown of the U.S. consular service during the Grant administration. He was a Yale graduate with a law degree from Columbia University and one of the first doctors of philosophy in the United States. A linguist as well as a lawyer, he had sought a position abroad to further his study of languages. In 1867 he was appointed vice consul to Moscow and was later transferred to Revel (now Tallin) in Estonia, then part of Russia. Still later he served as secretary of legation in St. Petersburg before being sent to Constantinople as the consul general and secretary of legation. Although he was only 36, his depth of experience and his academic achievements were outstanding. A drawback to Schuyler's appointment to Constantinople was that his long service in Russia had given him a pro-Russian, anti-Turkish bias.

Horace Maynard, the American minister in Constantinople, had no instructions on how to confront the rumored "Bulgarian horrors." When urged by two well-known Americans living in Turkey, the president of Robert College (founded by missionaries) and a former missionary to Bulgaria, he agreed to let the new consul general go to Bulgaria to investigate the rumors if Schuyler was willing. He was 43, and was accompanied by Januarius Aloysius MacGahan, a well-traveled American journalist working for the British *Daily Mail*. Schuyler left for Bulgaria in July 1876 to develop a thorough report. Before leaving, Schuyler wrote his daughter:

> My mission is nominally to see about the establishment of vice-consulates. I am armed with vizerial letters, so that the [Turkish] governors will try to give me protection, but I fear they will put all sorts of difficulties in my way, to keep me from seeing the calamities and distress of the poor peasants. I mean, however, to give my guard the slip and penetrate into the country. I have with me a secretary and interpreter who speaks Bulgarian as well as Turkish, an educated young man from Robert College, an American institution here. I hope to come back alive, though I must admit that I run some risk – and what is more, I hope to bring back irrefragable proved facts which will show to the civilized

world what short of a Government is this of England's protégé in the east.[44]

Despite the initial bias of Schuyler's fact-finding mission, there was no denying the outrages that Turkish troop, regular and ir-regular, had committed against helpless Bulgarian Christians. The short insurrection was confined to only a few places, but the Turks had let their troops run riot.

Schuyler was appalled at what he saw. He wrote, for example, about what had happened in one town, Pana Gurishta:

[It] was attacked by a force of regular troops, together with bashi-bazouks, on the 11th of May. Apparently no message to surrender was sent. After a slight opposition on the part of the insurgents, the town was taken. Many of the inhabit-ants fled, but about 3,000 were massacred, the most of them being women and children.

The ruffians attacked children of eight and old women of eighty, sparing neither age nor sex. Old men had their eyes torn our and their limbs cut off, and were then left to die, lest some more charitably disposed man give them the final thrust. Pregnant women were ripped open and the un-born babes carried triumphantly on the points of bayonets and sabers, while little children were made to bear the drip-ping heads of their comrades. This scene of rapine, lust and murder was continued for three days, when the survivors, were made to bury the bodies of the dead.[45]

MacGahan was also sending such reports to his newspaper.

Although there was, and still is, a dispute over how many Bul-garians were killed by Turkish troops, and how many Turkish vil-lagers were killed by Christian insurgents, the effect of Schuyler's mission and report, which added authenticity to the lurid accounts of MacGahan's in the *Daily News*, had a powerful effect in Britain. The Foreign Office and its diplomats and consuls were suspect, doing what they could to put the best face on a policy becoming increasingly repugnant to the British public. Schuyler's account, that of a neutral American official, was a major factor in causing a change in the British government's policy towards Turkey.

As an indication of Schuyler's reputation in Britain, William E. Gladstone, former prime minister (1868–74) and that to served sev-eral more terms in that office, in early 1874 wrote to Schuyler about his report:

It is an appalling document. By its production you conferred a great service upon the people of my country, if not upon all of Christendom. I am glad to tell you confidentially that this service is known and felt all over England. The day before yesterday I had to address a public meeting at Taunton, one of our small towns in a rural and rather remote district. I mentioned your name partly to test the feeling and knowledge of a community of this class; and I wish you had heard the hearty cheering with which it was received.[46]

Because of public pressure over the Turkish atrocities in Bulgaria, the British government was forced to withdraw its hitherto firm support of Turkey during that country's continuing quarrel with Russia over the Balkans. The Russians shortly thereafter declared war on Turkey in 1877, and soon the Russian armies were threatening Constantinople. Consul General Schuyler was off to a poor start at his new post. In January 1877 the Turkish minister in Washington complained about Schuyler's activities, putting Secretary of State Fish in a difficult position. Although Horace Maynard, the American minister, had not sent Schuyler's official report to Washington until November 1876, the report had been in the British and American presses several months earlier. Fish was unhappy both with Schuyler for allowing the report to be leaked to the press and with Maynard for sitting on it for so long. Secretary Fish could not remove Schuyler from his position right away despite the Turkish annoyance, as it would appear that the U.S. government was siding with the Turkish oppression of the Bulgarian Christians, which would be politically disastrous.

Fish waited until 1878 before quietly transferring Schuyler, first to Birmingham as consul general, then to Rome, again as consul general. Schuyler's career was not badly hurt by his part in the "Balkan horrors" episode. He later became the first American diplomatic representative to Romania (1880), then served as minister to Greece, Romania, and Serbia (1882) with his residence in Athens. When, in an economic move, the Athens legation was abolished two years later, Schuyler left diplomatic service to write and lecture at Johns Hopkins and Cornell universities. In speaking out on the poor state of the diplomatic and consular services, he was undiplomatic in putting the blame on Congress for the degradation of those services. This criticism did not sit well with that legislative body. When he was named to be the assistant secretary of state, number two position in the department, the Senate rejected his nomination.[47] Schuyler was sent instead to Cairo as consul general in 1889, where he died shortly thereafter.

During the 1877 war between Russia and the Ottoman Empire the U.S. consul in Jerusalem illegally, but out of good heart, extended American protection to Russian Jews in Jerusalem because "many of them are old, and have come here from religious motives. They are not the subjects of any foreign power, but the remnant of God's chosen Israel in whom all the nations of the earth be blessed; and having no longer a King or government of their own, are as much Citizens of the U. States as of any other country."[48] After this good deed the consul departed, leaving his successor to untangle the mess with the Turkish authorities.

It will come as no surprise that American consuls were dragged into the unending bitter relationship between the Irish and the British. In the British Isles and Canada the consuls had to deal with the Fenian movement involving Irish-Americans. This group was trying to free Ireland by attacking the English, not only in Ireland but in England and Canada. American consuls found that the British were not cooperative in letting the consuls see those Irish-Americans caught and jailed for their activities. British police regarded these prisoners as British subjects and of no concern to the United States. Even if he were persistent in getting to see the prisoner, the consul usually found that he could give little help except to ensure that the prisoner received normal treatment under British law.

The indignation of Irish-Americans at the arrest of their compatriots put consuls in difficult positions. Because of political pressure at home consuls were forced to appear to be doing something, but under the British judicial system consuls could do little except now and then get a minor offender released and returned to the United States.

Consul John Young, of Indiana but Irish-born, stationed in Belfast, seemed oblivious of the political dynamite in the Fenian prisoner problem. Minister Charles Francis Adams in London discovered that Young had not been reporting the arrests of Irish-Americans in Belfast, because he thought that the U.S. government was not interested.[49] Shortly thereafter Young was relieved of his post. Consular intervention by other U.S. consuls, however, did not help the American Fenians and they served their sentences, often under harsh conditions.

12

Cuban Problems and
Consular Corruption
(1870s–1890s)

The U.S. consular posts on the Spanish island of Cuba were among the most difficult in the system throughout the nineteenth century. Spanish colonial officials and officers of the Spanish army and navy considered Americans stationed in their colony as agents of a country that had long desired Cuba. Although the American consuls were not under instructions to undermine the Spanish rule, some individual consuls tended to be sympathetic to the insurrectionary forces that made sporadic attempts to free Cuba from Spain.

Prior to the Civil War U.S. consuls found themselves enmeshed in the unsuccessful efforts of Cuban filibusters, American citizens who attempted to foment insurrections in the mid-19th century to overthrow Spanish rule on that island. The U.S. government tried to stop such expeditions from recruiting and setting out from American ports, but with little effect despite a public announcement that any American filibuster would forfeit his nationality. The consuls still tried to protect most of their fellow countrymen who were captured from the results of their foolhardiness, but they ran up against the obduracy of the Spanish captain-general and his military. One consul, Allen Owen, newly appointed to Havana, took the public expression regarding loss of nationality by the U.S. government too literally and did nothing when fifty Americans were executed in 1851 as a result of a disastrous expedition led by General Narciso Lopez. As a result Owen was burned in effigy in Baltimore and was quickly removed from office.

After the American Civil War, U.S. consuls sent to Cuba were quite understandably opposed to the state of slavery that existed on the island until 1880, a position that alienated the powerful planter class. Had relations between Spain and the United States been close, the consul's lot in Cuba might have been less unhappy, but Spanish colonial officials continued to refer to Madrid almost all matters dealing with foreigners instead of trying to settle them quickly on the spot. Despite such difficulties Cuba and the United States had important commercial relations. As American merchant ships often visited Cuban ports, there were several consular posts on the island, not only in Havana but in Santiago de Cuba, Cardenas, Cienfuegos, Matanzas, and elsewhere. Consular agencies scattered about the smaller towns on the island during much of the latter half of the nineteenth century were concerned with the commerce of the many American businessmen and firms.

Cuba's Ten Years' War, 1868–78, was one of the most difficult periods for U.S. consuls and American residents on the island when, in a series of insurrections against the authoritarian colonial government, they were often caught in the crossfire. In these times of unrest consuls looked for U.S. naval ships to restore calm for the U.S. consular agents in coastal towns, who were not allowed to fly the American flag over their offices, a privilege that gave regular consuls some measure of protection.

It was a dangerous time; Americans were being killed. Those who sided with the insurrectionaries and were caught could be executed, and even innocent Americans who happened to be at the wrong place at the wrong time were vulnerable. Planters and Spanish military men from families that had been driven out of other parts of the Spanish empire in South America earlier in the century were bitter, tough people who were not going to be driven from their last bastion in the New World. Thus, when the fighting got hot and feelings ran high, there was little a U.S. consul could do without a warship to back him up.

American newspapers showed little understanding or appreciation of the problems of their consuls in Cuba. The *New York Sun* on 5 October 1869 under the headline "Another American Assassinated," reported that an American, Robert Wells, had been shot by Spanish troops in Cienfuegos when he had not halted when challenged by a guard. He was not only shot but bayonetted and died three days later from his wounds. As the reporter put it:

Nothing to be done, we find on making inquiries at the consul-general's office [Havana]. The great United States does nothing but exchange consular notes when an American is murdered in a foreign land. How different with the Britons! When young Ferguson was arrested at Manzanillo, the English consul there hastened and sent a sailing vessel to Nassau to inform the British commander there that a British subject was in danger. The result was that two British men-of-war were sent to Manzanillo to take Ferguson, either peacefully or forcibly. He was taken away. When the Spanish commander there hesitated to surrender him, the commander of the British frigate sent him word he must do so or he would bombard the city.[1]

The American press and public would continue to contrast the example of vigorous British consular action in defense of their subjects with the indifferent and ineffective response of American consuls trying to protect their citizens well into the next century. These examples were often gross exaggerations or even fictions. The British and American consuls and their naval counterparts were working under similar instructions, which did not include gratuitous bombardments of towns, and which required the use of legal procedures with perhaps a bit of naval bluff and bluster if this were deemed useful.

An American consul who would not take no for an answer, even from the secretary of state, when the protection of Americans was concerned, was H. R. de la Reintrie, vice consul general in Havana. After the murder of Samuel Alexander Cohner, a U.S. citizen, by Spanish "volunteers" (bully-boys supporting the Spanish colonial rule), de la Reintrie asked Washington for help. When the vice consul general's request for a permanent naval force off Cuba was turned down by Secretary Seward and the secretary of the navy, he wrote Seward: "I now, through you, would appeal directly to the Congress of the United States at Washington and in session, and say to them that at this time the lives and property of citizens of the United States are not safe here."[2]

The vice consul general found some support. Navy ships put in from time to time at Cuban ports, but could not stay too long in any particular place because of other duties. Several months after de la Reintrie had asked Seward to go to Congress for assistance, the

Navy Department instructed the rear admiral in command of the ships in Cuban waters: "You must exercise your best judgment but all citizens of the United States, native-born or naturalized, in Cuba, engaged in lawful pursuits, respecting the laws of the country, and taking no part in the measures to overthrow the government, are entitled to your protection as fully as you are able to extend it."[3] The presence of an occasional naval vessel could, however, do only so much in a country in turmoil. Moreover, there was the problem that sometimes Americans in trouble had not respected the laws of the country or had been attacked by vigilante groups of Spanish volunteers not answerable to their government. Such attacks often happened away from the guns of a U.S. naval ship and unknown to the consul.

An inherent danger in being the diplomat or consul for an open democracy such as the United States is the chance that what one writes in confidence can suddenly appear in a burst of publicity, leaving the author alone and vulnerable on a foreign shore. Such an occurrence happened to A. E. Phillips, acting consul in Santiago.

In June 1869 Phillips reported to the Department of State the capture of three Americans by the Spanish. The Americans had landed in Cuba to support an insurrection and within twelve hours were publicly shot without trial or notification to the consul. When Phillips heard of the executions, he protested at once this hasty action on the part of the Spanish to the governor, who apologized, a rare deference by a colonial official.

But a few days later the governor informed Phillips that another American had been caught and would be shot the next morning as a pirate, the term the Spanish used for insurrectionaries who came by sea. The acting consul hurried to the prison and talked to the captured American, Charles Speakman of Indiana, who protested his innocence, claiming that he was only a sailor on a ship chartered by Cuban insurrectionaries and that he had been compelled to help them. Phillips asked for more time to help prove Speakman's case. The English vice consul in Santiago had come to the prison to offer his assistance, and the two consular officers tried to persuade the governor to postpone the execution, but to no avail. "Our efforts were useless. His excellency gave us to understand that he was impotent in his position: dissension had broken out in the army; his troops reluctantly obeyed his orders; he had no confidence in his officers; he feared a counter revolution, and he was compelled to appease the wrath of the Catalans [Spanish volunteer troops] for his own safety."[4]

Phillips reported on alleged plots to assassinate the governor and commanding officers of the troops by the hard-line Spanish settlers. The consul went on to note: "The country is in complete disarray; the Catalonian volunteers do not allow the governor to render justice, and he cannot publicly resist them, as he has seen in the case of the unfortunate Speakman. We cannot enjoy personal safety here until some foreign power intervenes."[5]

The dispatch Phillips sent to Washington gave government policymakers a valuable picture of the unsettled and dangerous situation in Santiago. Unfortunately for the consul, the document was included in a report sent by President Grant to Congress, which had asked for correspondence concerning the situation in Cuba. The report was published in December 1869 and given to the press. By the spring of 1870, less than a year after the consul had penned his dispatch, it appeared in translation in the Cuban press.

The result of this early exercise in freedom of information was graphically described in the letter from Rear Admiral C. H. Poor, commander of the North Atlantic Fleet, to the Spanish colonel in command of troops in Santiago:

> As I understand the case from representations made by Mr. Phillips now on board this ship [USS Severn] he was compelled to leave Santiago de Cuba in the most hurried manner, in consequence of threats of assassination made to him on the part of certain volunteers composing a portion of the military force under your command, and instead of receiving the protection due to him as a citizen of a friendly nation having treaties of amity as with the government of Spain, and in virtue of his office at the time of American consul, he received an implied acknowledgment that the volunteers were beyond all control, and advice was conveyed to him from you to leave the island. It appears that the passions of the volunteers were aroused against Dr. Phillips because of the appearance in one of the Cuban papers of a translation of an official letter addressed by him to the State Department at Washington.[6]

Admiral Poor's report also was made public in February 1872.

During the early 1870s there was no vessel more infamous to the Spanish colonial rulers on Cuba or to U.S. consuls throughout the

Caribbean than the steamship *Virginius,* originally named inappropriately the *Virgin.* It had been a blockade-runner, built in Britain for that purpose during the Civil War.[7] Captured by the United States Navy, it was later sold on the open market. Its new owners, purportedly American but actually Cuban insurgents, were blockade-runners, slipping past Spanish naval patrols to deliver arms and men to the island insurrectionists.

Once the *Virginius* left port after its purchase in May 1870, she never put into any U.S. harbor but was careful to fly the Stars and Stripes. The *Virginius* quickly came to the attention of the American consul in Puerto Cabello on the Venezuelan coast, when the ship arrived in November 1870 with a Cuban insurgent "general," Manuel Quesada, who had come to Venezuela to help in a civil war then being waged between two parties known as the "Blues" and the "Yellows" in order to receive reciprocal support by Venezuelans in Cuba.[8]

The consul was suspicious of the activities and the actual ownership of the *Virginius.* He examined her American registration papers carefully but found them "in perfect order." This was not to be the last time U.S. consuls would look closely at that ship's papers. The consul in Puerto Cabello "warned the captain to be careful not to be guilty of any breach of our marine laws or he would be responsible."[9]

Two years later the presence of the *Virginius* again in Puerto Cabello came to the attention of the consul and the American minister in Caracas because of drawn-out legal proceedings over the possible sale of the ship. The case dragged on through Venezuelan courts. The consul again examined the ship's papers carefully. As the U.S. minister reported to the secretary of state:

> There has been an air of mystery and indications of "tinkering" about these proceedings, and, in fact, about all the doings of the Virginius and her people, that is very unpleasant, not to say suspicious; but as I can learn nothing certainly establishing fraud or bad faith, I see no alternative but to recognize the apparent facts and treat the vessel as any other American vessel, except in the matter of exercising more than ordinary care in dispatching her. A Spanish man-of-war is watching the vessel, and may capture or sink her. If so, the facts will be promptly reported to the Department.[10]

It appears that the minister and consul would not have been unhappy had the Spanish caught and sunk the *Virginius*, provided she was out of their area of jurisdiction, but the ship, slipping away from the blockader, continued to bring men and arms from Venezuela and other Latin American countries to the Cuban insurgents. The Spanish were well informed of the nature of the ship's work by captured insurgents. Every Spanish naval officer wanted to be the one to have the glory of seizing the notorious *Virginius*. The captain of the Spanish warship *Pizarro* was nearly successful in June 1873 when the *Virginius* put into the port of Spinal, Panama, at that time part of Colombia. The *Pizarro* followed it in and anchored nearby.

The U.S. consul in Aspinwall, James Torrington, a former congressman from Iowa, had been unhappy with his consular assignment even before the *Virginius* and *Pizarro* brought trouble to his port. A rebellion had been going on in Panama; troops on both sides were almost uncontrollable. With both a rebellion and a serious international incident imminent, Torrington sent for the United States Navy. The USS *Kansas* arrived in response to protect American interests in Aspinwall. Once again a consul examined the papers of the *Virginius* and again found them in order; the responsibility was his to see that this American ship was protected. But the Spanish captain of the *Pizarro* maintained that the ship was a pirate, had flown the Cuban flag, and was waging war against Spain. The captain of the *Kansas* replied that the *Virginius* was American and he was going to protect her.[11] The *Kansas* escorted the *Virginius* out to sea, taking precautions that the *Pizarro* did not immediately follow.

Despite its escape from Aspinwall, the *Virginius* was a marked ship and several months later, on 31 October 1873, was caught by a Spanish warship off Kingston, Jamaica, and taken to Santiago de Cuba. It arrived there at an awkward time, because the U.S. consul in Santiago, A. N. Young, was in Havana and the insurgents had cut the telegraph between Santiago and Havana. Access to a cable between Kingston and Santiago was controlled by the Spanish military governor. The American in charge was E. G. Schmitt, a longtime resident businessman in Santiago, who had been named vice consul only to cover the post when the consul was away. He was paid no salary and could only pick up a little extra money from fees collected while in charge. The vice consul's position was precarious because he must depend upon Spanish goodwill to carry on his business and continue to live on the island. Despite his temporary status, Vice Consul Schmitt responded to the crisis caused by the arrival of the *Virginius* with persistent courage.

When he heard about the arrival of the *Virginius,* Schmitt did his best to open a line of communication with Washington and his consul general in Havana. Discovering that he was blocked by the Spanish military governor from using the cable to Kingston, Schmitt sent off a message asking for instructions by way of the French consul, who was on his way to Havana.[12]

Feelings in Santiago were running high, with the colonists celebrating the capture of the notorious *Virginius.* Knowing that the lives of the 155 men on board the ship were in jeopardy, Schmitt insisted that he be allowed to see the American prisoners. General Juan D. Burriel, the military governor at Santiago, took his time before replying to Schmitt. When he answered, he referred ironically to the vice consul's "exquisite zeal" and explained that it took him two days to answer because of a holiday, that "officials do not come to the offices, being engaged as well as every one else in the meditation of the divine mysteries of All Saints and the commemoration of All Souls day as prescribed by our holy religion." He went on to say that he saw no reason for Schmitt to see the imprisoned Americans since they had not, the general claimed, asked for the vice consul.[13]

General Burriel had made up his mind to have some executions and was not to be thwarted by the American vice consul. Without waiting for instructions from Havana and taking advantage of the break in communications, he convened an immediate drumhead court martial, which speedily condemned to death 53 of the crew and passengers of the *Virginius.* The sentence was carried out in the next few days. Many on board the ship were of Cuban origin and American or British citizens by naturalization.

Schmitt became so insistent in his protests that Burriel told him that his conduct "obliges me to apply to the government, and propose that your exequatur to perform the duties of your vice-consulate may be withdrawn, as an officer who addresses protests so slightly founded."[14] Despite his annoyance at the persistence of the vice consul, the general posted guards at the U.S. consulate, apparently to protect Schmitt from the inflamed populace.

News of the capture of the *Virginius* did not reach Havana until 5 November. Immediately on hearing the news, the acting U.S. consul general, Henry C. Hall, wrote the captain-general of the island, asking that no sentence of death be carried out until the case could be carefully examined by both governments to establish the facts. By the time Hall was making his request, the first executions had taken place; those that followed could not have been prevented because of the four-to-five-day time delay before messages could get through to Santiago, a fact that General Burriel had taken full advantage of.

Hall, the acting consul general, was a New Yorker who had lived in Mexico and Cuba since the age of eighteen. He had been the consul in Matanzas, Cuba, prior to moving to Havana. It was fortunate that Hall was an experienced consular officer, familiar with the Cuban political scene. The open cable and telegraph lines from Havana to Washington enabled Hall to report directly to Secretary of State Hamilton Fish, who asked Hall to give a full report on the situation in Havana and directed the American minister in Madrid, General Daniel Sickles, to protest to the Spanish government there the Cuban authorities' actions.

On 12 November 1873 Secretary Fish instructed Hall in Havana to "demand of authorities the most ample rights secured by treaty or law of nations for all Americans citizens on the *Virginius*. Instruct consul at Santiago to see that they have counsel and advocate, and that he report as to all judicial or other proceedings."[15] Hall replied that Schmitt had done "everything possible to save lives and secure the rights of our citizens under treaty. His right of protest was ignored. Before the news of capture reached here, first four were shot. Before instructions to the consul could reach Santiago de Cuba, those reported yesterday were also shot. Evidently it was determined to carry out the massacre before instructions could reach there from Spain to spare life."[6]

It was not the protests of the American consuls or those of the British consuls in Havana and Santiago that stopped the executions, but the guns of the British navy. When news of the capture of the *Virginius* reached Kingston, the British governor immediately dispatched the steamer of war *Niobe* to Santiago to protect the British subjects on the ship. When the *Niobe* arrived in the port of Santiago on 7 November, the commanding officer immediately protested to General Burriel, who replied: "I am not in the habit of allowing myself to be overawed," but when the guns of the *Niobe* were trained on the city, the executions ceased. The consular protests may also have played a part in keeping Burriel from executing all his prisoners out of hand in the first few days.

Although the executions had stopped, the mood of the populace of Santiago continued to be hostile toward Americans. At Vice Consul Schmitt's request that the United States Navy keep a ship in the harbor for the protection of Americans, the USS *Juanita* was sent to reinforce the USS *Wyoming, which* had been sent to Cuba previously. Before sailing for Santiago, the commander of the *Juanita* was ready for any developments. He devised a telegraph code to use if the situation worsened. The following extracts from that code illustrate the gravity of the expectations:

SUN – prisoners executed
DOCK –I have taken possession of Spanish vessel by force
PARK – Spanish volunteers control the situation
GRASS – Am about to shell the city
DUST – Shall engage Spanish man-of-war
STEP – Have conference with Commandant [Spanish]
LAMB – Tone belligerent
HOUSE – Tone peaceful
CARPET – Spaniards have surrendered their vessel[17]

In the United States and in Spain and Cuba there were demonstrations against the Spanish and against Americans. As the diplomats on both sides took over to reach a peaceful settlement, the warlike mood subsided. The *Joanna's* captain did not have to send GRASS or DUST.

Within a few weeks the Spanish turned the surviving prisoners and the *Virginius* over to the United States Navy. On its return to the United States the *Virginius* sank, much to the relief of American consuls in the Caribbean. As a sop to the Spanish volunteers on the island, General Burriel was promoted.

The American consular establishment in Santiago de Cuba and Havana managed the *Virginius* crisis well, responding with initiative and courage when there was no naval force immediately available to back them up. Had Schmitt and the British consul not continued their protests despite the resistance of General Burriel and the dangerous hostility of the mob, matters could have been much worse. The consuls had applied something like a brake on local Spanish action. A wholesale shooting of the entire crew and passengers, 155 in total, might have been more than public opinion in America could have borne; a war between Spain and the United States was distinctly possible. At the very least these consuls helped postpone a war for twenty-five years, until events around another ship, this time of undoubted American ownership, the USS *Maine,* led to hostilities that eventually freed Cuba.

CONSULAR CORRUPTION

Although some able men were appointed consuls, the period between the Civil War and the Spanish-American War was the nadir of the U.S. consular system. President Ulysses S. Grant (1869–77) set the tone for the period with his almost complete indifference to competence in his consular appointments. Secretary of State Hamilton Fish, an upright, capable New York lawyer, stopped some of the more absurd Grant appointments to diplomatic positions and forays into foreign policy matters, such as the attempted annexation of Santo Domingo, but he made little effort to control consular appointments, saving his influence for more important matters. Secretary Fish had no feeling for the importance of having the right person in a foreign consular post, having never been abroad himself, nor had he had much interest in foreign affairs before his appointment as secretary of state.

Grant sought to reward friends and take care of the many veterans of the Union armies, now disbanded, with many of the ex-officers requesting jobs overseas. As their former leader, Grant felt his obligation. Consular ranks soon became full of former generals, colonels, and even men of lesser rank. Politicians and family friends also found Grant a soft touch for political preference. Although diplomatic appointments suffered from lack of discrimination almost as much as the consular ones, Fish made an effort to keep scoundrels, incompetents, or grossly unsuitable men out of the more important legations.

One of Fish's friends described the period of appointments as resembling the rutting season among stags, with the amenities and decencies of civilization forgotten.[18] In the early days of the Grant administration, the Department of State's anterooms were full of office seekers hoping for a legation or consulate. Cards were presented to Secretary Fish signed by Grant with notations such as "Coxe, Leghorn," or "John W. Fuller, Toledo, O., recommend for consul to St. John, N.B." Allan Nevins described the process: "Apparently the procedure was to drop in at the White House, remind Grant of auld lang syne, get one of the scribbled cards, and present it at the State Department – as at a teller's window – as a voucher good for one diplomatic [or consular] office."[19]

The patronage plague affected everyone, including Senator Carl Schurz from Missouri, who opposed the political spoils system in principle and in public; but when it came to consulships he joined the line in vying for Secretary Fish's blessing. Schurz wrote Fish:

Before me stood Lindeman, the unfortunate applicant for a consulship, who was sacrificed to keep Genl. Asterhaus in his place. He pierced me with a sad reproachful glance; – he spoke and what did he speak of? Of services rendered, of claims slightingly disregarded, of hopes recklessly excited and cruelly dashed to pieces. Of all this he spoke with the terrible eloquence of injured virtue, of bitter disappointment. I ran for my life. I reached the quiet asylum of my office – safe, as I vainly imagined. Lo! There sat in my chair, waiting for me, the equally unfortunate Baker, who would have had his consulship. Suddenly I heard a sharp knock, and through the open door appeared the gray head of Pile. My blood ran cold. Shall I describe the tortures of that interview? I have supped full with horrors. Let me not harrow you with the dreadful recollection. I cry to you for relief. What do I want? "Consulships!" say I. Any consulship in France, Switzerland, Belgium or Germany (salaried, of course) for Lindeman. Rio de Janeiro, which, as I am reliably informed, is soon to be vacated, or Antwerp or something of the same rank for Baker. As for Pile, we are trying to place him in the revenue service, but should we not succeed, I shall be down upon you for the consulship at Honolulu or the Governorship of New Mexico.[20]

Grant's appreciation for the need of better consuls did not improve. At the start of his second term in 1873 he recommended a man Fish thought very little of, as, in fact, did Grant. In his diary Fish noted that he asked the president: "Do you really want George S. Fisher given a place?" "Yes," exclaimed the president, "I want to get him out of the country."[21] Fish relented and sent the gentleman from Georgia to the busy port of Beirut, where he lasted only a year before tangling with missionaries and being recalled.

Surely one of the worst men ever to hold a consular position was George H. Butler, nephew of General Benjamin Butler, a powerful politician who had held several important military commands, including one near Richmond during the war. His abysmal ineptness as a general may have prolonged the Civil War.On returning to civilian life, Benjamin Butler again became a power in Congress and a leader of the Radical Republicans, having therefore considerable political influence, which he used to procure his nephew's appointment as the consul general to Alexandria, Egypt, in 1869. George

Butler's outrageous consulship required an investigation, almost unheard of in the Grant administration, especially as the subject of the investigation was so politically well related. Secretary Fish sent General Frederick Starring to Alexandria to verify the allegations against Butler.

The report by General Starring came into the hands of the *Nation*, a weekly magazine, which published the following:

> It appears that Mr. George H. Butler went to Alexandria, not, as some charitable people have supposed, because he was fond of drunkenness, loose women, laziness and change of scene, but for those only incidentally; primarily he was what the gentlemen of his intimacy call "being on the make." He intended to get all the money he could. To this end he no sooner got to Egypt than he dismissed every agent or servant of the consulate, and let it be understood that the highest bidder – Christian, Turk, Jew, or pagan – could have a place if he had the money. The privilege of being an American or European deputy consul or consular agent in Eastern countries is very highly valued, especially by men who have means and prefer to keep them. Extraterritoriality is an incident of consulship, and the house of a consular agent is a strip of American soil upon which no bastinado can enter – at least if intended for the consular agent. Many elderly gentlemen, then, resorted to Mr. Butler and were accommodated with commissions, for which they paid sums of various sizes; and not only was Mammon unduly worshipped by Mr. Butler, but as was inevitable, he went on to hate godliness, and made public remarks about our missionaries in Egypt which procured for him the just indignation of those gentlemen, who were in addition not only scandalized as Christians by his conduct, but greatly mortified as American citizens, and who were obliged to protest strongly. For reply, Mr. Butler expressed his desire to have their heads shaved, and then so despatched out of the Orient to America again.
>
> Moreover, he [Starring] has a word to say about the purchase by Mr. Butler of some half-grown slave girls from up-country, "Altogether, we are glad to have an attempt at a civil service reform, and shall try as hard as we can to believe that the system that gives us the Butlers now is at an end."[22]

Had Consul General Butler kept his barely nubile Nubian slave girls discreetly behind the doors of the consulate general and been a bit more diplomatic to American missionaries, he might have been able to enjoy for some years all the privileges that came his way. As it was, his clash with the missionaries and the subsequent investigation cost him his job. He left Alexandria in 1872 after two years as consul general.

Two days before he left Alexandria, Butler was attacked. Perhaps the ill repute of his uncle in the South during the war years, coupled with his own dissolute reputation at the consulate general, prompted three former Confederate officers then in the service of the khedive of Egypt, General Loring, Colonel Reynolds, and Major Campbell, to accost the consul general. Reynolds and Campbell fired at Butler twice but missed. One of the three struck at him with a loaded cane. The officers were arrested by the Egyptians but later released.[23]

THE KEIM REPORT

The best overall view of the U.S. consular service after almost one hundred years was provided by De Benneville Randolph Keim, a former newspaperman who had accompanied General George A. Custer on one of his Indian campaigns. Keim was appointed an agent by the secretary of the treasury for the examination of consular affairs under the provisions of an act of Congress approved 11 July 1870. The object of the act, and of Keim's inspection trip, was to look at the accounts of consular officers and to find out how their affairs were conducted abroad. Until the twentieth century this was the only real effort to examine objectively the consulates as a working system.

Keim made a thorough job of it, spending slightly more than a year, from August 1870 to September 1871, visiting posts in Japan, China, the Malay Peninsula, Java, India, and Egypt, and on the east and west coasts of Latin America, including the Isthmus of Panama, Ecuador, Peru, Chile, Uruguay, and Brazil. Keim's thorough final report, befitting the serious nature of his assignment, gave details of his travels, which covered exactly 47,685 miles and cost the U.S. government $5,441.44.

Some reservations must be made in accepting all of Keim's judgments on the consular service, since the gods accountants worship are not the gods of ordinary men. In an accountant's eye unbalanced books rank somewhere between high treason and premeditated murder. A too-close examination of consular accounts could cause shortsightedness in seeing how well the main work of a consulate was being performed in the care and protection of Americans and their interests within a consular district. Considering the brevity of the visit at each post, for much of his time was spent in sea travel, Keim was able, nonetheless, to identify many of the problems of the consular service. He wrote:

> I hope the defects of our consular system may be brought to light so clearly that some action will be taken to lift it out of the disrepute into which it has been dragged after years of more or less peculation and personal impropriety. At some ports I have found gentlemen worthy of the name of consul of the United States struggling under a miserable pittance from the Government, and yet have now the respect of those around them by their personal demeanor. At other ports I have found men unworthy of the commission they held, living in elegance out of the moneys of the Government, or worse still, living upon the benefits of a humane law, which properly applied would lessen the sufferings of the American sailor, by the vicissitudes of fate or his own recklessness, thrown upon a foreign shore. Almost every consulate had some defects in its history, owing to the incompetency, low habits and vulgarity of some of its officers, during the endless round of evils incident to official rotation. Abuses had been committed in the collection of fees; in the exercise of judicial powers; in the adjustment of the business affairs of American citizens; in the settlement, where permitted, of the estates of intestate American citizens dying abroad; in selling the American flag; in "running out" ships; in discharging seamen; in affording relief or medical attendance to destitute or sick American seamen; in establishing American settlements abroad; in issuing illegal passports; in countenancing shipping masters; in taxing Chinese emigrants. Indeed the most important feature of my investigations was the ingenuity displayed by consular officers, since the action of 1856, particularly, in defrauding the Government and grasping gains from various outside sources beside.
>
> It has always struck me that a majority of the persons filling the consular offices, unable or unwilling to appreciate

the importance of their positions in the eyes of the community in which they reside, as soon as they get beyond the restraints of public opinion at home, cut loose from all moral obligations, and act in a manner as astonishing to themselves, I should say, as it is to the calm judgment of those who are able to preserve their self-respect without the influence and assistance of home opinion. I have repeatedly heard complaints from consular officers that they do not receive the common civilities of American travelers. Taking some officers that I have seen or heard of, this attitude of personal relations is not extraordinary.[24]

The "running out" of ships mentioned in Keim's report was an ingenious device by which the masters of American ships, with the paid-for collusion of U.S. consuls, could circumvent the laws protecting American crews. The master of a ship signed on a crew at the high wages demanded by American sailors in a U.S. port, but when the ship arrived in Far Eastern waters, deliberate cruel treatment by the ship's officers forced some of that crew to desert. The captain then replaced them with cheap Asian crewmen, thus avoiding paying the American seamen back wages or the three months' extra wages required by law to assure passage home to a seaman discharged abroad. A consul was supposed to examine all desertion and discharge cases to see that everything was proper, but often he did not. Keim said that he heard the allegation in Hong Kong that ships' captains paid the consul ten dollars for each documented deserter.[25]

Keim first went to Japan, where the American consular presence had developed rapidly in the thirteen years since Consul General Townsend Harris's lonely negotiations opened that country to the West. There were now American consulates in Hakodate, Kanagawa, Nagasaki, Osaka, and Tokyo, and a consular agency at Niigata. Keim first visited Kanagawa (Yokohama), not an auspicious initial impression for the inspector.

At the time of my visit I found an officer in charge who was not only utterly incapable, but had established for himself a considerable reputation for ill manners and gross habits. Without saying anything farther, I may merely state that this officer was relieved.

The consulate and consular court occupied two rooms, excessively bare and filthy. A rude table, bookcase, and improvised desk, and a few chairs, the worse for rough treatment adorned the consulate.[26]

The inspector discovered that the consul, Lemuel Lyon, was illegally charging for advice given on judicial and consular matters. Keim found Consul Lyon ignorant of the law, overbearing in manner, and suspect in his judgments because of his willingness to take unauthorized payments from concerned parties.[27] Other Japanese posts visited by the inspector were better run but not very busy.

The next stop on Keim's itinerary was China. In Shanghai, still under Consul General George F. Seward (the post became a consulate general in 1863), Keim found the books in order and consular business well handled, but

> at the consulate general I found a number of circumstances to conspire against a ready acceptance of the statements of the officer in charge as strictly correct. His compensation was $4,000 per annum. At the time of his arrival it was said that he possessed no means, and it was evident from his own statements that it was quite the reverse at the time of my visit. I was informed that he was the owner of a large amount of property in Shanghai; that he possessed a plantation in Louisiana, and also a farm in New York, in the United States. His style of living, too, indicated a larger revenue than $4,000 a year. I must say I was considerably at a loss to combine these diverse elements and bring the amounts within the sum legally the right of the consul general.[28]

Keim discovered that Seward was selling the privilege of flying the American flag to Chinese owners of junks, granting them certain immunities and advantages in the river and coastal trade, charging about $250 for this unauthorized service and pocketing the whole amount. Seward also sold licenses to bars and boardinghouses in the American part of Shanghai and kept the fee. These commercial establishments were, as the inspector termed them, "the seat of every species of vice and crime."[29] Keim further found other abuses, such as using the seamen's relief fund for speculation. Despite this damning report, George Seward was to stay in China until 1880, spending his final year as the U.S. minister in Peking.

At Canton the vice consul, in charge in the absence of the consul, had been a missionary: "He also had an eye to gain. One of the enterprises which he had on foot was the establishment of a cotton factory in the consular building."[30]

The consul in Amoy during Keim's inspection tour was General Charles W. LeGendre, whose biography reads like an adventure story. Born in France and educated at the University of Paris, he married an American and emigrated to New York in the 1850s. At the onset of the Civil War he helped recruit the Fifty-first New York Volunteer Infantry Regiment and soon became its colonel. In 1862 at the capture of New Bern in North Carolina he was badly wounded by a musket ball that carried away most of his jaw. Two years later at the battle of the Wilderness he was again wounded, losing the bridge of his nose and an eye. For his bravery he was made a brigadier general and honorably discharged; in 1866 he was appointed consul in Amoy, whose district included the island of Formosa.[31]

Formosa was dangerous for mariners, for although it was under Chinese sovereignty, there was little control over the natives who preyed on shipwrecked seamen. After the crew of a wrecked American ship had been massacred and a small punitive expedition by the United States Navy repulsed, LeGendre himself went to the island to deal with the Formosans. He was able, despite the danger, to establish contact with the principal tribes and reach agreements with them to provide for the safety of American sailors who might fall into their hands.[32]

Inspector Keim found that General LeGendre ran the consulate at Amoy efficiently. "The consular jail attracted my attention particularly, as the best and most economical I had seen in China."[33] Only two years later, Consul LeGendre was to be a prisoner in that same jail, put there by his successor as consul.

While LeGendre was passing through Japan in 1872 on his way to the United States, the American minister in Tokyo introduced him to the Japanese authorities. The Japanese were mounting a punitive expedition against the island of Formosa because of problems with their shipwrecked sailors and island natives. Because of his work on Formosa helping American sailors, the Japanese were eager to secure LeGendre's services as an advisor. Happy to have a chance to see some military action, General LeGendre accepted the Japanese offer, resigning his consular commission. Upon returning to Amoy to help the Japanese military, he was arrested by the new American consul, who considered that LeGendre was violating American neutrality laws forbidding U.S. citizens from participating in foreign military adventures.[34] When word of the arrest reached Washington, orders were sent back to release the ex-consul. LeGendre stayed on in Japanese service until 1890, when he moved to Korea to become an advisor to the Korean king, an office he maintained until his death in 1899.

In Hong Kong Keim found the consulate reasonably well run, but noted that the office had a bad history. There was a shipping office attached to the consulate, and "a shipping office is synonymous with rascality."[35] Former consuls in Hong Kong had been heavily involved in the "running out" of ships, mismanaging sailors' relief funds, and pocketing an illegal fee for every Chinese emigrating to the United States.

Stopping at Saigon on his way to Java and Singapore, Keim reported: "I landed and made some general inquiries concerning the port. I found it not unimportant generally, though American interests were small. The French population lived a life poorly adapted to the trying effects of the climate upon the human constitution. The peculiar and irregular mode of living at their capital (Paris) had been transported hither. The *café* and the *salons de danse* were patronized with the ardor incident to a more invigorating latitude."[36]

Singapore had a full-time, salaried ($2,500) consul performing well, according to Keim, but he noted that there had been an excessive turnover in consular officers, fifteen men in the past fifteen years; fewer than half of whom had been Americans. The rest were vice consuls, usually British subjects, filling in between American appointees.

British merchants in Singapore, Keim found, had done their best to keep U.S. consular officers from enforcing any American regulations that inhibited British trade. Singapore had never been a friendly post for American consuls. Commerce was tied to Britain, and the British wanted it kept that way.

Posts in Java and India maintained Keim's exacting standards for bookkeeping. They dealt with American sailors fairly. From India Keim continued on to Egypt, stopping over at the Red Sea port of Aden, a consular post not listed on the State Department register of consulates and consular agencies. There once had been an agency there under the supervision of the consulate in Calcutta. When the agent left about 1870, he passed along the consular seal and books to Burjorjee, a Parsee merchant, without informing the department of his action. "To my surprise the consular office was by no means discreditable, and had more the appearance of dignity and respectability than some of the offices of salaried consuls that I had seen. I was at a loss in determining whether this agency still legally existed."[37]

Keim speculated on the number of stray U.S. consular seals, flags, books, and other consular paraphernalia that must be scattered about the world, the detritus of former consuls when they left their posts. He was concerned over the serious abuses of such official equipment and recommended that the U.S. government have an accountability system over consular property.

In Alexandria, Egypt, Consul General George Butler was in a position that Keim considered more diplomatic than consular. He spent little time looking into Butler's operations. Although the books were well kept, Keim politely remonstrated at the practice of selling vice-consular offices to natives, mildly suggesting that there was little need for such posts. Without looking at consulates as he passed through Europe, Keim proceeded to South America, as he was eager to see the posts on the Pacific coast, where he knew there were "the most flagrant instances of neglect and evident dishonesty in the consular service of the United States."[38] Arriving in Panama, Keim crossed over the isthmus and sailed down the Pacific coast to Payta, Peru, a port with no trade with the United States, but where thirty American whaling ships had put in during 1870. The consul claimed that he had dispersed $4,000 to destitute seamen, an unlikely call upon government money. As Inspector Keim put it: "It would be difficult to convince me, taking all the circumstances into consideration, that the consul kept an eye to the interests of the government."[39] At the port of Tumbez in Peru, Keim found that

> the flag and consular arms were over the entrance. As I stepped inside upon the bare ground and gazed around upon mud walls, my eyes were attached to a formidable array of empty vermout [vermouth] bottles, arranged with martial precision on the upper shelves of a rude frame, while upon the lower stood a line of bottles well filled with annissao and pisio, the most redoubtable of the native beverages. My first impression was that I had mistaken the place, or had entered by the wrong door. I was, however, speedily informed that I was in the Consulate of the United States.[40]

Consul Ralph Abercrombie, according to Keim, was an "utterly hopeless inebriate" who often slept in the market stall of the public square after a drunken spree. The consul was quite upset at the unexpected appearance of the inspector, which disrupted his business and caused the departure of his customers, "the drinking portion of the community."[41]

After examining the account books at consulates on the Pacific coast, Keim concluded that the U.S. government should not recognize vouchers for seamen's relief for more than $100 at Guayaquil in Ecuador or $300 from the consulates of Tumbez, Payta, and Talcahuano. He doubted that more than one voucher in ten was honest. Keim went then to the Atlantic coast of South America, calling at Montevideo, Rio de Janeiro, and the northern consulates of Brazil, Bahia, Pernambuco, and Para, where he found no particular problems.

Back in the United States after his globe-circling inspection tour, Keim in his final report pointed emphatically to the want of a consular organization in Washington, "the utter absence of any bureau organization having special charge of the affairs of consuls."[42] He noted how it would be next to impossible to define the jurisdiction of the State and Treasury departments over consuls because the consuls were accounting officers of the government. They received fees for official services and were disbursing considerable sums to destitute sailors, activities Keim judged to be concerns belonging more to the Treasury than to the State Department. It was obvious to him that a consular bureau should be formed under the secretary of the treasury (who, incidentally, was his employer), with only those consuls having quasi-diplomatic roles, as in Egypt, being responsible to the secretary of state.[43]

Despite his generally negative view of the U.S. consular system, Keim conceded that progress had been made in the past decade in bringing the system under control. An examination of consular service accounts in 1861 had shown that the consul in Liverpool had perhaps plundered some $200,000 and that the 4 infamous Pacific coast posts in South America accounted for the disbursement of $114,800 to supposedly destitute seamen, $8,000 more than such disbursements by all the other consulates, some 200 in the same year. In 1859 the U.S. government had paid $222,469.32 to help seamen, but only $31,503.02 in 1871.

Keim drew up an elaborate proposal for professionalizing the consular service. He called for a consular bureau in the Department of the Treasury under which those who desired to be consuls would be required to pass an examination before being appointed and must present testimonials of good character, a request that would have disqualified a number of consuls in years past. Upon passing the screening of the examination board, the applicant would be nominated to be a consul of the third class; to be promoted to the next grade he must serve at least one year in before going to the higher rank. There were other detailed provisions, the most important being the appointment of two permanent consular inspectors who would have considerable power to investigate consuls and their consulates.[44]

After Keim's report was published, Congress considered the idea of a merit system for both the diplomatic and consular services of the State Department, but nothing came of various proposals. The Senate had passed a bill in 1872 to make the two services more professional, but the House would not go along, preferring to keep patronage positions available for members' constituents.

In 1883 Congress took a major step toward reform in the government by passing the Civil Service Act, known as the Pendleton Act, which established the principle of selection by competitive examination for certain positions within the civil service. Unfortunately for the consular and diplomatic services, this positive development did not inspire Congress to take immediate measures to extend the competitive principle to those organizations. Moreover, because the Pendleton Act removed so many positions in the domestic civil service from the patronage system, Congress was not ready to close off consular and diplomatic jobs too from patronage requests.

Without waiting for an obviously reluctant Congress to pass an antipatronage act, President Cleveland in September 1895 took action regarding the consular service by issuing an executive order providing that any vacant consular position of which the salary was between $1,000 and $2,500 a year should be filled by a person designated by the president for examination and having successfully passed it. The salary provision covered more than 60 percent of the consular posts, 196 positions (53 were above $2,500, 71 below $1,000). The examination was both written, covering knowledge of consular regulations, and oral, including a test in a foreign language. In the first series of examinations, ending in March 1896, eight passed and five were rejected. The remaining positions were filled by transfers from other posts or from the department.[45]

There were flaws in this seemingly auspicious beginning of consular reform. Cleveland, prior to issuing his executive order, entered his second term as president with a thorough sweep of the consular service – one of the most drastic in its history – by throwing out many serving consuls and putting in deserving Democrats.

Having fulfilled his patronage responsibilities, he talked reform. The Republicans responded in kind when McKinley replaced Cleveland in 1897.

McKinley left the executive order in place but recalled 259 of the 320 serving consuls to replace them with men sponsored by the Republican Party. The examination process became a farce: 1 candidate was rejected out of the 112 tested in the first round.[46]

Although reform was not forthcoming from the leadership in Washington, there were stirrings within the consular corps to rid itself of some of the worst practices. Most men appointed to the consular service were honest and hard workers and risked their lives to further and protect American interests. These honest men resented the public assertion that the consular system was infested with corruption. As Keim noted in his inspection, he found many consuls cleaning up the messes left behind by less scrupulous predecessors and trying to run straightforward operations with balanced and accurate books.

MOSBY IN CHINA

Despite Keim's perceptive and highly critical 1872 report, the worst blot on the consular map remained the China coast, where the opportunities for consuls to make money on the side were still great. Washington was far away. From top to bottom the Chinese system thrived on the "squeeze" (bribery); the Western merchants accommodated themselves comfortably to that system. After all, the merchant community had been founded on the illegal drug trade of opium and was still trading in that product. There was a certain understanding among consuls at the various China coast ports, including Hong Kong and Bangkok, about fees charged for services, fees seldom legally sanctioned. Consuls had developed other arrangements in their districts for payments or investments by persons needing consular services that could only be interpreted as outright bribes.

They had more power in that area of the world; consular cooperation was necessary for merchants, shipping firms, and captains to carry on their businesses. Thus there were many opportunities for Yankee consuls to apply their own "squeeze." Into this cozy little world presided over by George F. Seward, the consul general in Shanghai, was tossed a rebel wildcat.

In 1878 newly elected President Rutherford B. Hayes, a former major general in the Union army, nominated a most unlikely candidate to be the consul in Hong Kong, John S. Mosby, the former Grey Ghost of the Confederacy. Mosby, a Virginia lawyer prior to the Civil War, had become one of the most successful guerrilla leaders in American history. That part of northern Virginia reaching into the suburbs of the Union capital was known as "Mosby's Confederacy" because Mosby and his small band of irregular cavalry had struck almost at will there in spite of seemingly overwhelming Yankee forces.

After the war Colonel Mosby, always a maverick among Southern military leaders, ran true to form in the postwar South, settling with his wife and six children as a lawyer in Warrenton, a town in his old guerrilla territory in northern Virginia. He kept out of politics and concentrated on his profession. By 1872, after a meeting with his old antagonist, General and now President Grant, Mosby publicly supported Grant's reelection and four years later supported Rutherford Hayes for the presidency.

Mosby's political efforts paid off. President Hayes offered him the consulate in Hong Kong, which Mosby accepted. He had hoped for a government position in Virginia, but his wartime exploits and peacetime political activities had alienated too many people in Virginia and Washington. It was safer for President Hayes to send the fiery ex-partisan leader abroad.

Now a widower, Mosby was forced to leave behind his six children, the eldest nineteen, the youngest seven, in the care of family and friends. The new consul arrived at the crown colony of Hong Kong in early 1879, where he made his presence felt. In carefully examining the books of David H. Bailey, his predecessor, he found that the former consul and his vice consul had been cheating the U.S. government. According to Mosby, Bailey had been able to make at least $30,000 over the past eight years by illegally collecting and pocketing various fees.[47]

Mosby's charges came at an awkward time for the China coast network of consuls. In 1876 George Seward had become American minister to China, with his residence in Peking. His successor in Shanghai as consul general was John C. Myers of Reading, Pennsylvania, who soon reported to Washington that Seward and Seward's vice consul, Oliver B. Bradford, had been involved in various illegal schemes and speculations in China, allegations hinted at by Keim five years before but not investigated. Seward was well protected through his political influence, and Myers was summarily dismissed from his position in June 1877, only a year after his appointment. Myers was followed by G. Wiley Wells, a former congressman from Mississippi, who also wanted to reform consular practices on the China coast. He was quickly removed. The new consul general designate to Shanghai was none other than David H. Bailey, who had already proved himself adept at corrupt activities while he was in Hong Kong.[48]

By the time Mosby took charge of the consulate in Hong Kong in 1879, both Myers and Wells had made known to Congress their complaints against George Seward. In his statement to the United States Senate, Myers wrote that Seward owned extensive property in Shanghai, including "about 40 houses which were regularly occupied by Chinese women as prostitutes."[49] He estimated that Seward had property worth at least a quarter of a million dollars in China, a sizeable acquisition for a man with a salary of only $4,000 a year and no outside means.

The Senate was already gathering evidence about Seward when Mosby's charges against Bailey were sent to the State Department. Mosby was obviously aware that his report on illegal operations in Hong Kong would only aggravate the attacks on Seward and his illegal operations in Shanghai. Mosby's report went to his direct superior, Assistant secretary of State Frederick W. Seward, son of Lincoln's secretary of state. He would not be happy with any attack on the China coast consuls, especially accusations against his cousin George Seward.

Assistant Secretary Seward sat on Mosby's report on Bailey. As a result the Senate routinely confirmed Bailey as consul general to Shanghai. After sending in the Bailey report, Mosby, carrying on his investigations in the Asian consular swamp, found that the consul in Bangkok, David B. Sickels, had a scheme of his own, which was to have the consulate's marshal, a special policeman in areas where there was extraterritorial jurisdiction, arrest Chinese on trumped-up charges and fine them $100 to $500 each, which Sickels pocketed.[50]

Having learned his lesson from his approach to Assistant Secretary Seward, Mosby passed this new information directly to President Hayes. Because of the reports coming from Mosby and the statements of Myers and Wells to the Senate, the State Department was finally forced to take action. David Sickels resigned from his post in Bangkok before formal charges were made against him.

Seward sent an inspector to Hong Kong to look at Bailey's books and evaluate Mosby's charges. The man selected to carry on the investigation was General Julius P. Stahel, the consul at Huogo and Osaka in Japan. During the Civil War Lincoln had put the then Major General Stahel in charge of the Union cavalry in Fairfax County, Virginia, to stop Colonel Mosby, an assignment that had not been successful. Seward may have deliberately selected Stahel to carry out the inspection, believing that Stahel would be sufficiently prejudiced against Mosby to blunt the charges against Bailey.

But in Hong Kong the two old antagonists got along splendidly. Stahel found indeed that Bailey had been up to no good and so reported to the secretary of state, William M. Evarts, who tried unsuccessfully to keep the report quiet.[51] In the resulting scandal that Mosby, Myers, Wells, and Stahel exposed and forcibly brought to the attention of Congress and the public,

George Seward was recalled from Peking and Bailey from Shanghai. Frederick Seward was obliged to resign from office in 1879. As in most cases where U.S. consuls and diplomats were suspected of corrupt practices, no legal steps were taken against the erring China consuls; they were simply allowed to resign.

After helping take care of Messrs. Seward, Sickels, and Bailey, Colonel Mosby remained in Hong Kong through Hayes's administration and those of his successors, James Garfield and Chester Arthur. Not content with his successful exposures, Mosby then questioned a consular practice that had been accepted by the State Department for the past twenty years, the charging of a fee to examine Chinese emigrants going to the United States on non-American ships. The inspection was intended to verify that the passengers were not part of the coolie trade and were going as acceptable immigrants.

The department, under Mosby's prodding, acknowledged that a consul had the right under the law to examine Chinese on American vessels only. This effort on Mosby's part to make his duties clear actually cut down on the fees that he and other consuls could receive from performing the inspections. While Mosby's action may have eased his legal mind and scruples, it certainly annoyed other China coast consuls, who did not like to see their powers curtailed or a significant source of revenue cut off.

The examination process for Chinese emigrants got Consul Mosby into a controversy with the authorities at San Francisco, where almost all the Chinese would land. There were complaints about the type of women Mosby allowed to emigrate; customs officials claimed that many of the women, few in number compared to men, were prostitutes. Mosby replied to the collector of customs in San Francisco, who was in charge of receiving immigrants, that in Hong Kong strict standards were maintained for screening Chinese females going to the United States. Mosby required character witnesses for each. He continued: "The women who get my certificates are much better than a majority of white women who come from San Francisco to Hong Kong. The China coast is overrun with California prostitutes who are much more demoralizing in China than Chinese cheap labor and lewd women in California. I am no more responsible for the number of Chinese going to the United States than you are for the number of San Francisco whores continually coming to Hong Kong."[52]

When Grover Cleveland became president in 1885, Mosby was replaced by a Democratic appointee as consul to Hong Kong, Dr. Robert E. Withers, a former lieutenant governor of Virginia. Prior to his departure from Hong Kong, a Chinese governor asked Mosby, the former Confederate leader, to command his regional army, at that time being threatened by the French, who were moving into Vietnam. Mosby rejected the offer and returned to the United States and a less frenetic life as a lawyer for the Southern Pacific Railroad in San Francisco and later a special agent for the U.S. government in Nebraska and Colorado. Although corruption was not completely eliminated at consular posts by the end of the century, because of the efforts of men like John Mosby, the level of toleration for such activities had measurably lowered in Washington. There is a Chinese adage that one should not break his neighbor's rice bowl (not hurt his means of making a living), which Mosby ignored. When he left Hong Kong there was shattered consular crockery up and down the China coast, and the consular service was the better for it.

13
Consuls and Commerce:
Trouble in Samoa
(1865–1900)

In the early years of the Republic, the reports consuls were expected to send to the U.S. government for internal use contained mainly trade statistics. The Treasury Department used these reports primarily for establishing tariff rates on foreign imports, for tariffs were the government's principal source of revenue. But Congress also used the consuls' information as a base for legislation regarding foreign commerce.[1] From time to time the State Department issued and made available to the public digests of the commercial regulations at various foreign ports, which were useful for American exporters who did not have their own agents abroad and wanted to find export markets. By 1853 the U.S. government and American business had found these occasional consular commercial digests valuable enough to establish a regular system of such reporting.

These commercial reports from the various consular districts were, understandably, quite uneven. Their value depended largely upon the individual competence and interests of the consul and the length of time he had been at the post. Consuls usually stayed no longer than four years before being replaced by another, often inexperienced, appointee. The more fortunate consuls had local consular clerks knowledgeable in commerce who could supply timely and accurate information. Some new consuls, however, without an adequate staff, had to improvise their reports, often with dubious results.

Consuls were in an excellent position to give practical advice to American exporters. Most countries, as did the United States, relied on ways of taxing imports into their countries to support their governments. There were many pitfalls for the unwary American businessmen. The wording of orders could be extremely important. An order of stamped iron items labeled simply "stamped ware" was, for example, charged duty at a very high rate by the Brazilian customs authorities because the order contained the word "stamped"; hence it was considered to be printed materials and consequently was taxed at the rate for paper products, thus putting the ironware at a prohibitive cost.

The inability or unwillingness of American manufacturers to cater to local styles and prejudices caused frustrations for consular officers trying to promote American goods in their districts. Many buyers in the world market were accustomed to certain uniformity in sizes and patterns. The American supplier had to be aware of these local designations if he wished to be successful. In Sierra Leone, for example, textile goods were expected to be sold in 12- or 20-yard pieces; in Venezuela, 33-yard pieces must be exactly 23 inches wide. In Haiti the preferred width was 23 or 27 inches. Many of these measurements were set to avoid certain local duties. A consignment of cloth might be charged less duty if it were just under two feet in width, hence the demand for the 23-inch measure in some countries.[2] Consular suggestions for marketing strategies usually went unheeded by businessmen catering to the American market and unprepared or unwilling to make special provisions for Haitian or Venezuelan preferences.

Besides trying to help American manufacturers find and keep markets abroad, the consuls were required to establish the true cost of goods exported to the United States. Duties on goods exported to America were set according to the actual value of those goods. Naturally many foreign exporters placed false, lower values on their products to lessen American duty. It was difficult to establish the actual value of certain products, especially those from only one source, where prices could not be dictated by the market. Prior to shipping goods to America, exporters brought invoices stating the supposed value of their goods to the nearest consulate to have them certified. Few consuls were experienced in ascertaining the real value of most manufactured products, which producers often took great care to conceal. In 1869 one Treasury inspector estimated that the United States, over a period of years, had been defrauded of $9,000,000 in duties on silk products alone from the consular district of Lyons.[3] While untrained consuls were costing the United States significant amounts of potential revenue, nothing was done to raise the expertise of the service. Patronage was still the principal concern in consular selection and service in the Union Army during the Civil War was a prime qualifier.

***

One of the Civil War veterans who became a consular officer was the author's great grandfather, Edmund Jussen. His was a classic American story. Born in a small town in Prussian territory in 1830 where his father was the burgomaster, Edmund caught the spirit of revolution that was sweeping Germany in the 1840s. He was rebellious enough to be expelled from his Catholic high school at the age of seventeen just prior to the 1848 revolt. At loose ends and seeking adventure he voyaged to the United States with an uncle. Reaching Wisconsin, Edmund decided to stay, while his uncle continued traveling. He was a penniless seventeen-year-old, speaking only German, but managed to support himself by hunting small game and selling it to the local farmers. Picking up English, he soon joined a friend as the joint proprietor of a small store. Reading law at night he passed the law exam and found his career. Involved in local politics and a strong supporter of Lincoln in the 1860 election, Edmund was an ardent antislavery man. He helped raise a Wisconsin regiment of volunteers for the Union army and was elected as its second in command. After service in the Mississippi campaign he was invalided out and returned to law. Remaining active in politics, he switched from Republican to Democrat after the election of 1876. In 1885 he was appointed consul general in Vienna by Grover Cleveland.

Life in Vienna was not all Straussian waltzes at the Hapsburg Court. Consul General Jussen had the full range of problems that faced an American consul in a country with strong commercial ties to the United States. To give some idea of what such a consular officer did, here are some of the problems that crossed his desk:

Letters from Austrian-Hungarian china manufacturers complaining about new American import taxes

A notice that an American citizen had been put in a mental asylum

Letters regarding American citizenship

Letters from Austrians asking for help in claiming estates of deceased Americans

Reports on the Polish exporters of petroleum falsely claiming their product was of American origin

Correspondence with the consul in Crefeld regarding an American woman who married a German Baron; "She (the Baroness) has been the most outrageously abused of the many foolish American women who have married Continental nobility. She married a title and not a man." Modern consuls do not have this problem, but one somewhat similar, that of American women marrying into Islamic families where their children are not allowed to go with their mother if the marriage breaks up.

A letter from an American vine company that wants to be considered as an importer to Austria because it has heard that the Austrian government decided on importing 5 million American grapevines; given the snobbery of the European vintners it is hard to imagine in this period that there would be a market for American grapes.[4]

The consul general left his post in 1889 when the Cleveland administration was replaced by a Republican one. Jussen had been planning to write a book on the American consular service, but died in 1891 before doing so, leaving his great grandson to carry on the task.

One of the more troublesome consular posts of the United States in the latter part of the nineteenth century was that at Apia, Samoa. With the almost complete demise of the American whaling industry during the Civil War, few American ships called at the Samoan Islands. Trade with the United States was meager; the sparse American population consisted of a few entrepreneurs and beachcombers. Despite the lack of a pronounced U.S. interest in the island group during most of the nineteenth century, circumstances required that the American consular representatives assigned there play a large role in the governing of those islands, with mixed results.

Samoa was a group of islands ruled by tribal chiefs, often warring with each other; European observers sometimes called them "the Irish of the Pacific." The islands of the Samoan group lie somewhat to the north and between the Fiji Islands to the east and Tahiti to the west. There are nine main islands in the group, with the main city, Apia, on the island of Upolu. The British, American, and German consuls resided in Apia, where the interests of their governments and of the consuls themselves sometimes collided.

Starting in 1839, a series of commercial agents and, later, consuls served at the U.S. post in Apia until the islands were split into German and American colonies at the end of the century. The first commercial agent was appointed by a U.S. naval commander, Charles Wilkes (later of fame over the *Trent* case, which almost brought the United States and Great Britain to blows during the Civil War), who negotiated a treaty with the Samoans. There was a slight oversight in this appointment, for Wilkes forgot to mention to the Department of State that he had named John C. Williams, an Englishman, as their agent. For five years Williams carried on the modest business of representing the United States before writing the State Department to ask for a commission as a consul rather than as a commercial agent. In Washington the clerks in the State Department were somewhat puzzled. A query went out to Wilkes asking just who this Williams was. [5]

The State Department, when informed of Williams's identity, did not approve him as consul but confirmed his appointment as commercial agent without salary. When Williams learned that he would have to depend on whatever he could glean from consular work, he resigned. Because of the muddled state of consular administration, with little attention paid to affairs in a far-off Pacific island, no successor was appointed for a year. Williams continued to act as the American consul until he left the islands in 1850.

Following Williams, commercial agents and then consuls on Samoa were mainly traders or real estate promoters seeking a profit out of the office. Dr. Aaron Van Camp (1853–56), a so-called dentist with dubious medical credentials, used his authority as the U.S. commercial agent to declare unseaworthy ships of American registry when the vessels were actually sound. The ships were then auctioned off. The commercial agent split the profits with the ships' officers, defrauding the ships' owners.

Other agents/consuls were busy with land speculation, the major occupation of the non-Samoans. In selling land to copra planters, who produced palm oil, speculators, including American representatives, required the native people to cooperate in giving over their rights. This consequently involved the speculators in the natives' internecine warfare, as they were forced to back one side or another to gain property rights.

Although the British, American, and German consuls were constantly squabbling with each other due to conflicting interests, the danger to the Europeans and Americans on the islands from the constant fighting among the Samoans helped establish Apia as an enclave of relative security, which the consuls forbade the natives to use as a battleground. This shaky arrangement began to break down when the Germans set out to gain predominance in the island group in the 1870s and 1880s. Superiority depended upon which country happened to have a warship in the area. Some conflicts between consuls derived from national policies, others from personality differences of men cooped up in a small island town. The German prime minister, Otto von Bismarck, after reading reports from his consul general on Samoa, remarked about the *furor consularis* (consular fury) coming out of that distant island group.[6] By 1885 an American of German birth, Bertold Greenebaum, was appointed consul. He found it almost impossible to help run Apia's municipal government with British and German consuls continually opposing each other, leaving the Americans in the middle. Greenebaum was concerned that the Germans appeared to be moving toward assuming a protectorate over the islands, with could lead to the unsavory possibility of Germans limiting opportunities for American traders.[7]

Increasingly, consuls were drawn into the incessant civil war, with the British and Americans supporting one faction, and the German consul general supporting another. The Germans were the most aggressive, ready to call upon marines at a moment's notice. . But Greenebaum was equally zealous. When the USS *Mohican* was in port in May 1886, he used its presence to declare Samoa a U.S. protectorate, reporting back to Washington that "everything is quiet. Not a drop of blood shed. The Stars and Stripes floating over the Islands."[8] Many consuls became partisan to one side or the other in the endemic civil war on the Samoan islands. The more professional consular services of Germany and Great Britain did not do much better with their men on the spot to calm the situation.

In looking at the American consular service prior to the twentieth century, one is struck by its diversity, each post reacting to the peculiar circumstances of its own consular district. There was little direction from Washington; most consuls served at only one post before being replaced by another political appointee. Each worked in isolation from his American colleagues at other posts. There was nothing to unify these consuls, such as the shared experience of West Point army officers serving together at a variety of army posts. Because of rapid turnover there was little chance to build up any esprit de corps within consular ranks.

Had the men been required to serve for some months in the Department of State before shipping out, perhaps a better feel for the system and an appreciation of the problems caused by domestic pressure on the secretary of state would have been developed. Even a small permanent corps of inspectors to visit posts on a regular basis would have helped unify the system, for such inspectors could have served as mediums for exchange of experiences and advice among the various posts, a potentially valuable service, but nothing of the sort developed. For 130 years (1776–1906) each consul had to march to his own drumbeat.

14

The Spanish-American War
(1898)

The Spanish-American War, the last hurrah for the old consular service, was fought in the colonial territories, including Cuba, Puerto Rico, and the Philippines, with supporting roles by the consuls in Hong Kong, Singapore, Port Said, Alexandria, Cairo, and Gibraltar. Ironically the war was precipitated by a consular action, the sending for a warship in response to unrest in a port city.

Although the warship threat had been used, with mixed results, as long as there had been a consular service, it was essentially the only option available when civil order was degenerating. The danger when a foreign warship anchored off a restive harbor city was that something might go wrong. In the case of the USS *Maine* in Havana harbor, something most certainly did go wrong.

The *Maine* was in harbor at the request of the American consul general because of possible anti-American riots in that city. When the ship blew up, or was blown up, war between Spain and the United States was almost inevitable. Had the battleship not been destroyed, it is doubtful that the reluctant President McKinley and his equally reluctant counterparts in the Spanish government could have been prodded into war.

Prior to the sinking of the *Maine*, the citizenries in the United States and Spain had, for a second time, become inflamed over the situation in Cuba. The Cuban insurrection (1868–78), in which the capture of the *Virginius* had been one incident, had died down after the Spanish agreed to certain reforms, which went unfulfilled. Again in 1896 the cry of *"Cuba libre"* sparked an insurrectionary movement. This time the insurrectionists struck at the vital center of Spanish rule on the island, the Cuban economy, which was based almost entirely on sugar production. The rebels carried out a coordinated campaign of burning sugarcane fields, destroying sugar-processing equipment, and blowing up trains. Much of the property destroyed was American-owned; Americans had about fifty million dollars invested in Cuba, yet the American public sided almost exclusively with the Cuban insurrectionists and against the Spanish.[1]

The Spanish reaction to the 1896 insurrection was brutal reprisal and reconcentration, which was a program of forcing the rural population into camps to be isolated from the rebels, one of the first efforts of such kind to cope with a guerrilla movement, used later in South Africa by the British and in Vietnam by the Americans. The Spanish management of the reconcentration camps was disastrous. The supply of food was mismanaged; hygiene was completely lacking. Thousands were dying as conditions worsened. General Valeriano Weyler, the Spanish commander, earned the name of "Butcher" in the American press for doing little to ameliorate living conditions in the camps while he pursued the rebels. The U.S. consuls, from their posts throughout Cuba, sent to Congress vivid reports on the dreadful conditions in their consular districts. These reports were eventually published for the American people.

Consuls were again caught between the intransigent Spanish authorities and the American public demanding both consular protection for its citizens aiding the insurrection and consular action to remedy the inhumane conditions on the island. In the midst of the conflict was Fitzhugh Lee, the U.S. consul general in Havana.

Lee was the grandson of "Light Horse" Harry Lee, the preeminent cavalry leader of the revolutionary army, and the nephew of Robert E. Lee. At West Point Fitzhugh Lee was more renowned for his horsemanship and pranks than for academic attainments. He graduated forty-fifth in a class of forty-nine in 1856. During the Civil War Lee served under his uncle in the Army of Northern Virginia, rising to the rank of major general. Although family connections helped, Fitzhugh Lee was a fighting general and an outstanding cavalry leader, by the end of the Civil War becoming, after the death of Jeb Stuart, the senior cavalry commander of the Army of Northern Virginia.[2]

Lee was the antithesis of the other Virginian cavalry leader turned consul, John Mosby. Mosby was of modest family background, a lawyer by training, with no previous military experience. During the war both future consular officers fought with daring, but while the partisan leader Mosby was always an outsider, even to his fellow Confederates, Lee was a pillar of the establishment, both within the high command of the Confederacy and after the war in the South. He became governor of Virginia in 1885 and served a four-year term. In 1896 President Cleveland named him to the prestigious but difficult position of consul general to Havana. When the new Republican administration took power in 1897, President McKinley kept Lee on as the consul general. Lee's military experience and past record assured him of the confidence of the American public. There was irresistible pressure on any public official dealing with Cuba; a strong, credible man was needed to be "our man in Havana."

Lee tried to avoid being inflammatory in his reporting on developments in Cuba. He noted that both the Spanish and the insurrectionists were killing innocent women and children and that there were too many atrocities on both sides. When the rival sensational Hearst and Pulitzer newspapers in New York, the "yellow journals," made much of the strip searching of Cuban women on American ships by Spanish male officials, Lee pointed out that the searching incidents reported had actually involved matrons, but he later informed the State Department that there had been males searching women.[3] With feelings running high, facts given by a consular officer made little impression on the public. The American press exaggerated conditions regarding the disrobing of a few Cuban ladies, while the greater horror was that thousands were dying of starvation and disease in reconcentration camps.

It was a critical situation for the sixty-two-year-old Lee. He had to keep relations open with the Spanish authorities while convincing the president, secretary of state, Congress, and the press that he was doing his utmost to protect American interests. In one particular incident, the secretary of state reprimanded him for not protecting Dr. Ricardo Ruiz, a Cuban-born dentist. Dr. Ruiz had been naturalized in 1880 but had returned to Cuba and had been arrested by the Spanish. In 1897 Dr. Ruiz died in prison after extraordinarily brutal treatment. His case caused a sensation in the United States.[4]

Although the McKinley administration and a new government in Madrid wanted to reduce tensions and find a solution to the problem of Cuba, the situation was becoming unmanageable. The new Spanish government removed General "Butcher" Weyler, who had become the symbol of brutal suppression, and proposed a new policy of limited political autonomy for Cuba. Consul General Lee, sensitive to volatile conditions, did not think that half-measures would work. He wrote that "the insurgents would not accept autonomy" and that the new Spanish governor general would "not have the means to carry out" the relief of those in the reconcentration camps.[5] He continued to inform Washington of the wretchedness of the camps.

The removal of General Weyler actually worsened the situation because he was a hero to the diehard Spanish and their Cuban associates. The volunteers, or pro-Spanish militia, were almost out of control, increasing the concerns for American lives and property. After discussing the danger with the new captain-general, Ramon Blanco, who had promised the consul general that he could control the situation, Lee wrote to Washington in December 1897: "In consequence of all this, and the assurances of the governmental authorities that American life and property will, if necessary, be protected by them at a moment's notice, I have declined to make an application for the presence of one or more war ships in this harbor, and have advised those of our people who have wives and children here not to send them away, at least for the present, because such proceedings would not, in my opinion, be justifiable at this time, from the standpoint of personal security."[6] Lee, however, asked for warships to be kept on station at Key West in case they were suddenly needed.

Captain-General Blanco did not gain full control. By mid-January Lee reported that mobs led by Spanish officers were attacking opposition newspapers. Doubtful of Blanco's ability, Lee stated that if "he cannot maintain order, preserve life, and keep the peace, or if Americans and their interests are in danger, ships must be sent, and to that end should be prepared to move promptly. Excitement and uncertainty predominates everywhere."[7] This consular dispatch may have started a chain of events that led to the war.

Lee was prudent in his dispatch of 13 January. He reiterated his earlier request that the United States Navy be nearby should there be need to protect Americans or evacuate them, but he did not ask that a naval ship be sent to Havana, only that one stand by. The very next day he cabled, "Noon. All quiet," and on the following day, 15 January, "Quiet prevails." But it was too late; he had stirred Washington into action.

Washington, January 14, 1898
 It is the purpose of this Government to resume friendly [sic] naval visits at Cuban port. In that view the *Maine* will call at the port of Havana in a day or two. Please arrange for a friendly interchange of calls with authorities.

Havana, January 24, 1898
Advise visit be postponed six or seven days, to give last excitement more time to disappear. Will see authorities and let you know the result. Governor-General away for two weeks. I should know day and hour visit.

Washington, January 24, 1898
Maine has been ordered. Will probably arrive at Havana some time tomorrow. Can not tell hour; possibly early. Co-operate with authorities for friendly visits. Keep us advised by frequent telegrams.

Havana, January 25, 1898
At an interview authorities profess to think United States has ulterior purpose in sending ship. Say it will obstruct autonomy, produce excitement, and most probably a demonstration. Ask that it is not done until they can get instructions from Madrid, and say that if for friendly motives, as claimed, delay unimportant.

Havana, January 25, 1898
Ship quietly arrived 11 a.m. to-day. No demonstration so far.

Lee went on to describe cordial calls of the officers off the Maine with the Spanish authorities. Except for some heckling at a bullfight the captain and his staff attended, there was no trouble.
Because Havana harbor could be unhealthy due to tropical illnesses, the secretary of the navy asked whether the *Maine* could be withdrawn shortly, but Lee thought that now that it was there, the departure of the warship without the substitution of another would be disturbing. He wrote:

Havana, February 4, 1898
We should not relinquish position of peaceful control of the situation or conditions would be worse than if vessel had never been sent.

The *Maine* stayed at the consul general's insistence; two weeks later Lee sent the following telegram:

Havana, February 15, 1898
Maine blown up and destroyed to-night at 9.40 p.m. Explosion occurred well forward under quarters of crew:

consequence many were lost. It is believed that all officers were saved, but Jenkins and Merritt not yet accounted for. Cause of explosion yet to be investigated. Captain-General and Spanish army and navy officers have rendered every assistance.[8]

The whole *Maine* episode seems tragically inevitable. In retrospect, it would appear that Lee's first instincts were correct, to keep the U.S. ships out of the port of Havana but ready to steam over from Key West if they were needed. Putting a ship in harbor could be an intolerable irritant to the ultra Spanish volunteers and their followers and an invitation to extremists to do something, whether to the ship or to the crew on shore leave. Another possibility was that any accident to the ship or crew could be inflammatory to the already-outraged American public and Congress. Once the warship was in port, the consul general could not order its dismissal, for withdrawal would only be interpreted as a sign of weakness. This has always been the objection to using naval ships as instruments of diplomacy: they are hard to send away.

It appears today, long years after, that an accident caused the disaster.[9] But at the time, with extreme tensions and overriding passions of the adversaries and the relatively unsophisticated examination that could be made of the wreck in the muddy waters of Havana harbor, it was difficult for anyone in the United States to accept the explosion as an act of God rather than an act of Spanish extremists.

The captain of the *Maine* and the consul general were impressed with the obviously genuine shock to the Spanish authorities from the captain-general on down and their expressions of willingness to help in all regards. Captain Dwight Sigsbee of the *Maine* called for calm. In his first message to Washington immediately after the disaster he asked, "Public opinion should be suspended until further report." Lee also called for an inquiry with "hope [that] our people will repress excitement and calmly await decision."[10] Despite the horror of the disaster, with a major American warship sunk in an unfriendly harbor and 268 of the crew dead, Lee and Sigsbee acted in a professional and rational manner, without arrogance or patriotic histrionics, to care for the survivors and maintain businesslike relations with the Spanish while a U.S. naval board of inquiry investigated the explosion. The Spanish set up their own investigation. But in the United States the newspapers, especially the yellow press of New York, had already found the Spanish guilty.

The United State naval board of inquiry on 21 March 1898 found that the *Maine* had been blown up by a submarine mine, while the Spanish board stated that there was no evidence of a mine and that the explosion might have been the result of spontaneous combustion in one of the battleship's coal bunkers.[11] The United States Navy's report was accepted as the truth in the United States. With war imminent, Lee had to turn his attention to getting the many Americans in Cuba out of what was bound to be a war zone. By 10 April, Easter, Consul General Lee and most of the remaining Americans had left. The other American consuls in Cuba, Puerto Rico, the Philippines, and Spain were also on the move to neutral countries.

Back in Washington on 12 April Lee appeared before a Senate committee to testify on the *Maine* and on conditions in Cuba. He stated that he did not think that Captain-General Blanco had anything to do with the explosion. Lee had seen him almost immediately after the disaster, and Blanco was in tears, in a state of shock. Lee thought, however, that the explosion might have been arranged by followers of General Weyler and that "the man who did the work was an officer thoroughly acquainted with explosives of all sorts and who knew all about it. It was very well done." He said that a mine could have been dropped off a rowboat next to the *Maine* on a dark night.[12]

President McKinley on 11 April had already asked Congress to approve American military intervention to secure a stable government in Cuba, which meant war. Lee's testimony the day after as to the *Maine* disaster and the deplorable conditions on the island helped substantiate the congressional vote on 19 April that supported the president's call for intervention.

Lee's consular role ended with his Senate testimony, but he was slated for a larger part in the forthcoming war. In May he was commissioned a major general of volunteers and placed in command of the Seventh Army Corps, thus having the distinction of holding the rank of major general in both the Confederate and U.S. armies. His force was slated to lead the main invasion of Cuba at Havana, but the Spanish surrendered before this attack could be launched. The capture of Santiago de Cuba and the destruction of the Spanish fleet there caused the capitulation. Lee did bring his command to Cuba as part of the occupation, and so the former consul general returned to his consular district, Havana, much as had the former consul general in Tripoli, William Eaton, at the head of his troops. Lee later commanded the Military Department of the Missouri before his final retirement in 1901.

The contribution of other U.S. consuls in Cuba was almost negligible, as the U.S. military did not use them as political advisors. Because of the haphazard manner with which the Spanish-American War was organized, it is not surprising that the civilian expertise at hand was ignored by soldiers trying to mobilize for an unexpected campaign.

The American consul at San Juan, Puerto Rico, Philip C. Hanna, did help somewhat by giving the men planning the invasion of the island useful information as to the composition and quality of the defending Spanish forces. On the outbreak of hostilities Hanna had retired to the nearby island of St. Thomas; from there he telegraphed that "10,000 American soldiers landed in Puerto Rico can hold the island forever, because I am convinced that a large number of Puerto Ricans will arise and shake off the Spanish yoke as soon as they are assured of help."[13] This opinion was encouraging to Washington authorities who wanted to annex the island; the invasion in due course was accomplished as successfully as Hanna had predicted.

With the declaration of war, the American consuls in Spain left, as did the Spanish consuls in the United States. John H. Carroll, the American consul in Cadiz, went only to the British crown colony of Gibraltar, where he worked closely with Horatio Sprague, the long-time consul there (he served from 1848 to 1901).

The movements of the Spanish navy, even though it was somewhat inferior to that of the Americans, still posed a threat that had to be taken into account by military strategists in Washington. There were several possibilities for the Spanish fleet: to leave the major base of Cadiz for Cuba, to interdict American troop and supply ships between Florida and Cuba, to attack major U.S. ports, such as New York or Charleston, to attack American shipping on the high seas, or to go to the Philippines. As Gibraltar was a major shipping port, the consul was in a strategic position, able to observe and report on ships going through the straits on their way to the Suez Canal and possibly on to the Philippines. He could gather intelligence from neutral ships and, because Gibraltar was close to Cadiz, acquire information from the Spaniards who crossed the border every day. Cable connections with Washington were excellent for conveying intelligence from his observation post on the rock. During the Civil War Sprague reported on Confederate ship movements and helped prevent rebel raiders from restocking supplies, repairing engines, and coaling at Gibraltar. He was to render similar services in 1898.

The situation in the Philippines in 1898 somewhat paralleled that of Cuba: the Spanish were faced with a revolt that had started in 1896 and were unable either to completely quell it or institute the reforms that might have defused the spirit of rebellion. There was not, however, the American involvement that there had been in Cuba. American commercial interests there were minor. There was little news coming from the islands and little interest in trying to obtain that news. It is dubious that there was a single man in the State Department in 1898 who had ever been to the Philippines, and there was no Filipino-American community like the powerful Cuban-American one in the United States to exert pressure on Congress. With no political guidance from Washington, the American representatives on the spot, military and consular, were left to improvise, but with no surety that their decisions would be approved or supported by their government back home. Only one thing was sure: if war came, the United States Navy should attack the weaker Spanish naval force based in Manila. Once that was successfully accomplished, Commodore (later Admiral) Dewey, the Far Eastern commander, had to depend on his staff, the nearby American consuls, and his own judgment.

The 1896 revolt in the Philippines had been kept under reasonable control by the Spanish through a series of well-planned military operations supported by reinforcements from Spain. The principal surviving leader of the revolt was Emilio Aguinaldo, of mixed Tagalog and Chinese ancestry, who came from a moderately well-to-do family of Filipino landowners. Aguinaldo had called for the expulsion of the Spanish friars (who were a major propertied class in the islands), a large measure of autonomy from Spain, freedom of the press, religious toleration, and equal treatment for Filipinos vis-à-vis the Spanish.[14] The Spanish did not repeat their brutal and unsuccessful Cuban policy of the reconcentration of villagers in the rebellious Filipino provinces. They were able to beat the insurgent forces in the field and dangle moderate reforms and a payoff to the leaders for a cessation of hostilities in 1897. This carrot-and-stick policy worked for a short time. A general amnesty was declared in December 1897, and Aguinaldo agreed to accept banishment along with twenty-seven of his companions for a payment of 400,000 Mexican pesos.

Aguinaldo and his staff went with part of the 400,000 pesos to Hong Kong to bide their time, a time that came sooner than they had reason to expect because of an accident on an American battleship in a Cuban harbor. While Aguinaldo was out of the country, the insurgency did not completely cease, but instead broke out again in March 1898 on the islands of Luzon, Cebu, and Panay.

The Americans who dealt with the situation in the Philippines were the commander of the United States Asiatic Squadron of four small but modern cruisers and two gunboats, Commodore George Dewey, and the consuls in Hong Kong, Manila, and Singapore. Dewey was a sixty-one-year-old naval officer with a rather average career of over forty years and many routine assignments. He was a straightforward naval commander who would do what he was ordered without hesitation. The most important trait of Dewey in the Philippine episode was his willingness to listen to advice, consider it, and then to take direct action without undue worry. An indecisive commander of the Asiatic Squadron in 1898 could have changed the history of the United States in Asia. Dewey had not spent as much of his time on foreign cruises as had many of his contemporaries. He had developed little sense of diplomacy or sophistication in international affairs. A significant part of his service had been concerned with supervising the care and upkeep of lighthouses off the coast of the United States. The new commodore arrived in Nagasaki, Japan, on New Year's Day 1898 to take over his command. It was his first trip to the Far East.[15]

The beginning of 1898 also saw another new arrival to the Orient, Oscar F. Williams, the consul to Manila. Williams, fifty-four years old, had been born in upstate New York and had been the president of the first class to graduate from Cornell University. He had been a teacher and then through contacts in the Republican party had received an appointment by the Harrison administration in 1889 as the U.S. consul to Le Havre, France. After a four-year tour there an appointee of the new Democratic administration replaced him. When the Republicans were back in power under McKinley, Williams applied for another consular appointment and was given that in Manila. There had been no consideration in Washington that because of rising tensions between Spain and the United States it might be well to have a man with a military background at the post. Williams was just a run-of-the mill political appointee with no military experience, but he proved to be a solid performer, showing courage and intelligence under difficult conditions. He was of considerable use to Dewey as the commodore prepared for his attack on the Spanish.

Leaving his wife behind in Rochester, New York, Williams

arrived in the Philippines after a forty-seven-day voyage on 24 January 1898, just three weeks before the *Maine* was blown up. It normally could take months for a newly arrived consul to meet the right people in his district, cultivate their confidence, and develop a sensitivity to conditions at a new post, even a tranquil one. Williams did not have the time. The Spanish-Filipino environment was new to him. The insurgency had reached serious proportions, and it was obvious after the explosion in Havana harbor on 15 February that war between Spain and the United States could break out at any moment. Manila was an obvious target for the American naval forces in the Far East. The new consul, however, wasted no time bewailing his lack of time to learn his district. He began a series of reports on the political situation in the islands, anticipating that these could be of use to the policymakers back in Washington. In his 22 February report Williams wrote, "War exists. Battles are of almost daily occurrence. Ambulances bring in many wounded and hospitals are full. Prisoners are brought here and shot without trial, and Manila is under martial law. Insurgents are being armed and drilled, are rapidly increasing in numbers and efficiency, and all agree a general uprising will come as soon as the Governor General embarks for Spain, which is fixed for March."[16] In the short time he had been at his post, Williams had not fallen into the trap of letting himself be taken over by the colonial rulers or succumbing to their censorship. He had quickly developed his own sources of information beyond the ruling clique in Manila. Because of the controls over cable messages going in and out of the Philippines, Williams sent his dispatches out on British or other foreign ships, which usually would stop at Hong Kong, some 700 miles away, where the U.S. consul would have his information passed on to Washington.

Williams was not a cold, objective reporter and analyst of the kaleidoscope of political and military developments in the Philippines. Rumor, supposition, and exaggeration were included in his reports without being labeled as such. The insurrection was probably not as extensive as he reported it to be in early 1898. Williams was also a solid American patriot who believed that there was nothing that could not be solved by supplanting decadent Spanish rule with enlightened American rule, and this perception colored his dispatches.[17] Furthermore, matters on the islands were so unclear that even the best of reporters might not have been able to gather all the pertinent facts to make a well-balanced report until the war was over.

Although Williams's reports helped to keep Washington informed, of far greater importance was the line of communication that Williams developed with George Dewey in Hong Kong, where the commodore waited with his Far Eastern squadron for the war and the expected orders to attack the Spanish flotilla at Manila. Dewey had sent a message to Williams in Manila on February 17: "I beg that you inform me what Spanish war vessels are present and what, if any changes there have been in the land defenses of that port in recent years."

The Spanish were quite aware of Williams's potential as an intelligence agent. The Spanish consuls in the United States were reporting on American warlike preparations, and the Spanish consul in Hong Kong checked on the presence of Dewey's squadron almost hourly. Williams wrote to Dewey's flag secretary, his point of contact in Hong Kong, that spies watched him constantly and that he suspected that the key to the safe in the consulate had been duplicated and was in Spanish hands. Under the circumstances Williams did not rely on the immunity of the consular premises to secure important documents but carried them on his person or destroyed them after reading them.[19]

Although he had no military training, Williams responded enthusiastically to Dewey's request for information concerning Spanish warships and land defenses. Unencumbered by having a family at the post, Williams seemed to be working on a "twenty-five-hour day." In mid-March he informed the Department of State: "I have no instructions from you as to these delicate complications but so far have gotten on well. I fly our flag all the time. Give double hours to the consulate and have notified the Americans that they can find me at any hour at the Consulate, at my hotel or on the path between.[20]

Williams complained that he was not kept abreast of the developing situation between Spain and the United States and that he was "depending upon unofficial reports. I must act as if peace reigned." The consul was probably fortunate. Instructions from a Washington official with no idea of what the situation was like in Manila at that time would only have inhibited and confused him. Although the consulate stayed open double hours, Williams still traveled about the city performing his intelligence chores for Dewey. The consul wrote on 31 March, "For nearly the entire period of my incumbency every odd hour of the day and many evenings have been given to the inspections of forts, arsenals, and battleships to fully inform Commodore Dewey at Hong Kong."

The military information that he obtained from his rambles and from callers at his office was good. He reported that the defenses of Manila were weak and that "any two U.S. ships could enter the port, silence the forts, and capture the city."[21] Although he may have exaggerated somewhat the ease of capturing Manila itself by a naval force, Williams was correct about the harbor defenses. Of major importance were the consul's continuing observations on the possibility of mines in Manila Bay, which were of great concern to Dewey. Williams had become privy to sensitive information and was able to convey to the commodore, as late as 5 April, the vital information that the mines could not be armed because the necessary insulated wire had not yet arrived from Europe.[23]

On 7 April 1898 the Department of State cabled Williams to close down the consulate and place American interests in the hands of the British consul. Williams cabled back: "Go where, no steamer." The department replied that if worst came to worst he could go to a neutral consulate until the Spanish allowed him to board a steamer to leave what was apparently going to be hostile territory.

There was a touch of braggadocio in Williams's dispatch of 11 April, less than a fortnight before the declaration of war. He informed the Department of State that he would leave Manila only if ordered, "but unless you order me to leave I shall not go – but face the music to give all possible aid to American interests and all information to our commodore." Williams felt that staying on could save the United States millions of dollars and some lives, "so you let me alone. If the U.S. fleet comes here I believe Spain will lose all her battleships, here stationed, in one day, and before 48 hours after the attack, the Stars and Stripes will float over Manila and these marvelously rich and beautiful islands – about 2000 in number – will become colonies of the United States."[24]

Common sense finally prevailed. Williams had been harassed by constant surveillance; there had been threats against his life. Realizing that he could do more for the cause by briefing Dewey in Hong Kong than waiting for internment in Manila, he turned his consulate over to the protection of the British consul and left 23 April on the *Esmeralda*, a Hong Kong–bound steamer. Two days prior to his departure Williams took the time to send to the State Department a report on a new tobacco tax imposed by the Spanish.[25]

In Hong Kong Commodore Dewey made ready. His ships were painted, transforming them from the white with buff trim of peacetime to dull gray. British sympathies were on the American side, but by 24 April, because of the war threat, the British governor was forced to ask Dewey to leave in order to keep up the appearance of neutrality in accordance with international law. The commodore took his squadron to Mirs Bay, near Hong Kong but in Chinese waters. An extraordinary incident in the history of the American consular service took place in Mirs Bay. The entire striking force of the United States in Far Eastern waters waited two days until the consul from Manila could join them. Dewey had received orders to attack the Spanish at once but was willing to wait for Williams's last-minute information on the state of Spanish defenses.[26] Williams joined the squadron on 27 April, brought there by the Hong Kong tug *Fame*.

The consul was brought immediately on board the flagship *Olympia* to brief Dewey and his commanders. As soon as he had finished reporting the latest news from Manila, the squadron weighed anchor and sailed for the Philippines with Williams on board. During the passage he was allowed to exercise his own brand of "stem-winding" in a speech to the crew about the indignities he had suffered in Manila and how his life had been threatened and the United States and its flag had been insulted. According to a diarist on the *Olympia*, "When he got through every mother's son of us cheered and cursed the Spaniards."[27]

Prior to the battle at Manila Bay another commanders' conference was held and battle stations were taken. Williams was transferred to the cruiser Baltimore for the first part of the battle. Ironically, it was the only American ship hit, but the consul was not hurt. At one point Dewey's ships withdrew to check on ammunition and feed the crews. Williams was transferred back to the *Olympia* and on the bridge with Dewey saw the final destruction of the Spanish ships.

After the battle the United States Navy reigned in Manila Bay, but lacked land forces for a takeover of Manila. The Spanish still had a considerable garrison in the city and forces scattered throughout the archipelago. Of the approximately 26,000 Spanish regular troops and 14,000 militia in the islands, some 9,000 were in Manila. The Filipino insurgency, however, tied down most of this Spanish force, including that in the Manila area. Without sizeable United States Army reinforcements Dewey could not hope to take over and hold the city unless the Spanish were to cooperate fully and, in effect, garrison it for their American conquerors against the growing insurgency. This was not an immediate prospect. Dewey's ships floated unmolested in the bay, the Spanish waited in their city, and the Filipino insurgents gathered.

At this point events set in motion by three consular officers began to dominate the political and military scene in the Philippines and would have repercussions for years afterwards in those islands. The three American consuls from Singapore, Hong Kong, and Manila pushed Emilio Aguinaldo into returning immediately to the Philippines to take command of the insurgent forces, a political act initiated solely by the consuls. There was no direction from Washington in this matter, and it is doubtful if there could have been since there was no consensus within the U.S. government in April and May 1898 as to American policy in the Philippines. The consuls depended upon their instinct and judgment as to the Filipino reaction to American intervention in the affairs of the Philippines, a judgment that proved right at the time, but later sadly wrong. Though he was a great help to U.S. forces in ending Spanish rule, Aguinaldo became a major obstacle to the American takeover of the colony.

The prelude to the Aguinaldo problem took place in Singapore as the United States and Spain were going to war in mid-April 1898. Aguinaldo had gone first to Hong Kong on his well-paid exile, but because of legal problems in the crown colony (there was a quarrel over the disbursing of the pesos given Aguinaldo and his followers) he found it advisable to depart for Europe. On his way Aguinaldo stopped over in Singapore, where E. Spencer Pratt was consul general.

In Singapore an Englishman sympathetic to the Filipino cause arranged a meeting at a boardinghouse between the consul general and the insurgent leader. Pratt immediately saw the advantage of engaging Aguinaldo's cooperation with the American naval force, then preparing to attack the Spanish at Manila (this was on 24 April). Pratt had no instructions for such an approach; Aguinaldo's arrival was fortuitous, not anticipated by the State Department, where attention was on Cuba and Spain, not on the Far East.

Pratt, previously U.S. minister to Persia, was not a cautious diplomat, but a man willing to take on responsibility. The United States had several such men in the Far East. These American consuls were eager to show initiative and put together an ad hoc alliance with the Filipino insurgency without waiting for instructions from Washington.

Concerning his discussion with Aguinaldo, Pratt reported:

I took it upon myself whilst explaining that I had no authority to speak for the government, to point out the danger of continuing independent action at this state and convinced him of the expediency of cooperation with our fleet then at Hong Kong and [obtained] the assurances of his willingness to proceed hither and confer with Commodore Dewey.[28]

Pratt cabled Dewey, "Aguinaldo, insurgent leader here. Will come Hong Kong arrange with Commodore for general cooperation insurgents Manila if possible." Dewey replied immediately, "Tell Aguinaldo come as soon as possible."[29]

In a second meeting Pratt and Aguinaldo barely touched upon the political future of the Philippines. As Pratt described it, the "General further stated that he hoped the United States would assume protection of the Philippines for at least long enough to establish a Government of their own, in the organization of which he would desire the American Government's advice and assistance. Pratt was careful to inform the Department of State that "these questions I told him I had no authority to discuss."[30]

The conversations between Pratt and Aguinaldo were themselves a cause of controversy. The Filipino leader claimed that Pratt had committed the United States to Filipino independence, an absurdity that Aguinaldo must have known. Pratt had no authority to make such a commitment, and Aguinaldo made no effort in his dealings with other American officials in Hong Kong or Manila to confirm what he claimed had been offered him. It is quite possible that Pratt was more generous in his praise of the insurgency than he indicated in his dispatches to Washington. Also, Aguinaldo may have felt that the consul general had been more positive about the eventual independence of the Philippines than was actually indicated. Both Pratt and Aguinaldo wanted to keep their lines of communication open; it is doubtful whether any concessions were demanded or given.

When Pratt's dispatch regarding his second conversation with Aguinaldo arrived at the State Department seven weeks later, a note was made on it (22 June 1898) that Pratt was only following instructions to "get unconditional assistance of General Aguinaldo, but not to make any political pledges."[31] It is difficult to understand what these instructions were, if any. Perhaps the unknown person making the note thought that such instructions had been given to Pratt. It was only later, when relations between Aguinaldo's insurgents and American troops in Manila turned sour, that Pratt was accused of either misleading Aguinaldo or being his dupe.[32] In the early stages of the war in the Far East, Dewey, Pratt, Aguinaldo, and the State Department were quite satisfied with developments.

In Hong Kong, American consul Rounsevelle Wildman met Aguinaldo on his return from Singapore. As Dewey had already sailed, Wildman and the Filipino general had time to get acquainted while Aguinaldo waited for transport to the Philippines. Wildman was experienced in the Far East, having served as the consul in Singapore from 1890 to 1893 during the Harrison administration. He was out of the service during the Cleveland period, but back in for the McKinley administration, this time as the consul in Hong Kong.

Wildman had already had a brush with the Filipino insurrectionary movement and had been slightly burned. Prior to Aguinaldo's exile a Filipino, Felipe Agoncillo, had called on Consul Wildman in late 1897 to propose an alliance between the United States and the insurgent forces. Agoncillo was anticipating a war between Spain and the United States (this was several months prior to the sinking of the *Maine*) and wanted to ensure American help when hostilities began. Agoncillo asked that the United States provide the insurgents with guns. As surety for this aid he offered "two provinces and the customs house at Manila" until the debt was repaid.[33] Wildman passed this startling proposal on to Washington; some months later he was told by the State Department: "You should not encourage any advances on the part of Mr. Agoncillo, and should courteously decline to communicate with the Department further regarding his alleged mission."[34]

Wildman considered himself an expert on the Philippines, although it is unclear whether he ever visited the islands; he certainly had never served there. His knowledge was based on his having worked among the Malays in Singapore. Wildman maintained that since the Filipinos were of the same stock, what held true for one group would hold true for the other. With typical nineteenth-century condescension the consul wrote: "I rank them [Filipinos] among the semi-civilized nations of the earth."[35] He meant that as a compliment.

Consul Wildman in Hong Kong had been impressed by Aguinaldo, as had the consul in Singapore. In his discussions with Aguinaldo, Wildman heard only what he wanted to hear and reported on the aspirations of the insurgents: "I know they are fighting for annexation to the United States, first, and for independence secondly, if the United States decides to decline sovereignty of the islands."[36] Aguinaldo kept his own counsel about his plans for the future.

Aguinaldo left Hong Kong for Luzon on the USS *McCulloch*, a naval transport. As described by Wildman's brother Edwin, then vice consul in Hong Kong, getting Aguinaldo and his companions on board the *McCulloch* was like a comic opera scene. Because of the sensitive nature of sending an insurrectionary leader on an American warship from the neutral British port to the Philippines, the Wildmans wanted to keep the boarding as unobtrusive as possible. When Rounsevelle Wildman reached the wharf at midnight, to his horror he saw Aguinaldo accompanied by his friends strutting majestically up and down with an air of solemn greatness and wearing enormous Filipino hats with gorgeous republican cockades. "The Consul General was panic stricken – whisking the monstrous hats from the heads of the astonished Filipino generals, he hustled them on board with sharp words of indignation."[37]

Wildman had provided Aguinaldo far more than simply moral support in the early days of the war. With 50,000 Mexican pesos entrusted to him by the Filipino leader, the consul had purchased in China 2,282 Remington rifles and 176,550 cartridges, which were delivered to the insurgents in late May. He had also arranged for another such shipment that was supposedly paid for with 67,000 pesos but never arrived for reasons that are unclear.[38]

Once in the Philippines, Aguinaldo worked independently, organizing his forces for fighting a series of minor battles throughout the islands in an attempt to overcome the many garrisons and besiege Manila, where the Spanish still held strong. He took care not to antagonize the Americans, who were careful not to antagonize him. Both the Filipinos and Americans had one aim, to defeat the Spanish. For the time being they needed each other.

In the spring and summer of 1898 the United States had no policy as to the Philippine Islands' future, whether they were to be independent, be returned to Spain, become an American colony, or perhaps be turned over, all or in part, to a different European power, such as Germany. Not until the late fall of 1898 was the decision made by the McKinley administration to annex the islands.

With such a vacuum in American policy it is no wonder that the consuls were confused and sometimes outright incorrect. During the siege of Manila Oscar Williams, working on the USS *Baltimore*, acted as a de facto political advisor to Dewey, now an admiral. In June 1898 Williams wrote: "It has been my effort to maintain harmony with the insurgents – in order to exercise greater influence hereafter when we reorganize government."[39] At that point he had no idea how that reorganization would evolve. His main concern was that the insurgents treat captured Spaniards humanely, which in general was done.

As the siege of Manila moved toward a climax in late July, there was apprehension that Aguinaldo and his forces might assume control of their own destiny while American leaders in Washington were still trying to make up their minds. Dewey was concerned about clashes between United States Army troops sent to the Philippines and Filipino soldiers, who shared the siege lines around Manila with their American quasi-allies. For most of the war the Filipinos had borne the brunt of the fighting, with the Johnny-comelately United States Army forces appearing only for the last act. Despite the major effort of the insurgents, Admiral Dewey thought that Aguinaldo was not sufficiently deferential to American control.

When Wildman heard of the growing tension between Aguinaldo and the Americans, he wrote him: "Do not forget that the United States undertook this war for the sole purpose of relieving the Cubans from the cruelties under which they were suffering and not for the love of conquest or the hope of gain. Whatever the final disposition of the conquered territory may be, you can trust to the United States that justice and honor will control all their dealings with you."[40]

Wildman, not knowing that he was obviously out of touch or when to leave matters alone, wrote the Department of State: "I know I can influence Aguinaldo and can hold him and his provisional Government absolutely in line with American policy and American interests."[41] While open hostilities between the Americans and the insurgents had not yet broken out, it was too late, had it ever been at all possible, to talk Aguinaldo into acquiescing to American rule. Wildman, however, was not sitting on the sidelines in Hong Kong giving gratuitous advice; he was an active participant in the war. Hong Kong served somewhat the same function it was to serve during the Vietnam War (1960-75) as a supply center for the United States Navy and Army fighting in the Philippines. During the war Wildman kept his office open from six in the morning to eleven at night every day to handle mail for American soldiers and sailors, which was first sent to Hong Kong to be sorted and forwarded both to and from the United States and the war zone. He acted as a kind of social worker, answering hundreds of letters from anxious mothers and relatives of the men in uniform. He was also an unofficial purchasing agent for servicemen, as there was no PX or its equivalent in the Philippines. As he reported, "They have no one else to look to or to aid them. Hong Kong is their world. I do not complain, it is a pleasure for me, but there are only four of us and with the expected added work of a port like Hong Kong, in War Time, we cannot keep up the pace."[42] Wildman was eventually given more staff and was rewarded in due course for his conscientious service when his post was elevated to that of consulate general. In Manila Bay, sweltering in his temporary consular office on board the USS *Baltimore*, Oscar Williams began to worry about his future. The American army and the Filipino insurgent forces were poised to take Manila. As the summer of 1898 dragged on, a groundswell of public opinion was developing in the United States that once the islands were in American hands, they should not be let go. If the Philippines became a colony of the United States, there would be no job for a U.S. consul in Manila. Anticipating American rule, Williams wrote to the State Department, asking to be considered for the prospective position of general commissioner of customs for the Philippines or that of a lighthouse inspector or general commissioner for agriculture. If none of those, perhaps he might be appointed superintendent of public education. Williams pointed out that he had been a student of the tariff, a teacher, a farmer, and an author.[43] The Department of State informed the consul that he was being premature.

By 22 August, Williams had reopened his consulate in Manila. He continued as a point of contact with Aguinaldo and pushed to have the Filipino leaders invited to the United States to see its size, wonder, and power. Williams thought that the U.S. government would save money by paying the insurgent forces a hefty bonus before discharging them. If Aguinaldo and other Filipino leaders were given some recognition for their part in defeating the Spanish and a proper amount of money, the "independent government movement here will dissolve like ice under a tropical sun."[44] However, the U.S. military in the field and the government in Washington brushed aside his advice.

With the expulsion of the Spanish from the Philippines and the peace treaty (Treaty of Paris) of 10 December 1898, which turned the islands over to the United States, Williams was soon out of a job. The consulate in Manila was closed on 1 July 1899. By that time Aguinaldo had declared independence and had turned the insurrection against the brand-new colonial power, the United States of America. A bitter guerrilla war was fought from 1899 to 1901 before the Philippines were firmly in American hands.

Rounseville Wildman continued in his consular position in Hong Kong until 1901. He and his family were lost at sea in the same year on their way back to the United States. E. Spencer Pratt remained at his post as consul general in Singapore until June 1899, when he was replaced by another Alabamian, who died there after only six months. The next consul appointed to Singapore committed suicide in the United States. Chosen to replace the suicide of what appeared to be a hard-luck post was the ex-consul to Manila, Oscar F. Williams, who served as consul general from 1901 to 1905. He died in Singapore shortly after another appointee replaced him.

After the Philippine struggle was over, with the United States in firm control, Aguinaldo captured, and the insurgency dead, the American Congress held a hearing on the events that had led to fighting between American troops and the Filipino insurgents, at which Admiral Dewey was a major witness. He tried to put some distance between himself and the three consuls, Pratt, Williams, and Wildman. They had, according to Dewey, forced Aguinaldo upon him. When asked if the consuls had the power to make him accept the insurgent leader, Dewey replied:

> Yes, they had in a way. They had not the official power, but one will yield after a while to constant pressure. I did not expect anything of them [the Filipinos]; I did not think they would do anything; I would not have taken them; I did not want them; I did not believe in them; because, when I left Hong Kong, I was led to suppose that the country was in a state of insurrection, and that at my first gun, as Mr. Williams put it, there would be a general uprising, and I thought these half dozen or dozen refugees at Hong Kong would play a very small part in it.[45]

The admiral was disingenuous. After the cooperation between the American navy (and later the American army) and Aguinaldo's forces soured following the Spanish defeat and the peace treaty that awarded the Philippines to the United States, it was politically wise to diminish the importance of the insurgents in the conquest of the Philippines. Dewey, considering himself a possible candidate for the presidency, was politically cautious. No military leader would have turned down the potential help that Aguinaldo and his forces represented at the time of the attack on the Spanish in the Philippines.

The three consuls involved, complete amateurs in political-military matters, had not done badly for the United States. At considerable danger to himself, Oscar Williams had performed an invaluable service for Dewey in keeping him informed of the defenses of Manila Bay. Pratt, Wildman, and Williams had been instrumental in getting the cooperation of the Filipino insurrectionary movement. Wildman set up a useful military post office and post exchange service without needing elaborate instructions from Washington. Wildman did with four men for the soldiers and sailors fighting in the Philippines the same functions for U.S. forces in the field that during the Vietnam War took thousands of Americans and other nationals to perform. The generally effective ad hoc work of these consuls stands in stark contrast to the overstaffed, overmanaged, and overelaborate U.S. political and military systems in place throughout the world more than half a century later.

15

A Professional Consular Service
(1860–1914)

From the end of the Civil War until the turn of the century a noticeable change took place in the patronage pattern in the consular service. In the early years the service was often a refuge for men engaged in the arts, such as Nathaniel Hawthorne, James Fenimore Cooper, William Dean Howells, and others of lesser renown who looked to a consular post to ease their financial burdens or give them some social status abroad. In the postwar industrial age men of arts were pushed aside to make room for former generals and other military men who had served either the North or the South in the Civil War. Now the few writers attaining a consulship were more likely to have been newspapermen than novelists or essayists, indicating perhaps a new emphasis on the practical, the here and now.

One major American literary figure, however, managed to become a consul in the postwar years. Francis Bret Harte was not the prototype of the bluff, uncouth Westerner as portrayed in his stories but a transplanted Easterner, something of a dandy who cared little for the Californians. In fact, he had spent almost no time in any mining community.

Bret Harte gained renown from a number of short stories published between 1868 and 1870, notably "The Outcasts of Poker Flat" and "The Luck of Roaring Camp," and the poem "The Heathen Chinee." Having achieved success, Harte quickly returned to the East, where he seemed to have lost his literary fire, for his later writing, although prolific, never approached his early success. A magazine he had helped establish collapsed. By 1878 he was desperate, with a family to support and a paltry income. As had others in similar straits, he turned to the State Department for help. Harte's father had been a college classmate of former Secretary of State William Seward. Seward's son Frederick was the assistant secretary. Using this tenuous tie and his earlier literary fame, Harte (with only twenty dollars in his pocket) saw Frederick Seward and through him gained an interview with President Hayes, who promised him some sort of appointment. Harte had hoped to go to St. Petersburg as a secretary to the legation but realized he could not afford diplomatic life. Instead he accepted an appointment as commercial agent in Crefeld, Germany, and went, leaving his family behind.[1]

Crefeld, a small city on the Rhine near Dusseldorf, exported silk and velvet products. Through the collection of fees Harte was able to earn approximately $2,500 a year. Although the post eased his financial concerns, he was miserable in Crefeld. He was a cosmopolitan; a German bourgeois backwater was not for him. He spoke no German, had no liking for the trade of commercial agent, and cared little for Germans as a people. He escaped Crefeld when possible, traveling to Paris and London and leaving the consular work in the hands of his assistant, a German. Harte gave a series of lectures and readings of his work whenever he visited England, enjoying a congenial society wherein his literary reputation was appreciated. Success in England made it difficult to settle down in Crefeld and respond enthusiastically to such assignments as a request from the appraiser of the Port of New York to send on "as full and exact information as possible, respecting the price of hatbands."[2]

Harte's position as a commercial agent rather than as a consul rankled him. His status with the Germans seemed diminished because he was not "Herr Consul." He began calling himself a consul and his letters bore the title of U.S. consul, but the State Department records continued to list him as a commercial agent.

Pleading ill health because of the damp climate along the Rhine, Harte, with the influence of friends in Washington, was transferred to the Glasgow consulate in 1880. The climate in Scotland was no improvement over that of the Rhineland, but Harte was in a much more hospitable environment. He now officially had the title of consul; his salary was $3,000. He no longer had to cope with a foreign language and was recognized in Great Britain as an important literary figure.

During the five years from 1880 to 1885 Harte spent much of his time in London tending to his literary endeavors. As he explained to his wife, still in the United States, he left his office in Glasgow in the hands of his vice consul, "a hardheaded Scotch lawyer and devoted to my service. In fact, I'm rather a good Consul. All I believe they can say about me is that I don't go much into society, and that I escape the fogs of Glasgow whenever I can, but even when I am away, all my letters and documents pass under my eye, and I telegraph often twice a day."[3]

Despite criticism of him as a part-time consul, Harte was able to keep up his intermittent "tending of the store" until the new Democratic administration under Cleveland came into power in 1885, when Harte, along with most of the Republican-appointed consuls, was removed from office. Having found that London suited him, Bret Harte never returned to the United States but stayed on in Great Britain, earning his living more or less as a hack writer. His wife finally joined him in 1898. He died in 1902 of throat cancer.

More typical of the late nineteenth-century use of consular patronage was the giving of a few assignments to men active in archaeology and exploration, in which there was increasing American interest. Newspaper accounts of the great explorations of Africa and other far-off, exotic places had an avid readership. There were then few charitable foundations or wealthy individuals to finance archaeologists and explorers. Universities, with rare exceptions, were not equipped to support expeditions. The U.S. government was in a position to assist a few of these archaeologists and explorers as consular appointees.

Edward Herbert Thompson (1865–1934) was an explorer and archaeologist sponsored by the American Antiquarian Society. President Cleveland gave him the consulship at Merida in Yucatan, Mexico, with the understanding that the consul would be free to investigate the Mayan ruins there. Though he had no formal training in archaeology, Thompson was an ardent student of the ancient culture, learning the local languages and going for long exploratory trips into the interior of Yucatan, leaving the few consular chores in the hands of his vice consul. This archaeologist *cum* consul spent over forty years exploring, studying, and writing about Yucatan and the Mayans. He was the consul in Merida from 1885 to 1893, then consul in Progreso, Mexico, from 1897 to 1909.[4] Thompson was not the only archaeologist to enjoy the freedom to pursue his profession while more or less acting as a consul, but his career was one of the longest and most rewarding. Other archaeologists and explorers served off and on in consular positions in Baghdad, Jerusalem, and Cairo.

The consular service has not been without its share of adventurers and colorful characters. Such a person was John S. Crosby, who served in Florence, Italy, between 1876 and 1882. When a young man, he had made the rarely attempted crossing of South America from Valparaíso to Montevideo just for the thrill of it. During the Civil War he won promotion to lieutenant colonel mainly through acts of bravery as a special courier. After the war he served with General Philip Sheridan in his campaigns against the Indians. Congress awarded him a medal in recognition of his bravery in saving lives after a boat disaster. When he was appointed consul in Florence, Crosby did not confine himself to strolling through the art galleries and assisting American painters seeking inspiration in Tuscany. The king of Italy decorated the stalwart Crosby for having been responsible for capturing a band of notorious bandits that had plagued the countryside.

After leaving Florence as consul, Crosby became the territorial governor of Montana (1882–84), during which time he was credited with keeping Yellowstone Park free of commercial exploitation. His final job, considerably different from his adventurous career and perhaps the most daunting, was as a school commissioner in New York City. He died in 1914 some months after an attack by a crazed servant.[5]

From the administration of Grant (1869–1877) until the election of Woodrow Wilson in 1912 the Department of State had only sent black ministers to head the U.S. legations in Haiti and Liberia. In the consular service, however, a few African-Americans were sent routinely to posts in Europe, Asia, and Latin America. One such appointee was Richard T. Greener, the first black to receive a degree from Harvard, in 1870. After some years of teaching, law practice, and work for the United States Treasury, Greener turned to politics as a Republican. In 1898 McKinley appointed him to be the consul in Bombay, but because of plague there Greener did not go, but was sent instead to Vladivostok, Russia, where he served as the American commercial agent.

It seemed that the Consular Service was becoming more and more a hodgepodge of artistic, ethnic, military, scientific and political reward for deserving Americans in the latter quarter of the 19th Century. There really was little else in the presidential desk drawer to hand out that would not cost money.

One of the more distinguished men in American politics in the post–Civil War era was Thomas Nast, the cartoonist, who was born in Germany in 1840 and brought to New York when he was six. By his late teens he was already an established illustrator and cartoonist for Harper's Weekly and Frank Leslie's Illustrated Newspaper. From the 1860s to the 1880s Nast was one of the most powerful influences in journalism, attacking Southerners for their outrages against black ex-slaves and making Horace Greeley, the Democratic presidential candidate in 1872, a figure of fun. He was the man most responsible for destroying Boss Tweed and the Tammany gang in New York City. He invented the symbols of the Democratic donkey and the Republican elephant.[6]

By the 1890s Nast was burned out. His political force as a cartoonist was waning, and he was having difficulty earning a living. In 1902 he turned to President Theodore Roosevelt for help. Because of his past services to the Republican Party, the president appointed Nast consul at Guayaquil, the port city of Ecuador. Sadly, this appointment proved to be the death of the cartoonist. Shortly after his arrival in Guayaquil, a notorious pesthole, Nast died of fever.[7]

Nast joined an already-long list of consular officers who died abroad of yellow fever, plague, epidemic, and other diseases that they probably would not have been exposed to had they stayed safely at home. Catastrophes were not always due to venturing into areas known to be dangerous. Several consuls and their families were killed in earthquakes. A consul and his wife lost their lives after the volcano of Mount Pelge erupted on the island of Martinique in 1902. William Palfrey, the first consul to be named by Congress, died at sea before reaching France in 1780 among many others who died on their ways to and from their posts. The names of those who gave their lives in the service are engraved on a plaque in the State Department in Washington. The author had a moment of concern that he and his family might join the list when a severe earthquake in Naples shook the consular building and residence in 1980.

A harbinger of the new soon to be more professional consular service was the hiring in 1900 of a young expatriate American as consular clerk in Budapest at a salary of $1,000. The consul in Budapest was Frank D. Chester, a Boston-bred, Harvard-educated (BA, 1891; MA, 1892; PhD, 1894) student of Semitic languages. Chester presided over a staff of four or five young men, none trained in consular work. The newly recruited clerk, Fiorello La Guardia, only eighteen, started at the bottom but soon proved invaluable to the consul because of his energy, willingness, and a skill in learning languages that closely paralleled that of the consul himself.

Fiorello was the son of Achille La Guardia, an Italian-born United States Army bandmaster. His mother was from Trieste, then part of the Austro-Hungarian Empire. La Guardia spent most of his boyhood at a series of western military outposts in North Dakota and Arizona. During the Spanish-American War Achille La Guardia became ill, retired from the army on a pension of eight dollars per month, and took his family to Trieste to run a small hotel, where he died after a few years. While his father was struggling with the hotel business, Fiorello started his own career. Through a friend he obtained the consular clerk's position in Budapest, which is what was to be a brilliant career in New York and the U.S. government.

Undaunted by the lack of a formal university education, La Guardia spent three years in Budapest taking dictation, making out invoices, and preparing reports. Consul Chester found one fault in La Guardia's work – his handwriting was a scrawl. The consulate had no typewriter, and as the consul noted, his clerk "was deficient in penmanship." Despite this problem La Guardia so improved himself in other matters that Chester appointed him to the consular agency in Fiume.

La Guardia was the sole American representative in what had become a major point of exodus for the great wave of emigration from Central Europe to the United States at the beginning of the century. In the three years La Guardia served in Fiume, he gave consular clearance to about 20,000 Slavs, Magyars, Germans, Jews, and Italians embarking for New York, most of whom became his constituents when he was later mayor of that city.

Consuls did not begin issuing emigrant visas until the World War I period, but much earlier they were supposed to "certify to the health of all passengers and crews and give the ship a certificate that it had cleared from a port free from contagious diseases or illness subject to quarantine regulations and that bedding and other household goods had been properly fumigated."[10] These instructions were vague and were often overlooked or treated as a pro forma exercise by the U.S. consuls at embarkation points, but not by the new consular agent in Fiume.

La Guardia observed that a certain number of would-be immigrants out of every shipload that left Fiume were turned back at Ellis Island for medical reasons and forced to return to the embarkation port with their passage money forfeit and families often separated. What was true of Fiume was true of every port from which emigrants left for the New World. The consular agent in Fiume, now only twenty-one, decided to do something about this sad condition.

To spare families the possible anguish of being broken apart at Ellis Island and stripped of their finances, La Guardia insisted that the Cunard line and other shipping lines servicing Fiume medically examine all emigrants before they were given passage. The shipping companies were appalled at the delays and expense but could not refuse. No ship could land passengers in the United States without a consular clearance, and La Guardia would not sign unless there had been a medical examination. The shipping agents complained to Washington, but the consular agent was supported by the State Department.[11]

Although La Guardia certainly had the best interests of the emigrants at heart, he enjoyed tweaking the noses of those in authority, a trait that continued throughout his career. Clearly consular work was too limited for the dynamic young consular agent at Fiume, and La Guardia resigned from the consular service in 1906. He went on to become a congressman and later the most popular and successful mayor New York City ever had. He had a firsthand knowledge of the immigrant origins of many of his constituents. He knew their problems, could speak most of their languages, and never failed to bypass the bureaucrats, if necessary, to help ordinary citizens. His consular training could not have been put to better use.

But momentum was building to recruit similar young men who could look to a lifetime career as consuls without depending on political influence. Too many consuls who had earned their laurels in other fields entered the consular service looking upon their positions as rewards rather than challenges. Recruiting officers into the lowest ranks and moving them up an established career ladder was a way to ensure a certain uniformity of competence.

"That the organization of your consular system is irrational and antiquated, and that in many respects fails in its manifest purposes, is generally admitted." So began an article entitled "Consular Evils and the Remedy" in the Dry Goods Economist of 1893. This was the voice of the consumer, the American businessman, who was increasingly dependent on consular work for developing an overseas market and who did not like the unevenness of consular work abroad. The growth of urban business, industry, commerce, and finance in the United States was an imperative in the professionalizing of the American consular service.

The Dry Goods Economist noted the inability of some consuls

to "even speak or write English correctly." There was also the problem of sending the right person to a post, taking due regard for local prejudices, "however unreasonable those prejudices may seem to us." The writer noted that in some cities Jews or blacks would not be acceptable and their ability to work as consuls would be limited. Another point made was that it was not wise to send foreign emigrants back to their native land to work as American officials. This was a common State Department practice, but former emigrants were seldom received with much enthusiasm in their native countries, and their effectiveness was thus curtailed.

The Dry Goods Economist made several other points, including the obvious one that a consul should speak the language of his consular district; otherwise he "is quite helpless." Care should be taken not to appoint a man who needs the job because he is "dead broke" since he will run the post for revenue only and soon "acquire a more or less odious reputation for extortion and meanness."

Those interested in consular reform frequently noticed a peculiar consequence of the jerrybuilt service, the discrepancy in salaries, which varied from post to post. For example, the U.S. consul in the small German mountain town of Annaberg had a salary of $3,000 while the consul in the major port of Naples received only $1,500. The discrepancies were caused by a lack of Congressional evaluation after the initial salary was established. Or a salary might be high at an obscure consulate because a congressman wanted to help his constituent destined to open that post. The Naples post, in existence since the early days of the Republic, was kept at the eighteenth-century salary level. Quite naturally, such discrepancies often kept good men from accepting important posts, for they preferred to remain in a backwater where they would be better paid.

The article in the Dry Goods Economist indicated the business community's growing concern about the poor caliber of consuls. In a major economic depression in the United States in 1893 American manufacturers turned to exports as their salvation. A successful export campaign required good commercial information from consuls and their assistance in promoting American goods. American business doubted that it was getting the proper value from its consular service and wanted improvement.

Congressmen began to demonstrate how well aware of faults in the consular service. Bills were introduced in 1894, 1895, and 1896, all calling for reform in the system, but there was not enough public interest in such reform to successfully send any of these bills through the legislative process. Senator Henry Cabot Lodge of Massachusetts, a strong proponent of consular reform, gave support. Boston, a major shipping and banking center in an industrial state, depended heavily on overseas markets for many of its manufactured products. The Boston Merchants Association, actively pushing for a revamped and professional corps of consuls to help sell American goods abroad, was joined by the newly created National Association of Manufacturers, whose president complained to President McKinley about the wholesale political purge of consuls, saying that the replacement by "untrained men for tried and experienced efficiency, would mean enormous financial loss to those of our manufacturers who are interested in foreign trade."[13] McKinley, however, in 1897 continued to appoint good Republicans to most consular positions, just as Cleveland had done for Democrats four years before. Although enthusiasm for reform died down in Congress after McKinley took office, an organized campaign was being developed both inside and outside the government to improve the deficient consular system.

For the first time in 120 years the man in charge of consular work in the State Department went out into the field to inspect posts in Mexico, Europe, and the Far East. Robert S. Chilton, Jr., the chief of the consular bureau, made his precedent–breaking tour in 1896–97. What he saw was not encouraging; he found illegal or questionable practices at many posts, usually concerned with fee splitting or unauthorized occupation with nonconsular business.

In Durango, Mexico, Chilton forced the resignation of the consul. The officer had been a witness against several Americans accused of robbery by a business rival who was also a partner of the consul. Instead of dutifully helping the jailed Americans, the consul did his utmost to keep them confined. Chilton recommended to the secretary of state that the consuls in Mexico be fully salaried because too many had business connections "that are hardly compatible with the dignity of their official positions and which necessarily lessens their influence with the authorities."[14]

Periodic attempts to achieve better discipline in the service by having the consuls general inspect the posts in their respective countries, including consular agencies, proved of little value. The consuls general had no authority to remove ineffective consuls; their reports tended to be blandly optimistic statements that everything was fine in their areas of responsibility. In some places the distribution of consulates and consular agencies had become somewhat cumbersome. When the consul general in Montreal inspected the U.S. consular establishment in the province of Quebec in 1899, he had to cover twenty-five posts, a number of them in towns of population under a thousand. When he tried to visit the twenty-sixth post, supposedly in his district, he reported, "The consular agency at Polton was not inspected as it took some time to locate where the agency was situated. There is no such place as Polton, but the Agency is at some place near North Troy, Vermont which is on the border line."[15]

An influential ally of those in the department who wanted to make the consular service more effective was Harry Garfield, son of the assassinated president, James Garfield. He was a prominent lawyer in Cleveland and closely associated with business in that industrial center. The Cleveland Chamber of Commerce had been a strong advocate of strengthening the consular service and with Garfield's help it was willing to lead a campaign within the American business community for a reform of the consular system.[16]

Garfield enlisted other chambers of commerce to join in the battle for reform. Two important tactical decisions were made. The first was not to push for reform of the diplomatic service at the same time as that of the consular one. There was little understanding in the business community of exactly what diplomats did. The businessman was likely to regard the diplomatic service as a finishing school for the sons of the rich. There is an apocryphal story of a telegram sent to the Department of State from the American ambassador in Mexico City: "Assign polo playing third secretary, stop, Matter is urgent, stop." The chambers of commerce considered themselves to be composed of hardheaded businessmen, not interested in developing a service they considered an almost useless plaything of the wealthy.

Garfield's other tactical decision was to keep the good-government organizations and individuals (known by some as "goo goos") at arm's length. The professional reformers were interested mainly in the removal of public offices from the hands of the patronage dispensers. While in theory there should have been a close alliance between the do-gooders of better government and the chambers of commerce, in practice the chambers of commerce wanted no association with those who the business community felt would alienate Congress; they preferred to appeal for reform as a practical dollars-and-cents matter. Better consuls made for more trade and a more prosperous United States. Progress toward establishing the career principle in the consular service, however, remained excruciatingly slow. Another consular reform bill was introduced in 1900, but this too failed.

A major problem that beset any attempt to have Congress enact a law spelling out how men should be appointed to the consular service was the Constitution. Article 2, Section 2 of that basic document stated that the president "shall nominate, and by and with the advice and consent of the Senate, shall appoint ambassadors, other public ministers and consuls." Congress could arrange for the classification and pay of consuls, but arranging for the actual process of appointment seemed to be encroaching upon presidential prerogative.

In 1901 Congress and President Theodore Roosevelt, an advocate of consular reform, had to face up to the political facts of life. If there was no firm set of rules governing the selection of consuls, there would be almost intolerable pressure on any president, no matter how well meaning, to appoint good party members. There could be executive orders, such as those of Cleveland's and McKinley's, providing for consular entrance examinations, but without legal restraints and a career system these orders inevitably would be overturned by political expediency.

In Congress itself there was no groundswell for consular reform. Senators and congressmen of the party in power (at the turn of the century, Republican) by and large saw no pressing need to discard patronage rights. The Speaker of the House, David B. Henderson of Iowa, was an opponent of consular reform and was able to use his powers to effectively bottle up any consular bill.[17]

A new bill introduced in 1903 skirted the constitutional problem by stating "that the President is authorized to prescribe such regulations for the admission of persons into the classified consular service, and for promotions therein and for removals therefrom as will best promote the efficiency thereof." This bill, providing for the division of the service into classes, a salary scale, and transfers within the service, split the business community that had been supporting consular reform. Some organizations took the hard line, a no-compromise stance for complete legislative control over appointments. They wanted a law to spell out exact terms of selection, appointment, and transfer of consular officers. They did not trust the political process that left the president in control of most of the critical elements of the consular system. Other business groups pushed for the weakened bill as the best that could be obtained at the time. Again the result was no consular legislation at all.

One problem the consular reformers had to face was that Secretary of State John Hay, who served from 1898 to 1905, had poor relations with Congress and was unwilling to enter into the fight for a career service. He had been Abraham Lincoln's private secretary, then a historian, assistant secretary of state (1879–81), and ambassador to Great Britain (1897–98). He was indeed knowledgeable about diplomatic and consular shortcomings but had no desire to improve them, although he detested the patronage considerations that the consular system attracted. He wrote to a friend: "The other day the Consul at Berlin died. The President had made up his mind to promote Frank Mason – the best Consul in the Service; but before the other man's funeral, nearly every State in the Union claimed the place by Wire."[18] Still Hay was unwilling to fight to get rid of patronage.

When Hay died in 1905, he was succeeded by a more dynamic secretary, Elihu Root, a corporation lawyer interested also in making organizations efficient by reorganization. As secretary of war following the Spanish American War, he had made long-overdue changes in that department. Besides being an able administrator, Root had excellent relations with Congress and was quite willing to go to that body to present his case.

Teamed with Root was the quintessential Washington bureaucrat: A farm boy from Taylorsville, Ohio (population fifty-two), Wilbur John Carr was a typical self-made man of the era. He was graduated at eighteen from the Commercial College of Kentucky University, the equivalent of a commercial high school, where he studied bookkeeping and general business. He then attended Chaffee's Phonographic Institute in Oswego, New York, taking a course in shorthand and typewriting, skills that often helped men of no private means to enter the business and government world. In 1892 Carr passed the civil service examination for a position as a stenographer and took a clerk's position in the Department of State at a salary of $1,000.[19]

The State Department was Wilbur Carr's world for more than forty-five years. With no family or social backing, a most important ingredient in that branch of the government, and without political pull, sheer ability allowed Carr to make himself indispensable to secretaries of state from James C. Blaine under Benjamin Harrison to Cordell Hull under Franklin Roosevelt. Most of this time Carr was responsible for the direction of consular work, and he should be given much credit for finally developing a career consular service for the United States.

Carr had worked with members of Congress who were interested in reform by helping draft many of the various bills that were unsuccessful in the early years of the century. Although these bills were not passed, Carr, as chief of the consular bureau, had gained useful allies in Congress and learned what was most likely to be acceptable on Capitol Hill. When Secretary Root took office, Carr worked long hours to supply him with information and practical suggestions regarding consular reform.

Root used his authority over the existing consular structure to make several salutary changes without having to ask for legislation. He established an efficiency report record for consuls, which covered the "ability, promptness, and diligence displayed by each officer in the performance of all his official duties," with the emphasis necessarily on the officer's trade reports to Washington since there still was no authorization for regular inspections in the field. Root obtained the cooperation of the newly established Department of Commerce and Labor, the recipient of these reports, to pass back to the consular bureau comments on the value of reports submitted by individual consuls.[20]

Theodore Roosevelt, long an advocate of civil service reform, had supported efforts to apply the same principles to the consular service and found Root a man more congenial than the late Secretary Hay to administrative changes. Together the president and the new secretary examined the records of consular officers before deciding which ones to move on to better-paying posts or to make consuls general. Merit was the prime consideration, not party connections.

In the Senate Henry Cabot Lodge tried once again, toward the end of 1905, to put a bill through Congress regarding a career service. This time Secretary of State Root took an aggressive role in pushing for the consular bill. He had copies of the proposed bill sent to commercial groups and newspaper and magazine editors together with reasons for the necessity of putting consular work in the hands of professionals.[22]

The ultimate success of the consular bill was due to Root's willingness to appear before the Senate Foreign Relations Committee, an effort no previous secretary of state had made. Root's presence and tactful handling of the questions concerning the bill and his comparing the consular service to the military service with the need for both to be removed from politics won the support of the Senate, but the Senate amended the proposed bill by doing away with the examination process and with promotion on the basis of merit, leaving these in the hands of the president. This amendment almost destroyed the proposed reform, but it met the objections of those senators concerned about the constitutionality of passing a law that circumscribed the president's prerogative to appoint consular officers. The amended bill created a rank and pay structure for consular officers and an inspection corps. The Senate passed the amended version of the bill on 30 January 1906.

Some who had been most active in pushing for consular reform lost their fire upon seeing the watered-down version that had come out of the Senate, but the realists in the ranks of reform persevered. Root used Carr as his point man with the House's Foreign Affairs Committee as it considered the Senate's bill. Carr, with consular facts at his fingertips and a good sense for the political considerations that motivated congressmen, was the ideal person to help the committee write the House's version of the bill. At the same time businessmen aroused by the publicity machine were mobilized to approach their representatives and persuade them to do something about the consular service. The House inserted a clause in its draft to the effect that the Senate had to approve any transfer of consuls of comparable rank between posts. This clause added an unnecessary complication, but it was a political price that had to be paid.

After passage by Congress on 5 April 1906, a consular reorganization bill built round the core of what was needed for a career service was signed by President Roosevelt and became law. It classified consular officers into a rational system, dividing consuls general into seven classes with salaries ranging from $3,000 to $12,000 per annum and consuls into nine classes with a salary spread from $2,000 to $8,000. It established consular inspection corps, provided for five consular inspectors, and required each post to be inspected every two years. Consular clerks with salaries over $1,000 had to be American citizens. Consular officers earning over $1,000 could not engage in business or legal practice, and all consular officers, except consular agents, had to forward all fees received to the Treasury Department. The time-honored grade of commercial agent, which had been used off and on since 1776, was abolished.[23]

President Roosevelt plugged the most obvious hole in the consular act by issuing an executive order on 27 June 1906 requiring that all new appointments to the lower grades of the consular service be filled by those who passed an examination. A Board of Examiners was established, which included a representative from the Civil Service Commission to oversee the examination process.

Promotions up the new consular career ladder were to be based on efficiency "as shown by the work that the officer has accomplished, the ability, promptness and diligence displayed by him in the performance of all his official duties, his conduct, and his fitness for the consular service." (The masculine pronoun was apt in the executive order, since American women were not eligible to be consular officers until the 1920s.)

The president's executive order was the result of recommendations made by a board of the five consular officers whom Secretary Root considered the best in the service. The chairman of this board was Frank Mason, the consul general in Paris. Among the board's recommendations was the closing of many consulates and consular agencies, especially those in Canada and Germany, which had proliferated without any rational plan.

It was fortunate that Roosevelt's executive order regulating the appointment of new consular officers was issued in 1906 rather than some years later. A Republican administration continuing under William Howard Taft, who replaced Roosevelt in 1909, kept the consular examination system intact. By the time a Democratic president was elected in 1912 the consular entrance process by examination was well established. The new consular system had effectively frozen the consular service in the upper ranks as it was in 1906. Men, mainly Republican appointees, filled most of the positions until they died or left the service. Had a Democratic president come to power in 1909, he might have wanted to redress the balance. What one presidential executive order can do may be undone by another. The period between 1906 and 1913 allowed the new consular system to settle in and be accepted by all but the most partisan.

Looking at the staffing of the consular service in the spring of 1906, the secretary of state noted that there were few consuls from the Southern states. Of the 274 principal consular officers, only 9 came from the South. There was only 1 consul from Virginia, while Massachusetts, which Senator Lodge represented, had 16. This was not a surprising state of affairs, as the South was solidly Democratic and the Republicans had been making the consular appointments since 1897. In order to confront possible Democratic opposition to continuing consular reform, the State Department, under Carr's guidance, made special efforts to recruit Southerners to take the consular examinations.[24] By 1911, of the 63 consuls recruited under the new system, 31 were from the South and 32 from the North.

There was some control over who could take the examination. It was not fully competitive but open only to those "designated" by the president. As a matter of fact, Carr's office controlled the decisions on who could take the examination. Southerners were given some preference, especially those who had been recommended by senators from the South. Candidates still had to pass the examination.[25] The system somewhat resembled that of the entrance requirements to West Point and Annapolis where future military officers usually needed congressional sponsorship to take the entrance examinations.

The consular examinations were given in Washington, D. C., in two parts, oral and written. "The object of the oral examination will be to determine the candidate's ability, alertness, general contemporary information, and natural fitness for the service, including moral, mental and physical qualifications character, address, and general education and good command of English."[26] Due consideration was given to prior business experience.

The written examination included business letters in French, German, or Spanish to be translated into English and vice versa. There were broad questions, such as "State some of the requirements for the development of a large foreign commerce, and what countries are our chief competitors for foreign trade?" There were specific questions on international, maritime, and commercial law, such as "What is meant by (a) salvage, (b) demurrage, (c) general average, (d) bottomry?" There were also questions on American history and government as well as geography, including "What countries: independent or otherwise, border on the Mediterranean Sea?" The written examination concluded with tests in business arithmetic and in the modern history of Europe, South America, and the Far East. Lasting two days, it was an eminently practical examination, testing what a consul would need to know to go about his business, not necessarily how well he had been educated.

This procedure would obviously have screened out many of the more colorful and effective men who had graced the old consular service as well as eliminating some o the rogues and incompetents. William Cathcart, fresh from his slavery on the, Barbary Coast, would have failed; John Mosby, after putting the oral examiners in their place, certainly would have passed, while the two political nephews, George Seward of Shanghai and George Butler of Alexandria, would undoubtedly have been kept from their respective consul generalships.

The diplomatic service had not been ignored, but no attempt was made to include it in any congressional act. President Roosevelt issued an executive order on 10 November 1905 requiring that vacancies in the office of secretary of legation or embassy (the equivalents of consular officer rank) be filled by those who passed an examination. The examination included oral and written tests in international law, diplomatic usage, and modern languages. Another executive order by President Taft on 26 November 1909 brought the diplomatic service into closer line with the now-career consular service, but there still was no provision for transfers between the two State Department services without taking the set examination of the branch to be entered. The oral examination was the most important part of the process in that it helped keep the diplomatic service a home for men from the "right schools" and "right families." The new procedures at least provided for more qualified men than before, albeit still with the "right antecedents."

One of the more important actions of Congress in 1906 was approval of funds for the official transportation of diplomatic and consular officers to and from their posts. No longer would officers find themselves out of funds and out of office on some foreign shore with no way to return home. In 1915 Congress voted to pay also for the transport of the immediate families of diplomats and consuls and their household effects.

There were some problems with the new career service. The grade and compensation of a consular officer depended on the post to which he was assigned. To obtain a promotion a consul had to be transferred, with senatorial approval, to a different post, a provision obviously disruptive to the system if consuls were transferred too frequently or if there were a series of transfers awaiting the pleasure of the Senate. It was not until 1915, with the pressing necessities of World War I, that officers in either the diplomatic or consular service would be awarded ranks not dependent upon the post of assignment and would be allowed greater ease of transfer to meet the fast-changing overseas staffing requirements of the time.

Of greater importance than the examination process, which is an inexact science at best, were the provisions in the consular act for promotions from within the service and the establishment of an inspection corps. These two provisions made it possible to keep good men in the service without the worry about changes in administration and in a systematic way to keep an eye on the actual operations of the various posts. The five inspectors of the consular service were called consuls-general-at-large, which, as one of them remarked, made them appear to be fugitives from the law. They had their own consular circuits to ride:

1. North America, including Canada, Mexico, and Bermuda
2. Eastern Asia, including the Pacific Islands, Australia, and New Zealand
3. South and Central America, the West Indies, and Curacao
4. European Russia, the Balkan States, Greece, Asia Minor, Persia, India, and Africa
5. Europe, excluding those areas included in (4).[27]

In order to cover posts every two years, these five senior officers were always on the move (in 1910 there were 63 consulates general, 241 consulates, and 262 consular agencies). They not only pointed out problems at each consular post and gave hints on how to deal with them but also passed on news and a little gossip about other posts, gave sound career advice, and served somewhat as itinerate psychiatrists. These consuls-general-at-large helped bind the consular service into a cohesive organization, for they gave its members a sense of belonging and esprit de corps, something that had been lacking when every consul stood more or less isolated from his brother officers at other posts. These inspectors were the best that the service had to offer, and reading their reports gives one a vivid picture of devotion to their calling, their honesty in the appraisals of the consular officers they rated, compassion for human frailties, and their sense of humor.

One of the original five inspectors was Alfred L. M. Gottschalk, who first had the European Russia and Asia Minor circuits. In a tour through consular posts in Russia in 1911, he made the following notes about the consuls he observed:

> Warsaw – a man almost superannuated, does not speak more than a few ordinary phrases of Russian tho he has been 25 years in the country. [The consul was sent to Fiume the same year.]
>
> Riga – an ex-drayman, almost blind and very nervous. [Despite his infirmities this consul later served at Nassau, Cardiff, Stoke on Trent, St. Michaels in the Azores, and finally at Newcastle, where he retired in 1932.]
>
> St. Petersburg – a man who has the every appearance of being half crazy: quarrels with everybody and is universally

disliked. [He stayed on until 1914 before leaving the service.] [28]

In his African inspection Gottschalk described the consul in Algiers (1909): "He is what the Frenchmen call, among themselves, *'un cadavre'*, something that cannot be galvanized back into life even by the best of inspectors" (the consul was seventy years old and had served previously in Palermo. He was replaced shortly after the inspector's visit). Farther to the south, in Lourenco Marques in Portuguese territory, Gottschalk saw that the consul was a broken man. W. Stanley Hollis had served there since 1898. He also had been in business in the area for over twenty years with only two leaves of absence since coming to the colony. He was in debt, had to send his ill wife home, and was completely out of touch with developments in Washington. Gottschalk wrote that Hollis was a good officer but needed a change of post. The consul said that he would take "anything to get out of this place, which is a penitentiary to me in my present condition." [29] The Department of State obliged and sent Hollis to Dundee, Scotland, and later to Beirut, Lebanon, as consul general. Gottschalk drowned in 1918 while returning from an inspection trip aboard a U.S. naval ship that sank in a storm.

Despite their willingness to write what they saw in explicit terms, the inspectors were not unforgiving and behaved as political realists. They knew that they could not advocate the wholesale replacement of the pre-1906 consuls and that it would take many years to bring the consular service up to professional standards. The inspectors would have to tolerate the officer material at hand, but they tried to move the better men to more demanding consular posts and relegate the incompetents to quiet spots. With better young consuls coming in at the bottom of the career ladder, inspectors helping to ease incompetents out of the way, a stronger and more responsive consular bureau in the Department of State, and some further legislative changes, the consular service had become a much more professional body when it had to meet the challenges of World War I and its aftermath.

16

World War I and the Creation of the United States Foreign Service (1914–1924)

The start of World War I presented American consuls in continental Europe with the task of clearing the war zone of U.S. citizens. Fortunately, tourism was mainly limited to the wealthier classes, who had the means to get out of the way, and the war was generally restricted to areas lacking large tourist attractions. The spas of Germany and the beaches of France were far from the artillery of either side. A general exodus of Americans from Europe occurred, as consuls persistently urged their citizens to go home and helped them do so. In response to many telegraphed requests to locate family members, consuls worked with shipping authorities and the French police to keep the concerned Americans informed. The consuls also distributed pamphlets advising unaccompanied "young ladies" of safe ways to travel, where to stay, whom to ask for help, and the like.[1]

One consul who did not escape the horrors of war was Wesley Frost, serving in Queenstown (later Cork), Ireland. When the British luxury liner *Lusitania* was torpedoed and sunk off Ireland on May 7, 1915, with great loss of life, many Americans were on board and 128 of them drowned. Many bodies were washed ashore, and Frost was given the sad task of preparing death certificates for the bodies identified. In expressing his emotion on the certificates, at the "cause of death" section, instead of simply "drowning" he wrote, "willfully murdered by the crew of the German submarine."[2] The sinking of the *Lusitania* was one of the factors that eventually led the United States to declare war on Germany in 1917.

In 1915, in the midst of the war, American consuls witnessed what has later been termed the Armenian Genocide in Turkey.

Around the time World War I was raging, the United States had a number of consular posts in Turkey, mainly to help the numerous American missionaries active in the Ottoman Empire. While an Islamic state, the Ottomans were remarkably tolerant of Christian missionaries. At the time of the forced removal and killing of thousands of Armenians, America had seven consulates in the region. Consular reports became part of a massive archive of eyewitness accounts of atrocities committed by the Turkish authorities. The rationale for the slaughter was the belief on the part of the Turkish authorities that the Armenians were siding with the Russians, who were fighting the Turks. This rationale appeared to be an excuse to create an internal enemy to divert attention from Turkey's poor performance in the military field. Armenians, who had lived peacefully for millennia in Turkey, were forced from their homes and set on long marches to desert areas, where most died.

As late as March 2011, the Armenian National Committee quoted a consular report that U.S. consul Leslie Davis wrote on Armenian "deportees" passing through the Harpoot Plain on their way to Der Zor.

> All of them were in rags and many ... almost naked, ... emaciated, sick, diseased, filthy, covered with dirt and vermin...driven along for many weeks like herds of cattle, with little to eat....There were few men among them, most of the men having been killed by the Kurds before their arrival at Harpoot. Many of the women and children also had been killed and very many others had died on the way.... Of those who had started, only a small portion were still alive and they were rapidly dying....Many Turkish officers and other Turks visited the camps to select the prettiest girls and had their doctors present to examine them.... Several hundred of the dead and dying [were] scattered about the camp...[including] the body of a middle-aged man who had apparently just died or been killed. A number of dead bodies of women and children lay here and there....Old men sat there mumbling incoherently. Women with matted hair and sunken eyes sat staring like maniacs. One, whose face haunted my memory ever since, was so emaciated and the skin was drawn so tightly over her features that her head appeared to be only a lifeless skull. Others were in the spasms of death. Children with bloated bellies were on the ground wallowing in filth. Some were in convulsions. All in the camp were beyond help.

Consular Agent F. H. Leslie in Ourfa reported, "For six weeks we have witnessed the most terrible cruelties inflicted upon thousands of Christian exiles who have been daily passing though our city from the northern cities. All tell the same story and bear the same scars: the men were all killed on the first day's march from their cities, after which the women and girls were constantly robbed of their money, bedding, and clothing and beaten, criminally abused and abducted along the way. We were not only told these things, but the same things occurred right here in our own city before our very eyes and openly on the streets."[4]

There were many more such American consular accounts, along with those from German and Austrian observers. To date the Turkish government has refused to acknowledge that there was a systematic killing of Armenians, and it remains a bone of contention between the Western Powers and Turkey.

During the war, American consuls reported on the fast-moving political and military developments and represented one or another of the belligerents as the neutral protecting power prior up to the U.S. entry into the war in 1917. By 1916, for example, the consulate in Jerusalem was acting as the protecting power for Great Britain, Belgium, Serbia, Montenegro, Russia, and Italy in the Holy Land, since Turkey was at war with all these nations, while the United States maintained peaceful relations. Prior to joining the war in 1917, American consuls also represented the interests of Germany and Austria-Hungary in France, Russia, and parts of the British Empire. These consuls inspected the treatment of prisoners of war and civilian internees in prisons and internment camps and saw to the distribution of relief supplies in Europe and the Near East.

At the end of the First World War, some consuls stationed throughout Russia had to move quickly to keep out of the way of the contending Red and White armies. One consul, Roger C. Tredwell, was caught by the Red forces in Tashkent in 1918 and kept in strict confinement for some months before being released.

When Turkish nationalists violently expelled the Greek minority from Turkey, American consul general George Horton, at great risk to his life, helped thousands of Greek refugees escape through the port of Smyrna. Horton added to the growing accounts blackening the Turks for their treatment during World War I not only of the Armenians but also of the Greeks, who had lived in Turkish Anatolia for thousands of years. In 1922 the Greek government took advantage of Turkish weakness following their defeat as an ally of Germany in 1918. The Greek army invaded Turkey at the port of Smyrna, now Izmir, and after some initial success was soundly defeated and retreated back to Smyrna. Obviously under great emotional stress, Horton sent a long report to the Department of State:

> I wish now to point out the difference between the Greeks and the Turks. The Greeks have undoubtedly massacred Turks, but no nation has such a consistent history of massacres on a great scale or ever had in the world's history as the Turks. Greek politics are corrupt and vicious, but the Greek is capable of civilization along modern lines; he builds hospitals, universities, founds steamship lines, introduces modern agriculture and given liberty, he develops. I see a difference between the excesses of a furious and betrayed army, retreating through a country which it had held for several years and without its officers, and the conduct of the victorious Turkish army, which, instead of protecting the helpless people which it had in its power, deliberately set about massacring and outraging it. . . . . . .
>
> I have also the honor to point out to the Department that all massacres on a large scale perpetrated by Turks, and the history of the Turkish empire is largely a history of massacres, are always ordered by higher authorities. Anyone who believes that the forces of Mustapha Kemal got out of hand at Smyrna and that he controlled them as soon as he could knows nothing about the history of Turkey or events in the Near East. I believe also if the Allied fleets in Smyrna harbor, the French, Italians, British and Americans, had emphatically told Mustapha Kemal that there must be no massacring, none would have taken place. If they told him today that he must cease carrying off the men between eighteen and forty-five into the interior, he would stop, but when he sees the great powers of the world sitting by in security on their battleships watching his fearful procedures, he is emboldened to greater and still greater excesses. The sight of a massacre going on under the eyes of the great powers of Europe and with their seemingly tacit consent is one that I hope never to see again.[5]

This report is still quoted by those who bear the Turks ill will, mainly some Armenian and Greek descendants of the events in Turkey during and at the closing of World War I.

***

Consular work was not without its amusing moments. In postwar Germany young Robert Murphy, on his first job as a vice consul in Munich, had to deal with the usual, and unusual, situations of Americans in trouble.

> One day a young American student came into my office with a problem. He said someone had stepped on someone's foot in a trolley car, and a German major who felt he had been insulted had challenged the American student to a duel. The officer had formally presented his card, saying he would have his second call upon the American's second to arrange details.
>
> The young man sought my advice and we agreed that this matter should be treated unofficially. I could remember nothing in the regulations of the State Department forbidding consuls to act as seconds in duels, but I preferred to submit the question to higher authority. The student explained that he knew nothing about dueling, was not a good shot, and had never even handled a sword. So we studied his situation. I told him that under German dueling rules he had the choice of weapons, as the challenged party, and I asked if there was any kind of weapon he did know how to use. To my delight, he replied that he was an expert archer. Now I began to see daylight ahead, and I agreed to act as his second—in a strictly unofficial capacity.
>
> The next day, at my invitation, the major's second called on me. I informed him that we would be quite happy to have the duel occur at a time and place of their choosing, but of course my principal would assert his privilege of selecting the weapons. The major's second solemnly agreed, and asked what the weapons would be. "Bows and arrows," I replied blandly. My German visitor turned purple with indignation, protesting that nobody ever fought a duel with bows and arrows, weapons used only by savages and barbarians. I replied imperturbably that apparently he was unfamiliar with American dueling practices, since bows and arrows were standard weapons in my country, having been used by the inhabitants of the North American continent for centuries. The type of German who challenges to duels usually is deficient in a sense of humor, especially in matters regarding duels, so it required several days of discussions before I had an opportunity to meet the challenger himself. When the major finally called on me, he had already come to

the conclusion that I had devised an ingenious way to save his honor and my principal's skin. I invited all concerned to the Hofbrau Haus, where we engaged in a beer duel, which hurt nobody, and the German officer and the American student became friends.[6]

In charge of consular work in Bavaria, Murphy was later a close observer of the rise of an obscure nationalist agitator, Adolf Hitler. He attended some of the Nazi Party's early meetings and, "like almost all foreign observers in Munich then, I found it impossible to believe that the demagogue Hitler, so unconvincing to me, would ever amount to much."

At the beginning of World War II, Robert Murphy served as consul general in Algeria and was a key player in arranging for the Allied invasion of North Africa. He then became political advisor to General Eisenhower during the later stages of the war and the top professional diplomat in the Department of State in the early postwar years.

World War I and a subsequent change in American attitude toward immigration added another burden to the consular establishment—visas, immigrant and nonimmigrant. Although consuls had conducted some screening of visitors and immigrants for medical problems prior to World War I, immigrants and visitors to the United States had been examined for suitability at American ports, with Ellis Island the main reception center on the east coast. Because of wartime controls and subsequent legislation to limit immigration, the initial responsibility for examining the qualifications of emigrants abroad was transferred to the consuls, and this has remained a major task of the consular service to the present day.

In 1924, the Rogers Act combined the consular and diplomatic services into a single Foreign Service of the United States. By that point, with the exception of ambassadors and ministers of legation, career men filled both services. Those who had specialized in the diplomatic field had some concern that the more numerous consuls might dominate the new Foreign Service. This did not happen. The diplomatic officers, now called political officers (because they reported on political events in foreign capitals), quickly seized the levers of power in the State Department's assignment and promotion machinery and, in due time, completely submerged the consuls. Political officers kept promotions to senior rank and important positions in legations, embassies, and the Department of State under their own purview. Not until the late 1960s and 1970s was some redress made in this systematic discrimination, through revitalized leadership in the consular bureau and long-overdue congressional outrage at the state of affairs.

When one looks back on the long history of the U.S. consular service from 1776 to 1924, one finds it hard to understand why it took so long to turn it into a more professional service similar to the officer corps of the American army and navy. Other countries, notably France, Great Britain, and Russia, had career consuls long before the American Revolution. Although Congress might have been apprehensive about losing patronage, there were never more than three hundred jobs at stake, and a good number of those neither paid a salary nor afforded a prospect of making a living to any appointee.

There were sound commercial reasons to have competent consuls at major ports and industrial centers abroad; there were practical reasons to have good men at politically sensitive posts; but the president, Congress, and the American people were content for more than one hundred years to leave consular appointments to political chance. In some ways there has still been no improvement in the overseas representation of the United States. While today career men and women of the Foreign Service run consular posts almost exclusively, too many American embassies in the more important capitals around the world are headed by political appointees, many of whom are amateurs in the field of foreign policy. The saving grace is that today these diplomatic neophytes are backed up by a solid professional service in subordinate ranks.

Although the new breed of consuls better serves the American public, something has been lost. The old consular service had its incompetents, dishonest men, and timeservers. But it also had its share of men with drive and initiative able to deal with rapidly changing situations without waiting for instructions—not playing safe, resorting to bureaucratic niceties, or doing little.

Perhaps the old consular service was what the United States needed during its first 120 years. There was little direction from the president or Congress and scant understanding at home by the American public about foreign affairs. Communications were necessarily slow and frustrating and often failed disastrously. But the creaky system suited the American style of government. Assign a randomly chosen consul to a post and let him sink or swim. Throughout the history of the consular service, most consuls proved to be good swimmers.

Notes

1 Consular Antecedents

1. Herodotus, *The History of Herodotus*, ed. Manuel Komroff, trans. George Rawlinson (New York: Tudor, 1928), p. 144.
2. Graham H. Stuart, *American Diplomatic and Consular Practice* 2nd ed. (New York: Appleton-Century-Crofts, 1952), p. 32.
3. John B. Wolf, *The Barbary Coast: Algiers under the Turks*, 1500 to 1830 (New York: W. W. Norton & Co., 1979), p. 195.
4. Ibid., p. 205.
5. Ibid., p. 260.
6. Ibid., p. 314.
7. David B. Warden, *On the Origin, Nature, Progress, and Influence of Consular Establishments* (Paris: Smith, 1813), p. 181.
8. Wolf, *Barbary Coast*, p. 315.
9. Warden, *Consular Establishments*, p. 241.
10. Ibid., p. 244.
11. Ibid., pp. 247–48.

2 Revolution and Confederation

1. Henry Merritt Wriston, *Executive Agents in American Foreign Relations* (Baltimore: Johns Hopkins Press, 1929), p. 7.
2. Coy Hilton James, *Silas Deane: Patriot or Traitor?* (East Lansing: Michigan State University Press, 1975), p. 11.
3. Thomas A. Bailey, *A Diplomatic History of the American People*, 7th ed. (New York: Appleton-Century-Crofts, 1964), p. 30.
4. Ellis Paxson Oberholtzer, *Robert Morris: Patriot and Financier* (New York: Burt Franklin, 1903), p. 44.
5. Deane to President of Congress, 12 October 1778, in *The Diplomatic Correspondence of the American Revolution*, ed. Jared Sparks, 12 vols. (Boston: N. Hale and Gray & Bowen, 1829–30), 1:135.
6. Franklin, Adams, and Lee to Jonathan Williams, 25 May 1778, ibid., 1:397.

7. Lee to Committee of Foreign Affairs, 9 June 1778, ibid., 11:171.
8. Franklin, Lee, and Adams to President of Congress, 20 July 1778, ibid., V:410.
9. Franklin to Marine Committee of Congress, 2 June 1779, in *The Writings of Benjamin Franklin*, ed. Albert Henry Smyth, 10 vols. (New York: Frederick A. Stokes Co., 1929), VII:340–41.
10. Adams to President of Congress, 29 June 1780, *Diplomatic Correspondence of the Revolution*, V:228.
11. Jay to Samuel Huntington, 30 November 1780, in *John Jay: The Winning of the Peace: Unpublished Papers, 1780–1784*, 7 vols., ed. Richard B. Morris, (New York: Harper & Row, 1980), 11:41.
12. 21 June 1781, Continental Congress, in *Secret Journals of the Acts and Proceedings of Congress*, 4 vols. (Boston: Thomas B. Wait, 1820–21), 11:585.
13. Ibid., 11:586.
14. Elias Boudinot to Franklin, 1 November 1783, in *Letters of Members of the Continental Congress*, ed. Edmund. C. Burnett, 8 vols. (Washington, D.C.: Carnegie Institution, 1934), VII:361.
15. Julian P. Boyd, "Two Diplomats between Revolutions: John Jay and Thomas Jefferson," *Virginia Magazine of History and Biography*, April, 1958, pp. 139–42.
16. Jay to Congress, 4 July 1786, in *The Diplomatic Correspondence of the United States of America from the Signing of the Definitive Treaty of Peace, 10th September 1783 to the Adoption of the Constitution, March 4, 1789*, 7 vols. (Washington, D.C.: Francis Preston Blair, 1833), 111:71.
17. Jay to Jefferson, 18 August 1786, ibid., 111:422.
18. Jefferson to Montmorin, 20 June 1788, ibid., 111:422.
19. Bailey, *Diplomatic History*, p. 54.
20. 21 December 1785, *Journals of the Continental Congress*, 34 vols. (Washington, D.C.: Government Printing Office, 1904–37), XXIX:897.
21. Adams to Jay, 2 September 1785, ibid., IV:354.
22. Jay to Congress, 13 October 1785, ibid. XXIX:831–33.
23. Samuel Shaw to Jay, 19 May 1785, *Diplomatic Correspondence of the United States*, VII:429.
24. Brian V. Evans, "The First China Hand," *Foreign Service Journal*, May 1983, pp.28–31.
25. Shaw to Jay, 19 May 1785, *Diplomatic Correspondence of the United States*, VII:427.
26. Jay to Congress, 20 January 1786, ibid.
27. Robert Morris to Congress, 22 June 1781, in *Papers of Robert Morris, 1781–1784*, 7 vols. ed. E. James Ferguson (Pittsburgh: University of Pittsburgh Press, 1973), 1:166
28. 26 May 1783, *Journals of the Continental Congress*, XXIV:
29. John Temple to Jay, 7 June 1786, *Diplomatic Correspondence of the United States*, VI:29.
30. Ray W. Irwin, *The Diplomatic Relations of the United States with the Barbary Powers*, 1777–1816 (Chapel Hill: University of North Carolina Press, 1931), p. 187.

31. Ibid., p. 25.
32. *Consolidated Treaty Series*, ed. Clive Parry, 231 vols. (Oceana Publications, Dobbs Ferry, N.Y.:1969) L:33–46.
33. Jay to Congress, 12 October 1787, *Journals of the Continental Congress*, XXXIIL:685.

3 Birth of the Consular Service

1. Department of State, Historian's Office, "*American Consular Officers, 1789–1800*" (Unpublished paper, 1964).
2. Jefferson to Montmorin, 20 June 1788, in *The Diplomatic Correspondence of the United States of America from the Signing of the Definitive Treaty of Peace, 10th September 1783 to the Adoption of the Constitution, March 4, 1789*, 7 vols. 111:422–423.
3. *The Papers of Thomas Jefferson*, ed. Julian P. Boyd, 21 vols. (Princeton, N.J.: Princeton University Press, 1965), XVII:423.
4. Ibid.
5. Ibid.
6. *The Debates and Proceedings in the Congress of the United States*, 42 vols. (Washington: Government Printing Office: 1834–56), 11:1770.
7. 1 Stat. 254.
8. Henry Bartholomew Cox, *The Parisian American: Fulwar Skipwith of Virginia* (Washington, D.C.: Mount Vernon Publishing Co., 1964), p. 13.
9. Ibid., p. 26.
10. Ibid., pp. 29–30.
11. Ibid., p. 30.
12. Ibid., p. 37.
13. Ibid., p. 38.
14. Ibid., p. 42.
15. Bordeaux, 28 June 1793, Department of State, "Consular Despatches", Record Group 59, National Archives.
16. Bordeaux, 20 December 1793, ibid.
17. Bordeaux, 1 March 1794, ibid.
18. Bordeaux, 23 April 1794, ibid.
19. Secretary of State to President, 21 June 1797, *Naval Documents Related to the Quasi-War between the United States and France: Naval Operations from February 1797– December 1801*, 7 vols. (Washington: Government Printing Office, 1937), 1:6.
20. Marseilles, 31 May 1798, "Consular Despatches".
21. Secretary of State to Stevens, 20 April 1799, *Naval Documents Related to the Quasi-War*, 111:70.
22. Port-au-Prince, 16 August 1799, ibid., IV:84.
23 Port-au-Prince, 9 December 1799, ibid., IV:504.
24. Port-au-Prince, 27 December 1799, ibid., IV:570.
25. Dudley W. Knox, *A History of the United States Navy* (New York: G. P. Putnam's Sons, 1936), p. 51.

26. Pickering to Stevens, 20 March 1800, *Naval Documents Related to the Quasi-War*, V:333.

4 The Barbary Consuls

1. U.S. Navy, *Naval Documents Related to the United States Wars with the Barbary Powers*, ed. Dudley W. Knox, 6 vols. (Washington D. C.: Government Printing Office, 1939–44), 1:36–41.
2. Ray W. Irwin, *The Diplomatic Relations of the United States with the Barbary Powers*, 1776–1816 (Chapel Hill: University of North Carolina Press, 1931), p. 61.
3. Ibid., p. 70.
4. Louis B. Wright and Julia H. Macleod, *The First Americans in North Africa: William Eaton's Struggle for a Vigorous Policy against the Barbary Pirates*, 1799–1805 (Princeton: Princeton University Press, 1945), p. 18.
5. Irwin, *Diplomatic Relations* p. 72.
6. *National Cyclopaedia of American Biography*, 75 vols. (New York: James T. White & Co., 1888–1984), 111:186.
7. Algiers, 18 March 1796, U.S. Navy, *Wars with the Barbary Powers*, 1:40.
8. Algiers, 3 April 1796, ibid., 1:142.
9. Algiers, 5 April 1.796, ibid., 1:142.
10. Irwin, *Diplomatic Relations*, p. 74.
11. Ibid., p. 75.
12. Ibid., p. 83.
13. Morocco, 18 August 1795, U.S. Navy, *Wars with the Barbary Powers*, 1:100.
14. *Dictionary of American Biography*, ed. Dumas Malone, 20 vols. (New York: Charles Scribner's Sons, 1934), XIII:611.
15. Irwin, *Diplomatic Relations*, p. 85.
16. *Consolidated Treaty Series*, ed. Clive Parry, 231 vols. (Dobbs Ferry, N.Y.: Oceana Publications, 1969), LIV:119.
17. Irwin, *Diplomatic Relations*, p. 200.
18. Ibid.
19. Ibid., p. 95.
20. Tripoli, 16 May 1801, U.S. Navy, *Wars with the Barbary Powers*, 1:485.
21. Irwin, *Diplomatic Relations*, p. 108.
22. Ibid., p. 111.
23. Morocco, 19 March 1802, U.S. Navy, *Wars with the Barbary Powers*, 11:91.
24. *Dictionary of American Biography*, XI:76.
25. Wright and Macleod, *First Americans*. pp. 172–76.
26. *Consolidated Treaty Series*, LVIII:145.
27. Irwin, *Diplomatic Relations*, p. 153.
28. *Dictionary of American Biography*, XVII:119.
29. Samuel Edwards, *Barbary General: The Life of William H. Eaton* (Englewood Cliffs, N.J.: Prentice-Hall, 1968), p. 230.

30. Irwin, *Diplomatic Relations*, p. 178.
31. Decatur brought recall orders for Mordecai Noah. Secretary of State James Monroe wrote Noah: "At the time of your appointment, as Consul at Tunis, it was not known that the RELIGION which you profess would form any obstacle to the exercise of your Consular functions. Recent information, however, on which entire reliance may be placed, proves that it would produce a very unfavourable effect." The 25 April 1815 dispatch went on to mention some problem with his accounts, but the thrust of this set of orders was that the fact that Noah was Jewish was the reason for his recall. Noah had been a newspaperman in Charleston, South Carolina, and had acquired political enemies (he was involved in a duel at one point), which may have some bearing on this odd decision on the part of Monroe. The fact that the consul was Jewish played very little part in Noah's effectiveness in Tunis and the cause for this abrupt action on the part of the secretary of state must be attributed to domestic American politics. Isaac Goldberg, *Major Noah: American Jewish Pioneer* (Philadelphia: Jewish Publication Society of America, 1936), p. 111.
32. Irwin, *Diplomatic Relations*, p. 181.
33. Ibid., p. 195.

5 Free Trade and Seamen's Rights

1. Clifford L. Egan, *Neither Peace Nor War: Franco-American Relations, 1803–1812* (Baton Rouge: Louisiana State University Press, 1983), p. 70.
2. Dumas Malone, *Jefferson the President: Second Term, 1805–1809* (Boston: Little, Brown & Co., 1974), p. 656.
3. Ibid., pp. 636–40.
4. Lee to Skipwith, 2 April 1805, Henry Bartholomew Cox, *The Parisian American: Fulwar Skipwith of Virginia* (Washington, D. C.: Mount Vernon Publishing Co., 1964), p. 94.
5. 28 May 1796, *Journals of Congress*, 1796–1797, 4th Cong., 2d sess., Appendix, p. 2919.
6. James Fulton Zimmerman, *Impressment of American Seamen* (New York: Columbia University Press, 1925), p. 147.
7. Frank Updyke, *The Diplomacy of the War of 1812* (Baltimore: Johns Hopkins Press, 1915), p. 20.
8. Zimmerman, *Impressment*, p. 64.
9. Ibid., p. 73.
10. Ibid., p. 108.
11. Bordeaux, 24 December 1801, Department of State, "Consular Despatches", Record Group 59, National Archives.
12. Bordeaux, 20 January 1802, ibid.
13. Bradford Perkins, *Prologue to War: England and the United States, 1805–1812*, (Berkeley: University of California Press, 1961), p. 305.

14. Bremen, 3 September 1808, "Consular Despatches".
15. Zimmerman, *Impressment*, p. 168.
16. St. Petersburg, 15/17 October 1812, "Consular Despatches."
17. St. Petersburg, 13 February 1813, ibid.
18. Bordeaux, 12 October 1812, ibid.
19. Lee to Director of Customs, Bordeaux, 28 June 1813, ibid.
20. Bordeaux, 16 July 1813, ibid.
21. Lee to Crawford (Paris), 16 July 1813, ibid.
22. French Minister of Customs to Lee, 19 July 1813, ibid.
23. Lee to Crawford (Paris), 26 July 1813, ibid.
24. *Dictionary of American Biography*, ed. Dumas Malone, 20 vols. (New York: Charles Scribner's Sons, 1934), XIX:443.
25. Crawford to Lee, Bordeaux, 20 August 1813, "Consular Despatches".

6 Yankee Consuls in Latin America

1. *Dictionary of American Biography*, ed. Dumas Malone, 20 vols. (New York: Charles Scribner's Sons, 1934), XV:30.
2. Washington, 28 June 1810, William R. Manning, *Diplomatic Correspondence of the United States Concerning Independence of the Latin American Nations*, 3 vols. (New York: Oxford University Press, 1925), 1:5.
3. Washington, 30 April 1811, ibid., 1:11.
4. La Guaira, 6 September 1810, ibid., 11:1144.
5. Caracas, 18 March 1811, ibid., 11:1148.
6. La Guaira 9 June 1811, ibid., 11:1157.
7. La Guaira, 5 June 1812, ibid., 11:1158.
8. Caracas, 1 December 1812, ibid., 11:1167.
9. St. Thomas, 17 February 1813, ibid., 11:1168.
10. La Guaira, 16 April 1822, ibid., 11 :1219.
11. Buenos Aires, 31 January 1818, ibid., 1:324.
12. *Dictionary of American Biography*, XIX:48.
13. Callao, 12 March 1824, Department of State, "Consular Despatches", Record Group 59, National Archives.
14. Callao, 3 May 1824, Manning, *Diplomatic Correspondence Concerning Independence*, ibid., 111:1751.
15. Ibid., 111:1757.
16. Callao, 24 August 1824, ibid., 111:1756.
17. Callao, 7 December 1824, ibid., 111:1774.
18. Callao, 22 December 1824, ibid., IIL1775.
19. Julius Goebel, Jr., *The Struggle for the Falkland Islands: A Study in Legal and Diplomatic History* (New Haven: Yale University Press, 1927), p. 438.
20. Ibid., p. 441.
21. Ibid., p. 444.
22. Mexico City, 25 October 1821, Manning, *Diplomatic Correspondence Concerning Independence*, 111:1600.

23. Vera Cruz, "Consular Despatches", 8 January 1832.
24. Vera Cruz, 7 March 1835, ibid.
25. Vera Cruz, 13 March 1835, ibid.
26. Galveston, 10 March 1835, ibid.
27. Mazatlán, 30 December 1837, ibid.
28. Neal Harlow, *California Conquered: War and Peace on the Pacific, 1846–1850* (Berkeley: University of California Press, 1982), p. 5.
29. Norman A. Graebner, *Empire on the Pacific: A Study in American Continental Expansion* (New York: Ronald Press, 1955), p. 72.
30. Harlow, California Conquered, p. 4.
31. Ibid., p. 7.
32. Ibid., p. 9.
33. Ibid., p. 13.
34. *Dictionary of American Biography*, X:617.
35. Graebner, *Empire on the Pacific*, p. 52.
36. Monterey, 10 April 1844, "Consular Despatches".
37. Leidesdorff, whose father was Danish and mother West Indian, is considered to be the first black to hold a consular title.
38. Monterey, 16 April 1844, "Consular Despatches".
39. Washington, 17 October 1845, William R. Manning, *Diplomatic Correspondence of the United States: Inter-American Affairs, 1831–1860*, 12 vols. (Washington, D. C.: Carnegie Endowment, 1939), X:170.
40. Harlow, *California Conquered*, p. 79.
41. Ibid., p. 64.
42. Ibid., p. 80.
43. Ibid., p. 117.
44. Washington, 17 September 1845, Manning, *Diplomatic Correspondence: Inter-American*, VIII:167.
45. Ward McAfee, "A Reconsideration of the Mexican-American War," *Southern California Quarterly*, 62 (1980): 49–65.
46. Mazatlán, 4 June 1846, "Consular Despatches".
47. Harlow, *California Conquered*, p. 123.
48. Ibid., p. 140.
49. Ibid., p. 196.
50. Vera Cruz, 23 May 1846, "Consular Despatches".
51. Mexico City, 6 July 1846, Manning, *Diplomatic Correspondence: Inter-American*, X:183.

7 Consuls in Europe – Consular Reform

1. William Barnes and John Heath Morgan, *The Foreign Service of the United States: Origins, Developments, and Functions* (Washington, D. C.: Government Printing Office, 1961), p. 70.
2. Ibid., p. 71.
3. Henry W. Boynton, *James Fenimore Cooper* (New York: Century Co., 1931), p. 141.

4. James Franklin Beard, ed., *The Letters and Journals of James Fenimore Cooper*, 6 vols. (Cambridge: Harvard University Press, 1960–1968), 1:137.
5. Antwerp, 18 August 1828, Department of State, *Consular Despatches*, Record Group 59, National Archives.
6. 18 September 1830, ibid.
7. 5 October 1830, ibid.
8. 2 November 1830, ibid.
9. 21st Cong., 2d sess., 1831, S. Doc. 57 (Serial 204), p. 2.
10. Ibid.
11. Ibid., p. 5.
12. Ibid., p.7
13. Ibid., p. 8.
14. Ibid., p. 10.
15. Charles Edwards Lester, *My Consulship*, 2 vols. (New York: Cored Lanpert & Co., 1853), 11:264.
16. 22d Cong., 2d sess., 1833, S. Doc. 83 (serial 230), p. 13.
17. Ibid., p.23.
18. 26th Cong., 1st sess. 1840, U.S. Stat., ch. 48, p. 397.
19. 29th Cong., 1st sess., 1846, H. Doc. 12, p. 3.
20. Ibid., p. 9.
21. Ibid.
22. *Dictionary of American Biography*, ed. Dumas Malone, 20 vols. (New York, Charles Scribner's Sons, 1934), XI:189.
23. Lester, *My Consulship*, 1:18.
24. Ibid., 1:37.
25. Ibid., 1:90.
26. Howard R. Marraro, *American Opinion on the Unification of Italy, 1846–1861* (New York: Columbia University Press, 1932), p. 33.
27. Palermo, 16 January 1848, *Consular Despatches*.
28. Marraro, *American Opinion*, p. 37.
29. Ibid., p. 155.
30. Howard R. Marraro, ed., *Diplomatic Relations between the United States and the Kingdom of the Two Sicilies: Instructions and Despatches, 1816–1861*, 2 vols. (New York: S. F. Vanni [Ragusa], 1951), p. 51.
31. Barnes and Morgan, *Foreign Service*, p. 100.
32. Nathaniel Hawthorne, *The English Notebooks*, ed. Randall Stewart (New York: Russell & Russell, 1962), p. 3.
33. Ibid. 86 The American Consul
34. Rose Hawthorne Lathrop, *Memories of Hawthorne* (Boston: Houghton, Mifflin & Co., 1897), p. 267.
35. Ibid., p. 269.
36. Ibid., p.282.
37. James O'Donald Mays, *Mr. Hawthorne Goes to England: The Adventures of a Reluctant Consul* (Burley, Hampshire: New Leaves, 1983), p. 110.
38. Ibid., p. 109.
39. James R. Mellow, *Nathaniel Hawthorne in His Times* (Boston: Houghton Mifflin, 1980), p. 433.

40. Lathrop, *Memories of Hawthorne*, p. 325.
41. II Stat. 52.
42. Mays, *Mr. Hawthorne Goes to England*, p. 184.

8 Consular Development in the Near East

1. Luella J. Hall, *The United States and Morocco, 1776–1956* (Metuchen, N. J.: Scarecrow Press, 1971), p. 91.
2. Ibid., p. 96
3. Ibid., p. 110.
4. Ibid., p. 112.
5. Ibid., p. 114.
6. Ibid.
7. Ibid., p. 116.
8. Ibid., p. 118.
9. Thomas A. Bryson, *An American Consular Officer in the Middle East in the Jackson Era: A Biography of William Brown Hodgson, 1801–1871* (Atlanta: Resurgens Publications, 1979), p. 8.
10. Ibid., p. 20.
11. Ibid., p. 37.
12. Lenoir C. Wright *United States Policy toward Egypt, 1830–1914* (New York: Exposition Press, 1969), p. 30.
13. Treaty of Amity and Commerce between the United States and Turkey, 1830, Art. IV.
14. *Dictionary of American Biography*, ed. Dumas Malone, 20 vols, (New York, Charles Scribner's Sons, 1934), XV:83.
15. Bryson, *American Consular Officer*, p. 59.
16. Ibid., p. 69.
17. Ibid., p. 86.
18. Ibid., p. 138.
19. James A. Field, Jr. *America and the Mediterranean World, 1776–1882*, (Princeton: Princeton University Press, 1969), p. 309.
20. *Dictionary of American Biography*, XIII:634.
21. David H. Finnie, *Pioneers East: The Early American Experience in the Middle East* (Cambridge: Harvard University Press, 1967), p. 27.
22. Ibid., p. 28.
23. Ibid., p. 37.
24. William F. Sands, *Undiplomatic Memoires* (New York: Whittlesey House, 1930), p. 92.
25. S. D. Ingham [Jackson's secretary of the Treasury, 1829–31], New Hope, Penna. to Calhoun, 25 May 1844, Department of State, "Domestic Letters," Record Group 59, National Archives.
26. Field, *Americans and the Mediterranean World*, p. 277.
27. *Dictionary of American Biography*, XIV:327.

9 Consular Operations in Africa, Asia and the Pacific

1. Department of State, Office of Public Affairs, "Establishment of Consular and Diplomatic Relations with India and South Africa" (Unpublished paper, September 1946).
2. *Dictionary of American Biography*, ed. Dumas Malone, 20 vols. (New York: Charles Scribner's Sons, 1934), XVI4.
3. Zanzibar, 6 March and 28 December 1846, Department of State, "Consular Despatches", Record Group 59, National Archives.
4. John Ross Browne, *Etching of a Whaling Cruise*, ed. John Seelye (Cambridge: Harvard University Press, 1968), p. 23.
5. Department of State, "Establishment of Relations."
6. Ibid.
7. Ibid.
8. Samuel Eliot Morison, *The Maritime History of Massachusetts, 1783–1860* (Boston: Houghton Mifflin Co., 1921), p. 219.
9. Ibid., p. 220.
10. Herman Melville's book *Typee* is an excellent account of seamen who deserted and lived in Polynesia at the time.
11. Rhoda E. A. Hackler, "Our Men in the Pacific: A Chronicle of United States Consular Officers at Seven Ports in the Pacific Islands and Australasia during the 19th Century" (Ph.D. diss., University of Hawaii, 1978), p. 106.
12. Ibid., p. 64.
13. Ralph S. Kuykendall and A. Grove Day, *Hawaii: A History: From Polynesian Kingdom to American Commonwealth* (New York: Prentice-Hall, 1948), p. 64.
14. Hackler, "Our Men in the Pacific," p. 291.
15. Ibid., p. 301.
16. Ibid., p. 306.
17. Tyler Dennett, *Americans in Eastern Asia: A Critical Study of the Policy of the United States with Reference to China, Japan, and Korea in the 19th Century* (New York: Macmillan Co., 1922), p. 50.
18. Eldon Griffin, *Clippers and Consuls: American Consular and Commercial Relations with Eastern Asia, 1845–1860* (Ann Arbor: Edwards Press, 1938), p. xix.
19. Foster Rhea Dulles, *China and America: The Story of Their Relations since 1784* (Princeton: Princeton University Press, 1946), p. 15.
20. Dennett, *Americans in Eastern Asia*, p. 93.
21. Ibid., p. 95.
22. Ibid.
23. Ibid., p. 97.
24. Kearny to Secretary of the Navy, 19 May 1843, East India Squadron Letters Received by Secretary of the Navy from Commanding Officers, Squadrons, Record Group 45, National Archives.

25. Dennett, *Americans in Eastern Asia*, p. 125.
26. John King Fairbank, *Trade and Diplomacy on the China Coast: The Opening of the Treaty Ports, 1842–1854*, 2 vols. (Cambridge: Harvard University Press, 1953), 1:121.
27. Dennett, *Americans in Eastern Asia*, p. 155.
28. Dulles, *China and America*, p. 28.
29. Ibid., p. 55.
30. 30th Cong., 1st sess. 11 August 1848, S. Ex. Doc. 43.
31. Ibid.
32. Griffin, *Clippers and Consuls*, p. 93.
33. Dennett, *Americans in Eastern Asia*, p. 188.
34. Ibid., p. 187.
35. Amelia Kay King, "James Kcenan, United States Consul to Hong Kong" (M.A. thesis, North Texas State University, 1978), pp. 30–33.
36. Ibid., p 40.
37. Ibid., p. 50.
38. Ibid., p. 64.
39. Ibid., p. 74.
40. Ibid., p. 83.
41. Griffin, *Clippers and Consuls*, p. 194.
42. Ibid.
43. Dulles, *China and America*, p. 54.
44. Carl Crow, *He Opened the Door of Japan* (New York: Harper & Bros., 1939), p. 19.
45. Ibid., p. 27.
46. Ibid., p. 28.
47. Ibid., p. 34.
48. Oliver Statler, *Shimoda Story* (New York: Random House, 1969), p. 31.
49. Townsend Harris, *The Complete Journal of Townsend Harris, First American Consul General and Minister to Japan* (New York: Doubleday & Doran & Co., 1930), p. 225.
50. Ibid., p. 205.
51. Ibid., p. 232.
52. Harris, *Some Unpublished Letters of Townsend Harris*, ed. Shio Sakanishi (New York: Japan Reference Library, 1941), p. 10.
53. Statler, *Shimoda Story*, p. 382.
54. Ibid., p. 383.
55. Ibid., p. 449.
56. Harris, *The Complete Journal*, p. 373.
57. Statler, *Shimoda Story*, p.274.
58. Harris, *The Complete Journal*, p. 576.
59. Statler, *Shimoda Story*, p. 569.

10 Consuls and the Civil War

1. Abraham Lincoln, *The Collected Works of Abraham Lincoln*, The Abraham Lincoln Association, Springfield, Ill., ed. Roy P. Basler, 9 vols. (New Brunswick, N.J.: Rutgers University Press, 1953), IV:284.
2. Ibid., IV:348.
3. Ibid., IV:460.
4. *Dictionary of American Biography*, ed. Dumas Malone, 20 vols. (New York, Charles Scribner's Sons, 1934), IX:306.
5. Frank L. Owsley, *King Cotton Diplomacy: Foreign Relations of the Confederate States of America* (Chicago: University of Chicago Press, 1931), p. 179.
6. Ibid., p. 105.
7. U.S. Department of State, *Foreign Relations of the United States: Diplomatic Papers*, 1862 (Washington, D. C.: Government Printing Office, 1963) 1:172.
8. Ibid., II:1350, 1371.
9. Frederick C. Drake, *The Empire of the Seas: A Biography of Rear Admiral Robert Wilson Shufeldt*, USN (Honolulu: University of Hawaii Press, 1984), p. 32.
10. Ibid., p. 31.
11. Ibid., p. 36.
12. *Dictionary of American Biography*, XVII:139.
13. Philip Van Doren Stern, *When the Guns Roared: World Aspects of the American Civil War* (Garden City, N. Y.: Doubleday & Co., 1965), p. 103.
14. Brian Jenkins, *Britain and the War for the Union*, 2 vols. (Montreal: McGill-Queen's University Press, 1974–1980), 2 vols., 1:120.
15. Stern, *When the Guns Roared*, p. 144.
16. Ibid., pp. 145–46.
17. Benjamin Moran, *The Journal of Benjamin Moran, 1857–1865*, ed. Sarah A. Wallace and Frances E. Gillespie, 2 vols. (Chicago: University of Chicago Press, 1948), 11:1024.
18. Jenkins, *Britain and the War for the Union*, II:292.
19. Moran, *Journal*, 11:1135.
20. Jenkins, *Britain and the War for the Union*, 11:291.
21. Ibid.
22. Stern, *When the Guns Roared*, p. 213.
23. Moran, Journal, 11:1078
24. Stern, *When the Guns Roared*, p. 197.
25. Ibid., p. 205.
26. Moran, *Journal*, 11 :1238.
27. Owsley, *King Cotton Diplomacy*, p. 318.
28. Stern, *When the Guns Roared*, p. 218.
29. Ibid., p. 317.
30. Jenkins, *Britain and the War for the Union*, 11: 118.

31. Foreign Relations of the United States, 1864, IV:322.
32. Ibid., 11:346.
33. Stern, *When the Guns Roared*, p. 106.

11 Post–Civil War Consular Activities

1. Act of 18 August 1856, Schedule B.
2. Edward Robinson, 19 December 1864, *Letters of Application and Recommendation during the Administration of Abraham Lincoln, 1861–1865,* National Archives, General Records of the Department of State, Record Group 59.
3. U.S. Department of State, *Foreign Relations of the United States, Diplomatic Papers, 1876* (Washington, D. C.: Government Printing Office, 1876), p. 142.
4. Hamburg, 22 January 1875, Department of State, *Consular Despatches,* Record Group 59, National Archives.
5. 20 March 1875, Ibis.
6. 7 June 1875, Ibis.
7. 1 April 1875, Ibis.
8. Berlin, 15 October 1877, *Consular Despatches.*
9. Department of State, *The United States Consul's Manual: A Practical Guide for Consular Officers, and Also for Merchants, Shipowners, and Masters of American Vessels in All Their Consular Transactions,* (Washington, D. C.: Hudson Taylor, 1863), 2d ed. p. 13.
10. 13 Stat. 137, 20 June 1864.
11. William Barnes and John Heath Morgan, *The Foreign Service of the United States: Origins, Developments, and Functions* (Washington, D. C.: Government Printing Office, 1961), p. 123.
12. 12 Stat. 340, 19 February 1862.
13. *Dictionary of American Biography,* ed. Dumas Malone, 20 vols. (New York, Charles Scribner's Sons, 1934), XVI:613.
14. *Foreign Relations of the United States, 1864,* 111:392.
15. Ibid., 111:419.
16. Ibid., 111:417.
17. Ibid.
18. Ibid., 111:400.
19. *Dictionary of American Biography,* XVIII:29.
20. William James Stillman, *The Autobiography of a Journalist,* 2 vols. (Boston: Houghton, Mifflin & Co., 1901), I:284.
21. Ibid., 1:301.
22. Ibid., 1:312.
23. Ibid., 1:315.
24. Ibid., 11:4.
25. Ibid., 11:27.
26. Ibid., 11:37.

27. Ibid., 11:42.
28. Ibid., 11:27.
29. Ibid., 11:63.
30. Ibid., 11:64.
31. James A. Field, Jr., *America and the Mediterranean World, 1776–1882* (Princeton: Princeton University Press, 1969), p. 320.
32. Stillman, *Autobiography, 11:62.*
33. Ibid., 11:68.
34. *Foreign Relations of the United States, 1872, p. 728.*
35. *Encyclopedia Judaica, 16 vols.* (Jerusalem: Keter Publishing House, 1972), XVII:214.
36. *Dictionary of American Biography,* XIV:407.
37. Vienna, 31 August 1872, *Foreign Relations of the United States, 1872, p. 63.*
38. Bucharest, 6 October 1871, Ibid., p. 681.
39. 10 February 1872, Ibid., p. 683.
40. *Encyclopedia Judaica,* XIIL214.
41. Arthur May Hyde, *A Diplomatic History of Bulgaria, 1870–1886* (Westport, Conn.: Greenwood Press, 1974), p. 48.
42. *Dictionary of American Biography,* XVI:471.
43. Field, *America and the Mediterranean World,* p. 366.
44. Eugene Schuyler, *Selected Essays: With Memoir by Evelyn Schuyler Schaeffer* (New York: Charles Scribner's Sons, 1901), p. 64.
45. Ibid., pp. 66–67.
46. Ibid., p. 101.
47. Field, *America and the Mediterranean World,* p. 372.
48. Jerusalem, 12 July 1877, *Consular Despatches.*
49. *Foreign Relations of the United States, 1866,* 1:86, 119, 148.

12 Cuban Problems and Consular Corruption

1. Mantanzas, 31 June 1870, *Foreign Relations of the United States, Diplomatic Papers, 1869* (Washington, D. C.: Government Printing Office, 1869)
2. Havana, 29 June 1869, ibid.
3. U.S. Navy to Rear Admiral Hoff in Havana, 7 April 1869, Spanish West Indies Report, Department of State, *War in Cuba: 1868–78 Correspondence,* (Washington, D. C.: Government Printing Office, 1872), p.30.
4. Santiago de Cuba, 19 June 1869, Department of State, "Consular Despatches," Record Group 59, National Archives.
5. Ibid.
6. 9 April 1870, ibid.
7. Richard H. Bradford, *The Virginius Affair* (Boulder Colorado: Associated University Press, 1980), p. 26.
8. Ibid., p. 27.
9. Puerto Cabello, 31 December 1870, "Consular Despatches".
10. Caracas, 9 September 1872, *Foreign Relations of the United States, 1872,* 1:715.

11. Aspinwall, 25 June 1872, *Consular Despatches.*
12. Santiago de Cuba, 2 November 1873, Ex. Doc. 30, re Steamer *Virginius,* 1st sess., 43d Cong. (Government Printing Office: 1874), p. 156.
13. Burriel to Schmitt, 4 November 1873, ibid., p. 158–9.
14. Ibid.
15. Washington to Havana, 12 November 1873, ibid., p.159.
16. Hall to Fish, Havana, 13 November 1873, ibid., p. 160.
17. Commodore Daniel L. Braine, USS *Juanita,* to Secretary of Navy, 21 November 1873. Record of Office of Naval Record and Library (Record Group 45). Letters from officers commanding expeditions, Letters from Commodore Daniel L. Braine. National Archives.
18. Allen Nevins, *Hamilton Fish: The Inner History of the Grant Administration* (New York: Dodd, Mead & Co., 1936), p. 119.
19. Ibid.
20. Ibid., pp. 119–20.
21. William Barnes and John Heath Morgan, *The Foreign Service of the United States: Origins, Developments, and Functions* (Washington, D. C.: Government Printing Office, 1961), p. 134.
22. *Nation,* 28 November 1872, pp. 341–42.
23. Alexandria, 19 July 1872, *Consular Despatches.*
24. De Benneville Randolph Keim, *A Report to the Hon. George S. Boutwell, Secretary of the Treasury, upon the Condition of the Consular Service,* (Washington, D. C.: Government Printing Office, 1872), p. 184.
25. Ibid., p. 174.
26. Ibid., p. 123.
27. Ibid., p. 162.
28. Ibid., p. 126.4
29. Ibid.
30. Ibid., p. 130.
31. *Dictionary of American Biography,* ed. Dumas Malone, 20 vols. (New York, Charles Scribner's Sons, 1934), XI:145.
32. *Foreign Relations of the United States, 1867,* 1:143.
33. Keim, *Report, p.* 78.
34. *Foreign Relations of the United Stales, 1874, p.* 331.
35. Ibid., p. 85.
36. Ibid., p. 37.
37. Ibid., p. 181.
38. Ibid., p. 133.
39. Ibid., p. 98.
40. Ibid., p. 135.
41. Ibid.
42. Ibid., p. 47.
43. Ibid.
44. Ibid., pp. 317–422.
45. Barnes and Morgan, *Foreign Service, p. 150.*
46. Ibid., p. 151.

47. Kevin H. Siepel, *Rebel: The Life and Times of John Singleton Mosby* (New York: St. Martin's Press, 1983), p. 202.

48. Ibid., p. 210.

49. John C. Myers, *Condensed Statement of John C. Myers* (Washington, D. C.: Government Printing Office, 1877), p. 17.

50. Siepel, *Rebel, p.* 212.

51. Ibid., p. 218.

52. Ibid., p. 236.

13 Consuls and Commerce

1. Chester Lloyd Jones, *The Consular Service of the United States: Its History and Activities* (Philadelphia: University of Pennsylvania, 1906), p. 64.

2. Ibid., p. 73.

3. Ibid., p. 79.

4. Consular letters, Vienna, 1885–1889.

5. Rhoda E. A. Hackler, "Our Men in the Pacific: A Chronicle of United States Consular Officers as Seven Ports in the Pacific Islands and Australasia during the 19th Century" (PhD diss., University of Hawaii, 1978), p. 437.

6. Louis L. Snyder, *Diplomacy in Iron: The Life of Herbert von Bismarck* (Malabar, Fla.: Robert E. Krieger Publishing Co., 1985), p. 102.

7. Hackler, "Our Men in the Pacific", p. 471.

8. Ibid.

14 The Spanish-American War

1. Thomas A. Bailey, *A Diplomatic History of the American People*, 7th ed. (New York: Appleton-Century-Crofts, 1964), p. 495.

2. *Dictionary of American Biography*, ed. Dumas Malone, 20 vols. (New York, Charles Scribner's Sons, 1934), XI:103.

3. G. J. A. O'Toole, *The Spanish War: An American Epic –1898* (New York: W. W. Norton & Co., 1984), p. 82.

4. Bailey, *Diplomatic History*, p. 497.

5. Havana, 23 November 1897, Department of State, "Consular Despatches", Record Group 59, National Archives.

6. 3 December 1897, ibid.

7. 13 January 1898, ibid.

8. U.S. Department of State, *Foreign Relations of the United States: Diplomatic Papers*, 1898 (Washington, D.C.: Government Printing Office, 1901) pp.1025–29

9. H. G. Rickover, How the Battleship *Maine* Was Destroyed (Washington, D. C.: United States Navy, 1976), p. 91.

10. Havana, 17 February 1898, "Consular Despatches".

11. O'Toole, *Spanish War*, p. 161.
12. U.S. Senate, 2d sess. 55 Cong. Affairs in Cuba, Report 885 (Washington D.C.: Government Printing Office, 1898) pp. 534–38.
13. San Juan, 4 April 1898, "Consular Despatches".
14. David F. Trask, The War with Spain in 1898 (New York: Macmillan, 1981), p. 395.
15. Ronald Spector, *Admiral of the New Empire: The Life and Career of George Dewey* (Baton Rouge: Louisiana State University Press, 1974), p. 40.
16. Manila, 22 February 1898, "Consular Despatches".
17. Rhoda E. A. Hackler, "Our Men in the Pacific: A Chronicle of United States Consular Officers at Seven Posts in the Pacific Islands and Australasia during the 19th Century" (Ph.D. diss., University of Hawaii, 1978), p. 72.
18. Spector, *Admiral of the New Empire*, p. 26.
19. Ibid., p. 44.
20. Manila, 19 March 1898, "Consular Despatches".
21. 31 March 1898, ibid.
22. Spector, *Admiral of the New Empire*, p. 46.
23. Manila, 5 April 1898, "Consular Despatches".
24. 11 April 1898, ibid.
25. 21 April 1898, ibid.
26. O'Toole, *Spanish War*, p. 177.
27. Spector, *Admiral of the New Empire*, p. 56.
28. Singapore, 28 April 1898, "Consular Despatches".
29. Trask, *War with Spain*, p. 399.
30. Singapore, 30 April 1898, "Consular Despatches".
31. Ibid.
32. Trask, *War with Spain*, p. 400.
33. Ibid., p. 398.
34. Ibid.
35. Hong Kong, 19 July 1898, "Consular Despatches".
36. Ibid.
37. Edwin Wildman, *Aguinaldo: A Narrative of Filipino Ambitions* (Boston: 1901), p. 74.
38. Trask, *War with Spain*, p. 405.
39. Manila, 16 June 1898, "Consular Despatches".
40. Walter Millis, *The Martial Spirit: A Study of Our War with Spain* (Boston: Houghton Mifflin Co., 1931), p. 334.
41. Hong Kong, 12 October 1898, "Consular Despatches".
42. 9 July 1898, ibid.
43. Manila, 4 August 1898, "Consular Despatches".
44. 2 September 1898, ibid.
45. Trask, *War with Spain*, p. 401.

15 A Professional Consular Service

1. George R. Stewart Jr., *Bret Harte: Argonaut and Exile* (Boston: Houghton Mifflin Co., 1931), p. 244.
2. Bret Harte, *The Letters of Bret Harte*, ed. Geoffrey Bret Harte (London: Hodder and Stoughton, n.d.), p. 85.
3. Ibid., p. 205.
4. *Dictionary of American Biography*, Supplement One, ed. Harris E. Starr (New York, Charles Scribner's Sons, 1944), XXI:685.
5. Ibid., IV:568.
6. Ibid., VII:578.
7. Ibid., XIII:391.
8. Arthur Mann, *La Guardia: A Fighter against His Times*, 1882–1933 (Philadelphia: J. B. Lippencott, 1959), p. 35.
9. Ibid., p. 36.
10. Ibid., p. 37.
11. Ibid.
12. "Consular Evils and the Remedy," *Dry Goods Economist*, pamph. (Dry Goods Economist Press: 1893), pp. 1–10.
13. Richard H. Werking, "The Master". *Architects: Building the United States Foreign Service, 1890–1913* (Lexington: University Press of Kentucky, 1977), p. 43.
14. Robert S. Chilton Jr., Inspection Report (1896–1897), Department of State, Inspection Reports on Foreign Service Posts, Record Group 59, National Archives.
15. John L. Bittinger, "Consul General," 29 June 1899, Inspection Reports of Consulates in Province of Quebec, ibid.
16. Werking, "Master." *Architects*, p. 48.
17. Ibid., p. 60.
18. William R. Thayer, *The Life and Letters of John Hay*, 2 vols. (Boston: Houghton Mifflin Co., 1908), II:192.
19. Katharine Crane, *Mr. Carr of State: Forty-Seven Years in the Department of State* (New York: St. Martin's Press, 1960), p. 9.
20. Werking, "Master". *Architects*, p. 94.
21. Ibid.
22. Ibid.
23. William Barnes and John Heath Morgan, *The Foreign Service of the United States: Origins, Developments, and Functions* (Washington, D. C.: Government Printing Office, 1961), p. 164.
24. Werking, "Master," *Architects*, p. 105.
25. Ibid., p. 103.
26. Department of State, "Regulations Governing Examinations, 1906."
27. Werking, "Master," *Architects*, p. 109.
28. Inspection Reports, Alfred L. M. Gottschalk.
29. Ibid.

16 World War I and the Creation of the United States Foreign Service

1. RG 84, Stack Area 350, 36/2/3, Volume 560
2. Consular letter, Queenstown, June 22, 1915.
3. Consular letter, Aleppo, June 5, 1915.
4. Consular letter, Ourfa, August 6, 1915.
5. Consular letter, Smyrna, September 26 and 27, 1922.
6. Murphy, Robert, *Diplomat Among Warriors*, 1964, p. 24.

Bibliography

Bailey, Thomas A. *A Diplomatic History of the American People.* New York: Appleton-Century-Crofts, 7th edition, 1964.

Barnes, William, and John Heath Morgan. *The Foreign Service of the United States: Origins, Development, and Functions.* Washington, D.C.: Government Printing Office, 1961.

Beard, James Franklin, ed. *The Letters and Journals of James Fenimore Cooper.* 6 vols. Cambridge: Harvard University Press, 19601968.

Boyd, Julian P. "Two Diplomats between Revolutions: John Jay and Thomas Jefferson," *Virginia Magazine of History and Biography.* April 1958.

Boynton, Henry W., *James Fenimore Cooper.* New York: Century Co., 1931.

Bradford, Richard H. *The Virginius Affair.* Boulder Colorado: Associated University Press, 1980.

Browne, John Ross. *Etching of a Whaling Cruise.* Edited by John Seelye. Cambridge: Harvard University Press, 1968.

Bryson, Thomas A. *An American Consular Officer in the Middle East in the Jacksonian Era: A Biography of William Brown Hodgson, 1801–1871.* Atlanta: Resurgens Publications, 1979.

Burnett, Edmund C., ed. *Letters of Members of the Continental Congress.* 8 vols. Washington, D.C.: Carnegie Institution, 1934.

Consolidated Treaty Series. Edited by Clive Parry, 231 vols. Dobbs Ferry, N.Y.: Oceana Publications, 1969.

Continental Congress. *Secret Journals of the Acts and Proceedings of Congress.* 4 vols. Boston: Thomas B. Wait, 1820–1821.

Cox, Henry Bartholomew. *The Parisian American: Fulwar Skipwith of Virginia.* Washington: Mount Vernon Publishing Co., 1964.

Crane, Katharine. *Mr. Carr of State: Forty-Seven Years in the Department of State.* New York: St. Martin's Press, 1960.

Crow, Carl. *He Opened the Door of Japan.* New York: Harper & Bros., 1939.

Debates and Proceedings of the United States. Washington, D.C.: Gales and Seator, 1834.

Dennett, Tyler. *Americans in Eastern Asia: A Critical Study of the Policy of the United States with Reference to China, Japan, and Korea in the 19th Century.* New York: Macmillan Co., 1922.

Department of State. *Consular Despatches, 1776–1906*. RG 59, National Archives. *American Consular Officers, 1789–1800*. Historian's Office. 1964.
_____. *Inspection Reports on Foreign Service Posts, 1906–1939*. RG 59, National Archives.
_____. *Domestic Letters*. RG 59, National Archives.
_____. *Establishment of Consular and Diplomatic Relations with India and South Africa*. Historian's Office. September 1946.
_____. *Regulations Governing Examinations, 1906*.
_____. *The United States Consul's Manual: A Practical Guide for Consular Officers, and Also for Merchants, Shipowners, and Masters of American Vessels in All Their Consular Transactions*. 2d edition. Washington, D.C.: Hudson Taylor, 1863.
_____. *War in Cuba: Correspondence*. Washington, D. C.: GPO, 1898.
Diplomatic Correspondence of the United States of America from the Signing of the Definitive Treaty of Peace, 10th September 1783, to the Adoption of the Constitution, March 4, 1789. 7 vols. Washington, D.C.: Francis Preston Blair, 1833.
Drake, Frederick C. *The Empire of the Seas: A Biography of Rear Admiral Robert Wilson Shufeldt, USN*. Honolulu: University of Hawaii Press, 1984.
Consular Evils and Their Remedy. New York: Dry Goods Economist Press, 1893.
Dulles, Foster Rhea. *China and America: The Story of Their Relations since 1784*. Princeton: Princeton University Press, 1946.
Edwards, Samuel. *Barbary General: The Life of William H. Eaton*. Englewood Cliffs, N.J.: Prentice-Hall, 1968.
Egan, Clifford L. *Neither Peace Nor War: Franco-American Relations, 1803–1812*. Baton Rouge: Louisiana State University Press, 1983.
Encyclopaedia Judaica. 16 vols. Jerusalem: Keter Publishing House, 1972.
Evans, Brian V. "The First China Hand." *Foreign Service Journal*, May 1983. pp. 28–31.
Executive Document 30, re: Steamer Virginius. 43d Cong.,1st sess. Government Printing Office: 1874.
Fairbank, John King. *Trade and Diplomacy on the China Coast: The Opening of the Treaty Ports, 1842–1854*. 2 vols. Cambridge: Harvard University Press, 1953.
Field, James A., Jr. *America and the Mediterranean World, 1776–1882*. Princeton: Princeton University Press, 1969.
Finnie, David H. *Pioneers East: The Early American Experience in the Middle East*. Cambridge: Harvard University Press, 1967.
Franklin, Benjamin. *The Writings of Benjamin Franklin*, edited by Albert Henry Smyth. 10 vols. New York: Frederick A. Stokes Co., 1929.
Goebel, Julius, Jr. *The Struggle for the Falkland Islands: A Study in Legal and Diplomatic History*. New Haven: Yale University Press, 1927.
Goldberg, Isaac. *Major Noah: American Jewish Pioneer*. Philadelphia: Jewish Publication Society of America, 1936.
Graebner, Norman A. *Empire on the Pacific: A Study in American Continental Expansion*. New York: Ronald Press, 1955.

Griffin, Eldon. *Clippers and Consuls: American Consular and Commercial Relations with Eastern Asia, 1845–1860.* Ann Arbor: Edwards Press, 1938.

Hackler, Rhoda E. A. "Our Men in the Pacific: A Chronicle of United States Consular Officers at Seven Ports in the Pacific Islands and Australasia during the 19th Century." Ph.D diss., University of Hawaii 1978.

Hall, Luella J. *The United States and Morocco, 1776–1956.* Metuchen, N.J.: Scarecrow Press, 1971.

Harlow, Neal. *California Conquered, War and Peace on the Pacific: 1846–1850.* Berkeley: University of California Press, 1982.

Harris, Townsend. *The Complete Journal of Townsend Harris, First American Consul General and Minister to Japan.* New York: Doubleday & Doran & Co., 1930.

_____. *Some Unpublished Letters of Townsend Harris,* edited by Shio Sakanishi. New York: Japan Reference Library, 1941.

Harte, Bret. *The Letters of Bret Harte,* edited by Geoffrey Bret Harte. London Hodder & Sloughton, n.d.

Hawthorne, Nathaniel. *The English Notebooks,* edited by Randall Stewart. New York: Russell & Russell, 1962.

Henry, Robert Selph. *The Story of the Mexican War.* Indianapolis: Bobbs-Merrill, 1950.

Herodotus. *The History of Herodotus,* edited by Manuel Komroff and translated by George Rawlinson. New York: Tudor, 1928.

Hyde, Arthur May. *A Diplomatic History of Bulgaria, 1870–1886.* Westport, Conn.: Greenwood Press, 1974.

Irwin, Robert W. *The Diplomatic Relations of the United States with the Barbary Powers, 1777–1816.* Chapel Hill: University of North Carolina Press, 1931.

James, Coy Hilton. *Silas Deane: Patriot or Traitor?* East Lansing: Michigan State University Press, 1975.

Jay, John. *John Jay: The Winning of the Peace: Unpublished Papers, 1780–1784,* edited by Richard B. Morris. New York: Harper & Row, 1980.

Jefferson, Thomas. *The Papers of Thomas Jefferson,* edited by Julian P. Boyd. 21 vols. Princeton, N.J.: Princeton University Press, 1965. XVII:423.

Jenkins, Brian. *Britain and the War for the Union.* 2 vols. Montreal: McGill-Queen's University Press, 1974–1980.

Jones, Chester Lloyd. *The Consular Service of the United States: Its History and Activities.* Philadelphia: University of Pennsylvania, 1906.

Journals of the Continental Congress. 34 vols. Washington, D.C.: GPO, 1903–37.

Keim, De Benneville Randolph. *A Report to the Hon. George S. Boutwell, Secretary of the Treasury, upon the Condition of the Consular Service.* Washington, D.C.: GPO, 1872.

King, Amelia Kay. "James Keenan, United States Consul to Hong Kong." M.A. thesis, North Texas State University, 1978.

King, Charles K., ed. *The Life and Correspondence of Rufus King: Comprising His Letters, Private and Official, His Public Documents and His Speeches.* 10 vols. New York: G. P. Putnam's Sons, 1894–1900.

302   Bibliography

Knox, Dudley W. *A History of the United States Navy*. New York: G. P. Putnam's Sons, 1936.
Kuykendall, Ralph S., and A. Grove Day. *Hawaii: A History: From Polynesian Kingdom to American Commonwealth*. New York: Prentice-Hall, 1948.
Lathrop, Rose Hawthorne. *Memories of Hawthorne*. Boston: Houghton, Mifflin & Co., 1897.
Lester, Charles Edwards. *My Consulship*. 2 vols. New York: Cored, Lanpert & Co., 1853.
Lincoln, Abraham. *Collected Works of Abraham Lincoln*, edited by Roy P. Basler. The Abraham Lincoln Association, Springfield, Illinois. 3 vols. New Brunswick, N.J.: Rutgers University Press, 1953.
Lonn, Ella. *Foreigners in the Union Army and Navy*. Baton Rouge: Louisiana State University Press, 1951.
Malone, Dumas, ed. *Dictionary of American Biography*. 20 vols. New York: Charles Scribner's Sons, 1928–36.
Mann, Arthur. *La Guardia: A Fighter against His Times, 1882–1933*. Philadelphia: J. B. Lippencott, 1959.
Manning, William R., ed. *Diplomatic Correspondence of the United States Concerning Independence of the Latin-American Nations*. 3 vols. New York: Oxford University Press, 1925.
_____. *Diplomatic Correspondence of the United States: Inter American Affairs, 1831–1860*. 12 vols. Washington, D.C.: Carnegie Endowment for International Peace, 1932.
Marraro, Howard R. *American Opinion on the Unification of Italy, 1846–1861*. New York: Columbia University Press, 1932.
_____. *Diplomatic Relations between the United States and the Kingdom of the Two Sicilies: Instructions and Despatches, 1816–1861*. 2 vols. New York: S. F. Vanni (Ragusa), 1951.
Mays, James O'Donald. *Mr. Hawthorne Goes to England: The Adventures of a Reluctant Consul*. Burley, Hampshire: New Forest Leaves, 1983.
McAfee, Ward. "A Reconsideration of the Mexican-American War." *Southern California Quarterly*, 62 (1980):49–65.
Mellow, James R. *Nathaniel Hawthorne in His Times*. Boston: Houghton Mifflin, 1980.
Millis, Walter. *The Martial Spirit: A Study of Our War with Spain*. Boston: Houghton Mifflin Co., 1931.
Moran, Benjamin. *The Journal of Benjamin Moran: 1857–1865*, edited by Sarah A. Wallace and Frances E. Gillespie. Chicago: University of Chicago Press, 1948.
Morison, Samuel Eliot. *The Maritime History of Massachusetts, 1783–1860*. Boston: Houghton Mifflin Co., 1921.
Morris, Robert. *Papers of Robert Morris, 1781–1784*, edited by E. James Ferguson. 7 vols. Pittsburgh: University of Pittsburgh Press, 1973.
Myers, John C. *Condensed Statement of John C. Myers*. Washington, D.C.: GPO, 1877.

National Cyclopaedia of American Biography. 75 vols. New York: James T. White & Co., 1888–1984.

Naval Documents Related to the Quasi-War between the United States and France. Washington, D.C.: GPO, 1937.

Nevins, Allan. *Hamilton Fish: The Inner History of the Grant Administration.* New York: Dodd, Mead & Co., 1936.

Oberholtzer, Ellis Paxson. *Robert Morris: Patriot and Financer.* New York: Burt Franklin, 1903.

O'Toole, G. J. A. *The Spanish War: An American Epic – 1898.* New York: W. W. Norton & Co., 1984.

Owsley, Frank L. *King Cotton Diplomacy: Foreign Relations of the Confederate States of America.* Chicago: University of Chicago Press, 1931.

Parton, James. *General Butler in New Orleans.* Boston: Houghton, Mifflin & Co., 1868.

Perkins, Bradford. *Prologue to War: England and the United States, 1805–1812.* Berkeley: University of California Press, 1961.

Phillipson, Coleman. *The International Law and Custom of Ancient Greece and Rome.* 2 vols. London: Macmillan & Co., 1911.

Rauch, Basil. *American Interest in Cuba, 1848–1855.* New York: Columbia University Press, 1948.

Sands, William F. *Undiplomatic Memoires.* New York: Whittlesey House, 1930.

Schuyler, Eugene. *Selected Essays: With Memoir by Evelyn Schuyler Schaeffer.* New York: Charles Scribner's Sons, 1901.

Siepel, Kevin H. *Rebel: The Life and Times of John Singleton Mosby.* New York: St. Martin's Press, 1983.

Smith, Walter. *The American Diplomats and Consuls of 1776–1865: A Geographic and Biographic Directory of the Foreign Service from the Declaration of Independence to the End of the Civil War.* Washington, D.C.: Department of State, 1986.

Snyder, Louis L. *Diplomacy in Iron: The Life of Herbert von Bismarck.* Malabar, Fla.: Robert E. Krieger Publishing Co., 1985.

Sparks, Jared, ed. *The Diplomatic Correspondence of the American Revolution.* 12 vols. N. Hale and Gray & Bowen, 1829–30.

Spector, Ronald. *Admiral of the New Empire: The Life and Career of George Dewey.* Baton Rouge: Louisiana State University Press, 1974.

Starr, Harris E., ed. *Dictionary of American Biography: Supplement One.* New York: Charles Scribner's Sons, 1944.

Statler, Oliver. *Shimoda Story.* New York: Random House, 1969.

Stern, Philip Van Doren. *When the Guns Roared: World Aspects of the American Civil War.* Garden City, N.Y.: Doubleday & Co., 1965.

Stillman, William James. *The Autobiography of a Journalist.* 2 vols. Boston: Houghton, Mifflin & Co., 1901.

Stewart, George R., Jr. *Bret Harte: Argonaut and Exile.* Boston: Houghton Mifflin Co., 1931.

Stinchcombe, William C. *The American Revolution and the French Alliance.* Syracuse: Syracuse University Press, 1969.

Stuart, Graham H. *American Diplomatic and Consular Practice*. 2nd ed. New York: Appleton-Century-Crofts, 1952.

Thayer, William R. *The Life and Letters of John Hay*. 2 vols. Boston: Houghton Mifflin Co., 1908.

Trask, David F. *The War with Spain in 1898*. New York: Macmillan, 1981.

Updyke, Frank. *The Diplomacy of the War of 1812*. Baltimore: Johns Hopkins Press, 1915.

Warden, David B. *On the Origin, Nature, Progress, and Influence of Consular Establishments*. Paris: Smith, 1813.

Webster, Charles K., ed. *Britain and the Independence of Latin America 1812–1830*. 2 vols. London: Oxford University Press, 1938.

Werking, Richard H. *The Master Architects: Building the United States Foreign Service: 1890–1913*. Lexington: University Press of Kentucky, 1977.

Wildman, Edwin. *Aguinaldo: A Narrative of Filipino Ambitions*. Boston: Lathrop, 1901.

Wolf, John B. *The Barbary Coast: Algiers under the Turks, 1500 to 1830*. New York: W. W. Norton & Co., 1979.

Wright, Lenoir C. *United States Policy toward Egypt, 1830–1914*. New York: Exposition Press, 1969.

Wriston, Henry Merritt. *Executive Agents in American Foreign Relations*. Baltimore: Johns Hopkins Press, 1929.

Zimmerman, James Fulton. *Impressment of American Seamen*. New York: Columbia University Press, 1925.

Index

www.ingramcontent.com/pod-product-compliance
Lightning Source LLC
Chambersburg PA
CBHW020656270326
41928CB00005B/146